ACQUIRING SKILL IN SPORT

[Second Edition]

Bob Sharp

First published in 2004 by
Sports Dynamics.

Available in the UK and Europe from:
Sports Dynamics
8 Skillicorne Mews
Queens Road
Cheltenham
GL50 2NJ

Tel/fax: 01242 522 638

www.sportsdynamics.co.uk
orders@sportsdynamics.co.uk

©Sports Dynamics

A catalogue record for this book is available
from the British Library.

ISBN 0 9519543 42

Designed and typeset by J. Shambrook.
Cartoons by Ian Rodney, Senior Designer, University of Strathclyde
Photographs by Brian Lochrin, Senior Photographer, University of Strathclyde
Printed and bound by Fotodirect Ltd. Brighton, UK.

ACKNOWLEDGEMENT

This book is dedicated to my former mentors ~
Professors Bob Wilberg and John Whiting.

"Bob opened the door and John led me through."

Thanks are extended to the pupils of Jordanhill School, Glasgow, and the Principal Teacher of Physical Education, John Summers, for their help with the photographs that appear in this book.

Bob Sharp is a Reader in Sport Studies at the Faculty of Education (formerly Jordanhill College of Education), University of Strathclyde. His key teaching subjects are statistics, research methods and the psychology of skill acquisition. He has delivered courses in these subjects to sport, physical education and outdoor education students for almost 30 years. He has written widely in professional, academic and commercial publications and served on numerous educational and national governing bodies over the years.

He is a strong believer in the philosophy of experiential learning and learning through practical experience. As a lifelong sportsperson he achieved success in trampolining and athletics in his earlier years. For the past 30 years he has focused his interests in the outdoors as a climber, walker and skier. He leads one of the UK's mountain rescue teams and chairs the governing body for mountain rescue in Scotland.

CONTENTS

PREFACE

"I sometimes think that running has given me a glimpse of the greatest freedom a man can ever know, because it results in the simultaneous liberation of both body and mind."
~ *Roger Bannister*

Roger Bannister's words are a very appropriate introduction to this book because they underline not only the central role that movement plays in all our lives, but also the fascinating interplay between movement and the brain. The fact is that skilled movements don't simply 'happen'. We may not consciously think about our movements or think too deeply about how we learn, but the brain is intimately involved in these processes. Ultimately, the ability to perform skilfully is based on the joint influence of inheritance and experience. Whilst it is well established that genetic make-up has a key part to play in all we do, including how we learn and perform, this book focuses on the role of experience. Specifically, it looks at how people acquire skills and the changes that take place during learning. It also focuses on what coaches and teachers can do to enable skill acquisition.

In many ways, learning and teaching are related. For example, as people learn, their capacity to understand complex terminology and to work for longer periods increases. Good coaches and teachers take advantage of these changes to facilitate learning and develop skills even further. This book is concerned with both the process of learning and the process of teaching/coaching.

A fundamental principle of learning is that it never stops. This is an important feature that is often overlooked. From the moment of birth we acquire knowledge and develop skills which help us meet work, recreation and daily challenges; this continues throughout our lives. Of all the things we learn, much is physical in nature. Indeed, most of what we know, understand and learn is reflected in physical movement. Attitudes, feelings, values and knowledge are expressed through movement, via facial expression, gestures, speech and bodily activity.

Movement clearly plays a critical part in our lives. It is reflected in mundane tasks such as closing doors and tying shoe laces to more complicated skills such as playing a musical instrument, driving a car or playing volleyball. In all of these activities people display different levels of performance and varying techniques or styles. There are many reasons for such differences. People have different genetic backgrounds, levels of interest, experience and learning opportunities. Most importantly, people are introduced to new skills in different ways and receive different experiences depending on how they are coached or taught. It is well known that coaches and teachers can have a profound effect on how people learn and their eventual level of performance.

It follows that coaching, teaching and learning are all inter-dependent. But it should be noted that skill acquisition is just a single (albeit important) facet of the work of teachers and coaches. Many authors have described the complex role of teachers and coach (e.g., Lyle, 1999; Martens, 1997; Miles, 2003). Miles (2003) suggests that coaches are involved in the technical, physical, social, psychological and personal development of people. Furthermore, they act as managers, trainers, teachers, scientists and motivators as the occasion demands. This holistic view is reflected in his comment that:

> *"... a coach is someone whose actions take other people forwards in some aspects of their lives. In a sporting context, a coach is someone who uses sport as a vehicle for the development of individuals, both as performers and as people."*

In a similar vein, Martens (1997) indicates that coaches should have

> *"... the teaching skills of an educator, the training expertise of a physiologist, the administrative leadership of a business executive and the counselling wisdom of a psychologist..."*

Throughout this book, reference is made to a number of different people concerned with skill learning, viz., coaches, teachers, instructors, etc. Whilst there is often a clear distinction in the role of these people, the present text attempts to cut across these boundaries and focus on principles that apply to all. Not all the principles raised in the book apply to everyone and many ideas are not specific to sport. Indeed, much of what we know about the principles of skill acquisition apply to diverse areas such as creative skills, social learning and the acquisition of language. Consequently, in the context of this book, terms such as coaching, teaching and instructing should be considered equal and in most cases, interchangeable.

The overall strategy is to describe principles and ideas, discuss their merits and weaknesses and demonstrate how they may be applied to good effect in the teaching and coaching of sports skills. Clearly, the reader's background and experience will dictate how much is taken from the book. However, the intention is to change the reader's thinking in one of several ways. The book will introduce readers to ideas and topics they have not encountered before, remind them of methods or procedures which have been forgotten or reinforce principles which are currently used. The book will have achieved its overall aim if it makes the reader a more informed (and hopefully better) teacher or coach. To do this, the reader will have to take ideas from the book and experiment with them in the practical situation. Books by themselves do not make people better teachers or coaches. Ideas have to be considered and principles tested in practice. 'Learning by doing' is one of the first principles of skill acquisition!

The book has been divided into chapters that form reasonably independent sections. Whilst the first edition of this book has been completely re-written it still retains the same overall structure and emphasis. The reader does not have to read the entire text to make sense of individual chapters. However, readers should bear in mind that learning is a complex process influenced by many factors and that a complete picture of skill acquisition can only be understood by recognising the interactive nature of many factors. Cross-references between chapters should help the reader see important links.

The text is written for all those interested in skill acquisition, especially teachers and coaches, but notably school pupils in their final year ('A' level in England and Wales and 'H' grade in Scotland) and first year university students. The main intention is to present readers with ideas based on present research and thinking that has currency and practical application. The book has been written as a clear and practical treatise based on scientific findings, anecdotal evidence and acquired wisdom. Readers will not find themselves bogged down with excessive detail from scientific documents and esoteric journals. Each chapter includes summary and review sections as well as descriptions of practical tasks that can be carried out to exemplify key principles. Throughout, the pronouns she, he, her, him are meant to be interchangeable and inclusive of males and females. No gender bias is intended or implied. The strong view is taken throughout the book that in both the learning and performance of sports skills, men and women have equal status and opportunity.

Finally, it is worth recording the success of the first edition of this book. It was written as a successor to the classic texts by Barbara Knapp (Knapp, 1963) and John Whiting (Whiting, 1969) and eventually sold more copies than both of these. For this reason, whilst the book has been re-written in its entirety, the original aims remain the same.

Bob Sharp
January 2004

References

Knapp, B. (1963). Skill in sport. *The attainment of proficiency.* London: Routledge & Kegan Paul.

Lyle, J. (2002). *Sports coaching concepts: A framework for coaches' behaviour.* London: Routledge.

Martens, R. (1997). *Successful coaching.* Champaign, Illinois: Human Kinetics.

Miles, A. (2003). *What is sports coaching?* Leeds: Coachwise Solutions.

Whiting, H.T.A. (1969). *Acquiring ball skill. A psychological interpretation.* London: G. Bell and Sons Ltd.

CHAPTER 1 – THE CONCEPT OF SKILL

"Skill is an inherent part of every sport. Performers use skill to achieve their objectives (e.g., score a goal, execute a somersault, hit a forehand winner). Skilful performances make sport exciting to watch ~ for some performers it can be their main objective for competing."

Foxon (1999)

WHY TAKE PART IN SPORT?

Considering the mass of people involved in sport, the number and variety of sports as well as the different motives that guide people to participate, it is hardly surprising that the analysis of skill – from whatever perspective – is a complex topic. It is also a topic that is investigated by a wide variety of people including psychologists, sport scientists, coaches, neuro-biologists and teachers. Let's look at some of the reasons why people take part in sport and why many work so hard to improve their performance. Such knowledge should be very helpful to teachers and coaches who wish to assist the skill development of those in their charge.

There are a variety of factors. Some people take part just to make friends; skill improvement and performing well is secondary. Sport, of course, is a rich medium for meeting people and making friends. Sport also provides a means of improving fitness, losing weight and taking one's mind off the pressures of daily life and work. People join local walking clubs and aerobics classes simply to improve their health and fitness levels.

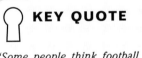

KEY QUOTE

"Some people think football is a matter of life and death. I don't like that attitude. I can assure them it is much more serious than that."
Bill Shankly
(former football manager)

Others find they have a particular ability in sport and take part to nurture their inherent talents; they desire to do well, maximise their potential and achieve their very best.

Some people are good at those sports that emphasise the control of one's body, e.g., gymnastics, skiing, diving. Others tend to favour sports that require making adjustments to an ever changing display as in soccer or volleyball. And many people rise to the challenge of the outdoor environment and climb, canoe, sail, orienteer, etc. By and large, people take part in sports and activities which they enjoy, provide satisfaction and contribute to self esteem. And, of course, many people take part in sport for financial gain or national prestige.

It is probably difficult to assess the reasons why any one person enjoys sport. Some may not be able to articulate their feelings and for others there may be a number of reasons. However, the acquisition of skill and improvement in performance are central to the efforts of most people involved in sport.

SKILL EXPRESSIONS

A variety of labels are used to describe the kinds of topics central to this book. Researchers, teachers and coaches tend to use the following – skill acquisition, motor development, skill learning, psychology of skill, motor learning, motor control, skill development, perceptual motor skill. These are some of the most common expressions, but there are others. The term used at any given point depends on the audience in question (e.g., coaches might prefer the term skill development). There is also a cultural factor; in North America the expression motor learning is common whereas in the UK the corresponding expression is skill acquisition. Typically, the expression used tends to describe the subject focus – learning, control or development. Expressions such as motor learning and skill acquisition refer to the body of knowledge that focuses on learning – how we improve and practice. The terms perceptual motor skill and motor control are used when the focus is on how skills are co-ordinated or controlled. This area of knowledge is more concerned with skilled performance per se, rather than how skilled movements are acquired. Motor development is concerned with changes in performance not directly related to the learning process. Rather, motor development examines changes in performance as a function of time (the aging process), especially changes in early childhood rather than old age.

The present book focuses on the learning process as applied to sporting and physical activities. It is concerned with how people learn sports skills. It should be said that whilst the emphasis is on learning, many issues are equally relevant to motor control and skill development. For example, reaction time is a factor that has a bearing on how skilled someone performs in certain sports, e.g., 100 metre sprint. In the area of motor learning, attempts have been made to reduce a person's reaction time through various practice regimes. And in developmental terms, it is known that reaction time changes as people grow older. So, there is an overlap in subject knowledge between the three areas.

Let's now focus in more detail by looking at the multi-dimensional nature of skill.

THREE DIMENSIONS TO SKILL

Although a simplification, *Figure 1* serves to highlight the complexity of human learning. The relevance of the three dimensions shown will be mentioned many times

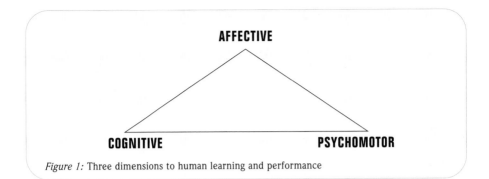

AFFECTIVE

COGNITIVE   **PSYCHOMOTOR**

Figure 1: Three dimensions to human learning and performance

throughout this book. The affective dimension (to feel) concerns the emotional or attitudinal side of our personality. We reveal emotions when confronted with say a pleasant sight or hear of a terrible accident and we all respond differently to such situations. Similarly, we all have different aspirations in our professional lives and are motivated to pursue leisure interests in our free time for varying reasons. The affective facet is, if you like, the 'qualitative' side of our personality. The cognitive dimension (to know) is concerned with our intellect and memory – how intelligent we are, how good we are at discussion and reasoning, how well we remember and converse with others. The last dimension – psychomotor (to do) – is concerned with our movements. Here again, we all differ in the manner in which we say walk or run, the sports that we are attracted to and the level of performance we reach.

This tri-partite way of looking at the individual is intuitive and general. If the reader cares to think of any situation in everyday life such as watching a football match on television, going for a walk at the weekend or discussing the latest politics with a neighbour, then it is possible to see an element (to varying degrees) of all three dimensions in each example. Thus, watching a football match on television requires careful perception of the game in progress (Cognitive) and it stimulates emotional feelings (Affective) which are reflected in facial expressions and whole body movements (Psychomotor). The intensity and importance of each of these will depend entirely on the nature of the situation.

Sometimes there is a mismatch between attitude and skill!

This three-way approach reinforces the complexity and richness of skill learning. Performing well in sport is more than just a matter of acquiring a repertoire of movement patterns. To be good at ball games demands that the player knows and understands the rules of the sport and understands the value and nature of complex strategies. Players may keep a precise log of their training, know something of their sport's development and history and also possess a keen awareness of their opponents. These are all intellectual elements. Excellence also depends on mental attitude, setting correct goals, dedication and application to hard training, sportsmanship, motivation, the need to achieve and possibly the 'right' sort of personality. The affective dimension is without doubt a critical ingredient in sport, and one which has taken on much greater prominence in sport during the last quarter of a century through the influence of sports psychology. Both athlete and coach must be aware of attitudinal, motivational and emotional aspects if athletes and learners are to meet their potential. We will return to some of these topics in Chapter 7. Finally, the learner acquires the techniques of their sport; the precise movement patterns which, if executed at the right time and in the right manner, reveal fluent, skilled performance. In this regard, technology may make a highly significant contribution. McCarthy (1990) has shown ways in which performance in a number of sports can be enhanced through improvements in equipment design, weight, material type, etc. The last 10/15 years has seen remarkable progress in the design, manufacture and materials used to make sports equipment and these have had a significant impact on human performance (Williams, 1998).

Skilled performance then, is an interplay between attitudes, knowledge and movements and reflects the extent to which each of these three elements makes a contribution. It follows that the development of skill and the pursuit of excellence should recognise these three ingredients. This is highlighted in a comment from John Shedden (1986), a former national skiing coach. He says:

"There is a general misconception that skill is essentially technical excellence and whilst it's not possible to be skilled without a high level of technical excellence, it's also very important for the learner to realise that the control of his body is important, but so is the control of his emotions and the ability of his body to carry out the tasks that are set which requires certain levels of fitness.

Therefore, skill is a continuous interplay between the technical ability of the skier, the emotions of the skier, the perceptions and judgements that skier can make and the fitness or the degree of preparedness that the skier possesses. Skill is developed therefore by attending to all of these things either in turn or combinations of one or the other."

LEARNING AND PERFORMANCE

Learning, performance and skill – all three words are related. Performance is the observable behaviour that demonstrates a person's skill. When we watch someone perform a skill or play a game, we are watching them perform. This is fairly obvious. Performance is observable and transient. It shows how competent someone is at the time of the performance. It may or may not be a very reliable indicator of their underlying skill. A single performance may be an outstanding

success or a dismal failure. In both cases, it may not reflect the person's actual potential or stage of learning. That is why it is important to watch a person repeatedly to gain a full and more reliable picture of their true underlying skill. When we observe a person who has followed a period of practice over a period of time, we are in a good position to note whether or not learning has taken place. Learning is reflected in changes in performance; it cannot be predicted from a single or few observations of performance. The changes observed will often show that the learner passes through a sequence of identifiable stages. Martens (1997) identifies three stages, viz., mental, practice and automatic. We'll return to this in Chapter 2.

THE SHAPE OF LEARNING

It is worth repeating that learning is reflected in a change in performance (see *Figure 2*). We say that a person has learned something if their performance shows improvement from one occasion to the next. A young javelin thrower may improve their throw from say 25 metres to 45 metres over a period of weeks. Such an improvement must be stable and relatively permanent and not just a transient increase caused for example, by a change in fitness level, motivation from friends or improvement in health.

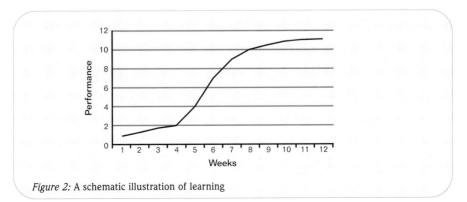

Figure 2: A schematic illustration of learning

Moreover, maturational or developmental changes that predispose a learner to better performance (e.g., increases in body weight, development of the central nervous system) are not responsible for learning. Learning takes place through practice and experience. It is worth mentioning here that whilst learning is recognised by observing changes in a learner's performance over time, lack of change does not imply learning is not taking place! This stems from what has already been said about the complexity of skill and how skilled performance depends not only on the ability to execute good technique but also the capacity to perceive, attend, make decisions, anticipate, etc. The learner may well be making internal changes with regard to these elements (e.g., learning to recognise which cues to attend to) but they are insufficiently developed to result in significant technical improvement. Changes like this account for the common experience of 'plateaus' in learning; periods when there are, apparently, no changes in performance. There are other reasons that will be dealt with when we address motivation in Chapter 7.

Examination of *Figure 2* shows a gradual improvement from one week to the next. An analysis of the exact shape tells us something about the nature of the underlying learning. The curve in *Figure 2* suggests the individual learns fairly slowly in the early weeks before embarking on a rapid period of improvement. In the later weeks

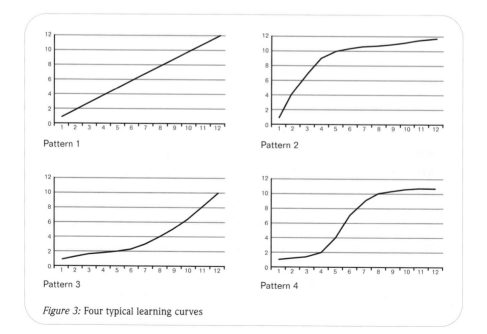

Pattern 1

Pattern 2

Pattern 3

Pattern 4

Figure 3: Four typical learning curves

progress is less rapid and performance finally seems to stabilise. The overall pattern may reflect some early difficulties in understanding the task followed by a substantial gain once these problems have been hurdled. Or it might be that the learner was held back initially through fitness or strength limitations. Learning curves like this will always show individual differences.

There are four typical curves which reflect most learning situations (Magill, 1993). These four patterns are shown in *Figure 3*. Pattern 1 shows 'linear' improvement where the gains are equidistant over time. Pattern 2 shows 'negative acceleration' – quick gains initially are followed by slower progress. Pattern 3 shows 'positive acceleration' – slow gains initially followed by speeding up. Pattern 4 shows an ogive ('S' shaped). Here gains initially are slow, then more rapid and finally slower. The curve shown in Pattern 1 would suggest the learner is progressing at a fairly even pace with stable gains seen on a regular basis. This kind of pattern is uncommon. Pattern 2 would occur with someone who progressed very quickly initially – possibly because they are a quick learner or because the task was fairly simple. Pattern 3 shows the progress of someone who takes time to improve in the early stages but picks up quickly thereafter. This might result because the task is difficult to understand or the learner unfamiliar with the demands. The final pattern shows the progress of someone who progresses slowly initially then picks up much faster and then slows down once more.

In practice, whilst learning tends to follow one of these four general patterns, any individual will probably reveal a more discontinuous pattern interspersed with periods where little progression takes place. As noted before, periods of no apparent learning are called 'plateaus' in learning. We will return to this matter in a later chapter when an examination of the solutions to these problems will be discussed.

A DEFINITION OF SKILL

Let us now examine what we mean by skill and skill acquisition. The word skill has many uses and is used by the layman as well as sports coaches and teachers. We talk about the skill of a lawyer or a skilled darts player. We refer to a person who speaks many languages as a skilled linguist. Someone who communicates easily with people and who makes friends readily possesses good social skills. A Formula 1 racing car driver has keen perceptual skills and an ability to make rapid body movements exceptionally quickly. There are common elements in all these examples. Within the context of sport the word skill is used in several ways:

• Skill is used when referring to a specific act or sequence of movements such as a chest pass in basketball, a somersault in gymnastics or a snowplough turn in skiing.

• Skill is also used to define the level of performance of an individual or team. For example, a volleyball team may play at district level or an athlete may be a good club runner. In this context an international athlete would be considered more skilled than a club standard athlete.

• Skill is also used in an absolute manner within the specific context of high level performance. In this case, one is either skilled or not skilled. Thus, a person is considered to be skilled only if, for example, they compete at Olympic level.

Given the different interpretations of skill, the present text adopts the view that skill is a quality that belongs to the

All four characteristics of skill are present in this activity

individual. It does not reside outside the person in the form of, say, a physical movement. Skill is something that facilitates the link between intention and action. We can be more precise and say that skill satisfies four criteria. Let us examine these criteria and then follow by showing how this knowledge can help the coach and teacher.

• Firstly, skill results in actions that have a clear end result. Skill is goal directed. Thus, one learns to spike a volleyball in order to reduce the time for the opposition to play a return shot. Or, one learns to navigate in a woodland area so as to develop confidence in more mountainous terrain. Similarly, one may learn to swim in order to meet friends, increase fitness or avoid drowning! Skill has direction and purpose.

• Secondly, skill is a learned characteristic. Skill requires practice and experience for proficiency. This means that skill is not acquired through hereditary influences. It also follows that skill improvement is not based on changes in age or increased fitness. A person's performance may improve because they improve their flexibility (say, in gymnastics), but it would be wrong to say that skill learning has taken place. Skill requires physical practice and other kinds of related experiences such as observation and feedback for improvements to occur. Skill acquisition is a relatively permanent state of affairs unlike, say, flexibility or endurance that are free to fluctuate depending on a person's fitness.

• Thirdly, skill results in movements that are economic and efficient in terms of their energy and time outlay. Skilled action is not clumsy to the eye. There are cases of good performers who look clumsy in the way they move (e.g., a soccer player may move awkwardly but still be an effective goal scorer) but, by and large, skilled action is pleasing to see, well timed, consistent, co-ordinated, and looks fluent, etc.

• Finally, skilled activity is the end result of a whole chain of central nervous system activity. For example, a skilled netball player selects and absorbs information about the game, opponents and teammates. When in possession of the ball she needs to decide what action to take. This will depend on the score in the game, her position on court, the position of other players, and so on. Only when her brain has processed this information can she initiate the most appropriate action. How skilled that action is, will depend on the success of the preceding nervous activity as well as the efficiency of the resulting movements. An illustration of this overall view of skill is the example of a squash player who may well be able to 'read' the game and know what shots to play but, through lack of co-ordination fails to make the right moves. Similarly, an aspiring soccer player may be a very competent 'juggler' of the ball but lack the perceptive awareness and decision making ability to translate such skills into the game proper. Shedden (1986) expresses this very well when describing skiing. He says:

> *"A skilful skier is one who has learned techniques, but more than that, one who can use those techniques by making sound judgements about his own level of performance on that day, about his own emotional disposition to the snow conditions and about the nature of the surface on which he is skiing – the snow textures and so on – in order to make the technical ability that he has effective."*

On the basis of these observations, the following definition of skill is proffered:

> *"Skill is the learned capacity to select and execute specific movement patterns that are effective and efficient"*

DEFINITION OF SKILL LEARNING – IMPLICATIONS

A premise that will run throughout this book is the importance of applying theory to practice. It is vital that readers should examine the various sections and chapters and adopt the very positive stance, "So what?" An attempt will be made to demonstrate the implications of each of the various principles and research findings raised within the book. So, let's make a start by examining the implications of the four criteria described above for coaching and learning.

Goal Direction

If skill is goal directed and aimed at achieving specific results, then the instructor/teacher/ coach must be aware of the goal and generally speaking so too must the learner. Both parties must have a clear idea why a movement or technique is being practiced and how it fits into a broader context. This means that the coach or teacher must plan ahead with clear strategies and direction to session content and instruction.

Similarly, the learner must be made aware – if it is not obvious – of the reasons why they are practising certain things and why practice is vital. Too often the reason for doing things is overlooked by the coach who, perhaps because they are wrapped up in their subject, assumes the learner knows what the objective is. Thus, one of the potential dangers of part practices where skills or games are broken down into constituent parts is that the learner is not given a chance to appreciate the overall effect of the sequence of parts. This can be solved by talking to learners and expressing the reasons for breaking actions down into smaller parts. An example from badminton illustrates this point. On introducing a backhand clear to learners, the coach could indicate why this is a good stroke to add to their repertoire. They could talk about the need to force opponents to the backcourt to gain extra time for recovery. The coach could illustrate this by setting up practice of a low drive and a high clear with a view to comparing the relative recovery times to base. This would reinforce the importance of the movement and help motivate the learner to greater effort. In subsequent practices, the coach would draw attention to occurrences of the backhand clear in the game situation in order to highlight its importance and application.

KEY POINT

SKILL IS :
• Goal directed
• Learned
• Efficient
• Reflected in a complex sequence of nervous activity

Learning

We shall elaborate later, but at this stage it is sufficient to point out two things. Firstly, the coach must consider what are the correct kinds of learning experiences needed to develop skill. S/he must, for example, devise the correct type and length of physical practice for the learner. How long should the gymnast practice a routine on the rings and how many unsuccessful attempts should they be allowed to make before moving onto something different? Should techniques be treated as 'wholes' or broken down into smaller parts? Should practice include a variety of new skills or should it be blocked to repeat practice on just one or two? How should the amount of time spent physically practising be balanced with different experiences such as watching others perform, discussing problems with fellow learners, critically evaluating ones own skill, mentally rehearsing and so on. Non-physical experiences like these are vital to learning. The old adage 'practice makes perfect' is not always correct. Valid practice must be mixed with other experiences and for different learners in different ways.

Secondly, the coach must be assured that learning has taken place. Learning cannot be assumed to take place simply because the learner understands what is to be done and performs well once or twice. The learner may perform well today but not the next time the action is attempted. There is a critical difference between performing well during practice and repeating that success at a later time. As noted before, learning is recognised by a permanent change in performance that remains relatively stable over time. The coach must be convinced that learning has taken place and this will involve not only structuring repeated practice, but also monitoring and evaluating progress in some way. Evaluation might be through direct visual observation or through more objective means such as using a skill or fitness test, videotaping the learner or encouraging the learner to keep a logbook that is monitored on a regular basis.

Efficiency

If skilled movement meets certain criteria concerned with effectiveness and economy of action then the coach or teacher must know what constitutes good performance. Coaches and teachers (perhaps to a lesser degree) must be 'technically articulate'. Judges in any competitive sport where technique is evaluated, e.g., gymnastics or ice skating know what skilled movement looks like and are able to make assessments of good and bad performance very quickly. They are able to compare what they see with an internal memory of the correct performance and spot errors immediately. The coach may not need to be quite so speedy in his or her judgement but they must be accurate. Only then will the coach be able to tell whether the learner is improving, consolidating a bad habit or progressing at a slow rate and thus be in a position to give feedback enabling learning to continue. The process of error detection and correction and the techniques available are considered in a later chapter.

> ### KEY QUOTE
>
> *"Although techniques may be regarded to conform to an accepted standard (eg., there is a technical blueprint for performing moves in gymnastics upon which they are judged), skilful movement is highly individual. A skilful tennis serve or basketball shot can be executed in a number of different ways; skilful swimmers or track athletes may have different styles; skaters performing the same compulsory figure have been shown to execute the action in slightly different ways. The same movement outcome can be achieved in a variety of ways by different people"*
> **Archontides et al** (1994)

Before leaving the matter of skill efficiency it should be understood that skilled movements are not always so rigid and well defined that a strict movement pattern should be followed in a precisely executed manner. The environment is relatively 'forgiving'. Skilled movement can be flexible in that a small degree of 'error' is usually possible whilst still allowing success. For example, the timing of catching a ball can be a little late or early but the ball will still be held. Research has shown that when catching a lawn tennis ball moving at 10 metres/sec the catcher has a time window of 60 msec in order to avoid timing errors in grasping (Alderson, Sully and Sully, 1974). *Figure 4*, over, illustrates this principle.

Using the same principle we can see that Olympic and club class athletes might well

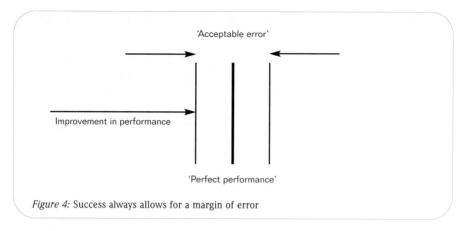

Figure 4: Success always allows for a margin of error

make the same general movement, but their technique and therefore the ultimate quality of that movement will be different. It is the same general movement but the technique is different. The same could be said for many other actions (e.g., tennis serve, triple jump, chest pass, sweep stroke in canoeing). The implication here is that the coach must teach and expect performance from people that is appropriate to their level of competence. It could be harmful for example, to expect a novice high jumper to practice a Fosbury flop on their first attempt. An easier/lower risk technique such as the western roll might be more appropriate. The same principle applies to individuals who differ in their body shape or fitness levels. A person's physical make-up may well dictate the manner in which they execute a movement. The sensitive coach acknowledges this by expecting performance only within the physical constraints of the learner's make-up.

Central Nervous System Processing

This final point is absolutely critical. The way in which movements are carried out is just the final outcome of what may be considered to be a whole sequence of processes including sensing and perceiving information, attending to the right things, making decisions at the correct time and anticipating when certain things will take place. To be proficient, a player has to be skilled not only in carrying out movements, but also skilled in these unseen processes which take place in the brain before the movement is executed. Let

> ⌐**KEY POINT**
>
> The four characteristics that define skill (goal direction, learned, efficient, complex sequence of nervous activity) each has implications for teaching skills and should be used by the teacher or coach to help shape practice.

us give some examples of this. If we take a rock climber ascending a new route, then he must plan movements that are mechanically efficient and 'matched' to fit the characteristics of the rock. He must also use his knowledge of the rock to identify possible hand and footholds and to anticipate combinations of moves that will put him in a balanced position. It is said that a rock climber 'climbs with his eyes'. He needs perceptual skills, decision making ability as well as motor skill. If proficient in all aspects he should be able to execute skilled movements and be seen by others to move skilfully. To take another example, consider a young girl learning to play soccer. Initially she will grapple with the physical movements of kicking, trapping the ball, etc., as well as the problem of learning rules and basic tactics such as where to pass the ball, who to pass it to and when to release it. To the beginner, there are perceptual, decision making and motor elements to worry about. As the child becomes more skilled then action depends less on ball control and trapping ability, etc., and more on cognitive aspects such as tactics, anticipation, decision making, confusing the opposition, etc. This example demonstrates not only the unseen internal factors involved in skill but also indicates how their relative balance may alter through learning. Thus, different skill levels present different kinds of problems.

Some aspects of skill may require emphasis at one stage of learning whilst others take over at a later stage. This is an issue about which the coach or teacher needs to be fully aware, for it is only logical that they present to the learner, skills and ideas which are pertinent to their level of expertise and understanding. Too often, instructors tend to get bogged down with the techniques of their sport at the expense of other important aspects. They must be aware of which points to emphasise, which cues to draw attention to and which techniques to introduce at each stage of development. This is a topic that we'll return to when dealing with the issue of breaking complex actions into smaller parts.

SKILLS, ABILITIES AND TECHNIQUES

It should be clear from what has already been said that there is a difference between skills and techniques. Techniques describe movement patterns. When you watch

Hand-eye co-ordination is a basic ability

someone perform you observe techniques being executed. Techniques reside outside the performer. Until they move there is no way of knowing if technique is good or bad. Techniques lend themselves to measurement. A coach might video a performer to provide precise data on temporal or spatial accuracy and patterning. This kind of analysis would be of particular interest to the bio-mechanist.

Skills are not techniques, but they underlie techniques. Skill is concerned with the application of good techniques at the correct time. A player may have a repertoire of good techniques (e.g., the expert football juggler), but be unable to use them in the game situation. Such a person would not be skilled. As already emphasised, it is vital through learning that learners understand how and when to apply techniques. Skill therefore is reflected in techniques and can only be judged through the execution of techniques.

A word that sometimes causes confusion is the word ability. We often refer to an able or skilled person and we may say that someone has lots of abilities. The words skill and ability are frequently used interchangeably, but they are not the same. To clarify the exact meaning it is useful to think of an ability as something which the learner possesses (as distinct from techniques which, as we have noted above happen outside the person) and which is more general than skill. In addition, abilities should be thought of as genetically determined whereas skill is learned. Abilities are inherited and relatively enduring characteristics that underlie a person's potential to acquire skill and perform a variety of skills.

It is suggested that to be skilful, say in gymnastics, the individual must possess a given profile of underlying abilities. In the case of gymnastics we might list such abilities as kinesthetic awareness (sensitivity to movement via internal feelings within the muscles and joints), manual dexterity (use of the hands and arms to carry out fine movements), control precision (highly controlled movement adjustment involving the use of large muscles) and co-ordination (the capacity to balance when moving quickly or poised in a still position). The important thing to note here is that such abilities are not specific to gymnastics; they may be intrinsic to other sports also. *Figure 5* is adapted from Scully (1996) and shows the kind of thinking on this subject.

Theoretically, it is possible to define the underlying abilities that contribute to any sport, but this is an area of research that has proved to be very difficult to assess. If it were possible to do this, then it could be reasoned that instruction should be devoted to enhancing people's abilities rather than skill in particular sports. And because some abilities are stronger in some people than with others, focus could be placed on only

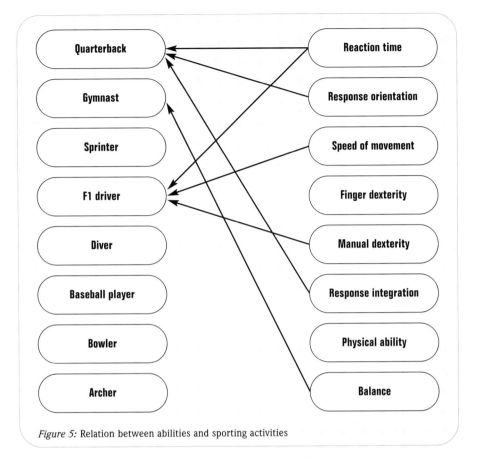

Figure 5: Relation between abilities and sporting activities

those requiring development. In this way, not only would time be saved but, learners might be more able to transfer their learning between sports that share common abilities. This kind of thinking applies in movement education where underlying movement concepts such as timing and flow are developed in the belief they will transfer to subsequent sports. More research is needed on this matter.

One topic that has received support from research is the idea that abilities important in early learning may not be the same as those required later. It is thought that the 'structure' or profile of abilities required in a particular sport changes as the learner becomes more competent. This idea would account for the common example of the youngster who 'stars' early on, but never achieves her expected performance: she possesses the correct mix of abilities as a beginner but not as an expert.

We shall return to this issue in a later chapter

when looking at teaching beginners and experts and also when considering the topic of task analysis. *Figure 6*, below, summarises the relationship between skill, ability and techniques. The interested reader may wish to refer to Schmidt and Wrisberg (2000) who provide a more detailed account of the relationship between skill and abilities.

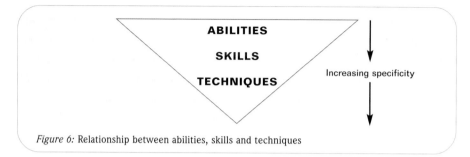

Figure 6: Relationship between abilities, skills and techniques

CLASSIFYING SKILLS

Just imagine how many different sports exist – individual sports, team sports, aquatic sports, outdoor sports, indoor sports, motor sports, combat sports and so on. A list of specific sports and activities would probably run into hundreds. How do researchers begin to analyse such a vast array of different activities? Is it possible to classify particular sports in a manner that

> ## ◯⃞KEY POINT
>
> Classifying skills into particular categories makes the task of understanding the [learning and teaching] demands of specific skills much easier.

makes it sensible to examine categories of sports rather than individual ones? For example, is it possible to group certain sports that are alike in terms of the problems they present for learning or the demands they place on fitness requirements? This topic has been looked at over the years. Today, we have a reasonably clear taxonomy or classification of skills which makes the task of teaching and instructing a lot easier as we can identify classes of skills which do present similar kinds of problems and challenges for the learner and teacher. Let's examine some of the major ways in which skills are classified. Davis, Bull, Roscoe and Roscoe (2000) give further examples of the following four classification systems. It is wise to think of each system as a continuum rather than a dichotomy.

Open and closed skills

This is the most common categorisation. All skills take place within an environment that is more or less variable. In some skills, the environment plays a significant part in how someone performs or learns. Team games such as football and hockey come into this category. Thus in football, the precise action of a player at any moment in time depends on their position on the field, who has possession of the ball and whether their team is defending or attacking. It might also depend on the weather, state of the pitch and the behaviour of the crowd. Climbing a mountain or kayaking a swollen river are similarly influenced by environmental conditions such as weather and temperature. Skills that are performed in an environment which is constantly changing and presents uncertainty about what to do, when to act and how to perform are referred to as open skills. Skills that take place in a relatively stable environment that is predictable are referred to as closed skills. Closed sports skills include trampolining, archery and gymnastics. It is important to note that it is not always correct to classify skills like this. In some circumstances, sports which are referred to as open, contain closed skills. Thus a free kick or penalty in football is a closed skill that takes place within an open sport. And a golfer playing a drive (closed skill) may be influenced from time to time by the wind speed and direction or the behaviour of the crowd. In this case, the closed skill becomes an open skill.

Discrete and continuous skills

Quite separate from the open/closed distinction is that between discrete and continuous skills. Here, attention focuses on the beginning and end points of the movements involved. Skills which take place very quickly and which are very well defined in terms of their technical description (e.g., golf swing, striking a cricket ball) are referred to as discrete skills. Skills that do not have a readily defined beginning and end point such as swimming, cycling and skating, but which still have a regular pattern embedded within them, are referred to as continuous skills. Continuous skills tend to be more slowly executed than discrete skills and can be stopped by the performer mid-way through. There are other skills that are neither discrete or continuous and these are called serial skills. Skills such as dribbling a hockey ball, a tumbling routine or figure skating are comprised of discrete skills that are linked together in a co-ordinated manner.

Gross and fine skills

Skills can be categorised in terms of movement precision. For example, handwriting, throwing a dart and typing require greater spatial precision than skills such as dribbling a ball and swimming. In the former examples, accuracy tends to depend on the action of small muscle groups. In the latter examples, it is larger muscle groups that tend to be involved. The former set of skills are called fine motor skills and the latter are called gross motor skills. Again, this distinction is not an exact one since there are many skills that require the action of large muscle groups to make a very precise movement. Take, for example, high jumping or the run-up in a triple jump. Whilst many large muscle groups are required (leg, arm, stomach muscles), skills hinges on their capacity to generate movements which require to be within an accuracy of millimetres.

Self-paced and externally-paced skills

It is possible to categorise skills according to whether the individual has control over the timing or pacing of the skill. Self-paced skills are those where the individual has control over these aspects. Examples include a golf swing, cycling and swimming. Here, the individual decides when to initiate movement and, in many cases, the pace or speed of movement. Externally-paced skills include, dribbling a football, sprint start and kayaking a rapid. Here, actions depend largely on events taking place in the environment. The challenge for the performer is their skill in choosing the right skill at the right moment to meet the given circumstances.

Simple and complex skills

Complexity is a function of a wide variety of variables that includes the accuracy required, the number of movements and muscles involved, the speed with which information has to be processed and the number of decisions required for performance to be successful. Thus, a gymnastic vault involving somersaults and twists is more complex than say casting with a fishing rod. And a footballer who attempts to dribble past three of four defenders before finally shooting for goal, executes a more complicated sequence of movements that a sprinter attempting to run 100 metres as fast as possible. The division between simple and complex is largely a function of the 'central' information-processing required of the individual rather than the shape or character of the technical performance although the two are often bound together. A practical analogy is to say that the simplicity or complexity of a skill is not unlike that between easy/difficult. However, whilst the difficulty of a skill may change with learning (a difficult skill becomes easy), the level of complexity remains constant.

Integrated and sequential skills

All skills involve a combination of movements. For example, at one level, a golf swing could be described as comprising the initial stance, backswing and foreswing and follow-through. Indeed, every movement has at least two phases; a preparatory phase and an action phase. The preparatory phase usually involves some kind of postural adjustment to place the performer in a mechanically efficient position to carry out the main action.

In many skills, the action of one movement is inextricably linked to the action of a movement before and/or the one afterwards. For example, a move in ice climbing involves planting two ice axes into the ice, moving up with one leg and then moving up with the other; there is a synchronicity and rhythm in the overall action. And with breast-stroke swimming, the arm action is timed precisely with both the leg action and the breathing. These are examples of highly organised or integrated skills.

In contrast, a simple forward roll is less organised since the actions of pushing forwards, tucking and opening are less time dependent; they are more sequential in nature. Whether the 'parts' of a skill are integrated or not has a significant bearing on how

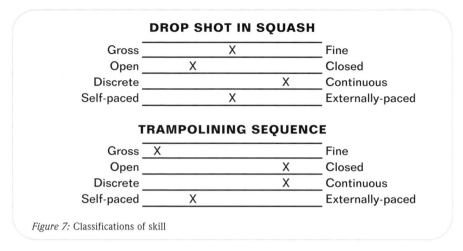

DROP SHOT IN SQUASH

Gross		X		Fine
Open	X			Closed
Discrete			X	Continuous
Self-paced		X		Externally-paced

TRAMPOLINING SEQUENCE

Gross	X			Fine
Open			X	Closed
Discrete			X	Continuous
Self-paced		X		Externally-paced

Figure 7: Classifications of skill

they should be practiced. Highly organised skills are best practices as a whole whereas less organised skills can be practiced in parts.

It should be noted that the various classifications of skills are not independent of one another. Any particular skill can be classified according to each of the above classification systems. Thus, a golf swing could be described as closed, discrete, self-paced and gross in nature. Some other examples are shown in *Figure 7*. The exact description of a skill has a bearing not only on its physical (fitness) requirements, but also how it is best taught and practiced. This point is underlined by Matheson and Mace (2001):

> *"By analysing the skill in this way, it is possible to devise teaching and learning strategies that will enhance the skill and improve the performance for an individual player. If the coach and performer can understand the nature of the task, then performance can be optimised through determining where the strengths and weaknesses of an individual performing a skill lie. Such an understanding will also improve knowledge of the perceptual requirements of the skill, i.e., what cues have to be attended to in order to complete the task successfully."*

RELATIVITY OF SKILL

It should be clear from the above notes that skill has a number of well-defined characteristics. Specifically, skill belongs to the individual. On the basis of these characteristics an individual may be considered skilled or not so skilled. However, there are circumstances when such a

> **KEY POINT**
>
> Skill is not absolute. Sometimes the skill of an individual depends on the skill of an onlooker!

judgement is less clear because it depends on the context in which the skill is displayed. Let's take a few examples by way of illustration. The author was once an amateur football player with aspirations to play at professional level. Within his circle of friends he was considered to be a 'competent' player with 'good' promise. When he emigrated to Canada and resumed his football (now called soccer) career, he found that he was a 'star' overnight; there were very few people with equal or better skills. On the downside, he also used to play basketball at University level. When he made moves to join the Canadian University squad, he failed to make the sixth team! These examples demonstrate that skill has a relative dimension. It depends on whom you play with and the context of your performance. Of course, this has a bearing on how good learners feel about themselves when performing in the company of others of equal competence. Those who are slightly more proficient than others (but still relatively unskilled) may feel as if they are real stars. The key for the teacher/coach is to encourage such interest and motivation without 'spilling the beans' about their real performance.

Another example of the relative nature of skill is seen in the competitive environment. There are many occasions when the skill of an individual, or team for that matter, depends on the judgement of others. A good example of this is seen in gymnastics. A number of judges decide the score awarded to a gymnast and consequently how well the gymnast is ranked against others in the competition. The fact that each judge may give a different score shows that skill is not absolute; it depends in part on the skill of the judges. The same problem arises when an umpire in cricket judges a batsman to be caught 'leg before wicket' or when a football referee gives a 'yellow' card to a player. In each case, the competence (or lack) of the player is decided by another person. Uncertain situations like this, where decisions by the referee can have drastic outcomes, are gradually being reduced through the use of video replay. In some sports such as rugby and cricket, the referee or umpire, now has recourse to film of the action before a final decision is made.

Finally, readers may care to consider the relative importance society places on sport and the value it accords to highly skilled sports people such as David Beckham and Paula Radcliffe. How does society value the importance of sporting talent against say the skill of a surgeon, painter, politician, musician or linguist? How are these values reflected in newspaper coverage of the different subjects, government financing for promotion and curricular time in schools to develop relevant skills? How important is physical education and sport in schools compared to say English or mathematics? Does the significant decline in number of playing fields, reduced funding for sports councils, declining standards in sport at international level, decreasing levels of fitness and the increasing levels of obesity in society, say something about the true value of sport in our society?

ARE YOU INTERESTED?

A brief but very important topic to finish this chapter. Here are some questions to think about. What are the key factors that contribute to skill? What limits a person's potential? Why are some people very good and others only mediocre? What is the single most important factor dictating ultimate skill level? There are no clear answers to any of these questions because so many factors combine and play a part – inherited abilities, practical experience, availability of good coaching, equipment and clothing factors, encouragement from peers and family members, fitness levels and so on.

However, one factor is fundamental to skill acquisition at all levels – level of interest. Most people agree that if a person is not interested in learning they will learn very little if anything at all! How many coaches and teachers have tried in vain to encourage children to take part or learn new skills, only to be thwarted at every stage? Quite simply, there has to be a will or motivation to learn. Interest in an activity and a desire to improve is the basis of all learning – a point emphasised by the cognitive/experiential school of learning (see Chapter 2).

The key question is how do you ensure that someone wants to learn? In a coaching situation this may not be a particular problem since, by and large, coaches deal with people who have chosen to take part in a particular sport/activity. They have already demonstrated an interest by choosing to take part in the first place. However, coaches come across people who, for reasons such as peer pressure, declining fitness and injuries, begin to loose interest. But, by and large, coaches work with people who show commitment and enthusiasm and there is little need to develop or encourage these qualities. In contrast, a physical education teacher faced with say 30 newcomers to a sport may have an uphill task convincing everyone of the need to take part and learn new skills.

Enjoyment is fundamental to learning

There are a number of key issues here. Firstly, it is vital for all those who want to help others develop their skill in sport to be aware that learner interest is a critical prerequisite to learning. Interest and enthusiasm is the foundation or bedrock of all learning. Secondly (and linked to the first) is the ability of teachers and coaches to know how to gauge levels of interest. How do you know those in your charge really want to learn the skills you wish to teach? Apart from obvious signs (negative signs of boredom and frustration or positive signs of excitement and eagerness) it is important to talk to learners and determine what are their goals and interests. Learners should be questioned about why

Gross errors are a feature of early learning. Interest is lost if the learner fails to move forwards (!) quickly.

they enjoy a particular sport/ activity, or what they wish to learn. They should also be questioned about any previous experience in related sports.

Understanding why people want to take part and what their aspirations are provides solid evidence of interest level. Those who do not wish to be involved will quickly be identified. Involving learners like this (as active participants in the learning process) is a key principle highlighted throughout this book. Indeed, the very process of talking to learners about their needs, wishes and problems is also a useful motivating strategy. The third issue centres on this very topic. How do you develop a person's level of interest and motivation to succeed? It might be impossible to generate an interest which is clearly lacking (the author has no interest in snooker or golf and no efforts to convince him would ever be successful!), but there are many ways to nurture enthusiasm, develop sporting potential and raise interest to a point well beyond initial levels.

These methods relate to the 'style' adopted by the teacher or coach, the manner in which practice is devised and structured, the kind of feedback given and how it is administered, how information is imparted to learners, how learning goals are established, motivational tools, and so on.

The main aim of this book is to show how these and other factors influence skill acquisition. But a secondary aim is to highlight how the manipulation of these variables can also exert a powerful influence on a person's level of interest. All teachers and coaches should always be mindful of the critical need to play to a 'captive audience'.

"An interest in your chosen sport or activity is vital if you are to remain motivated and inspired. Take, for example, hillwalking which is a popular leisure activity. Enthusiasm and commitment compel people to leave their beds at an ungodly hour, sweat up a mountain carrying a heavy pack, endure extreme cold

and heavy rain showers and sometimes risk life and limb on a precipitous rock face. Interest can drive people to great heights!"

Saunders (2003)
(Nina Saunders is an expedition leader)

SUMMARY OF KEY POINTS

• Skill is defined by four criteria. It is goal-directed. It is learned. Skill results in actions that are efficient in terms of their outlay in energy/time. Skill involves 'internal processing' as well as physical action.

• Learners should understand the aims of their learning experiences and be informed about why they are practicing or training in certain ways.

• Physical practice is only one way in which the learner acquires skill and knowledge. Other experiences such as watching athletes perform, viewing video film of themselves in action and mental practice are equally important.

• The performance of learners should be monitored in order to evaluate whether or not learning is taking place.

• The coach/teacher should know what skilled performance looks like and be able to detect and correct errors. Observation ability is based on technical knowledge, coaching/teaching experience as well as personal experience in sport.

• It should be acknowledged that different people perform the same movement in different ways and allowance should be made for variations in technique between people.

• Skill is relative in the sense that whilst two people may perform competently at their particular level of play (e.g., Olympic or club) they may both be judged as skilled players by their respective colleagues.

• The coach and teacher should know what are the important ingredients that contribute to skill. They should understand what are the perceptual aspects (e.g., what information to attend to, what information to ignore), the decision making aspects (e.g., when to time an action, how many ways of executing movements) as well as the motor aspects (nature of the movement pattern, importance of feedback). In addition, it should be clear when is the appropriate time for each element to be introduced to the learner.

• Skills can be categorised in particular ways – fine or gross, open or closed, etc. Understanding how a skill is categorised helps identify the key aspects relevant to practice.

- Techniques are movement patterns. Skill reflects itself in good technique. Abilities, which are enduring, inherited qualities form the basis of skill. To be skilled and hence demonstrate good technique requires the possession of appropriate underlying abilities.

- Interest level is fundamental to learning. Anyone helping learners to develop their skill should be aware of strategies to both develop and maintain interest.

PRACTICAL TASKS

- Gather together three or four friends and select a videotape of a sporting event – say an International athletics match or football match. If the film depicts an individual athlete (say a gymnast or athlete) watch them perform for say 10 minutes. This may involve watching a repeat of an individual performance such as a long jump or sprint race. If the film depicts a ball game then identify a 10 minute section of play. As a group, watch the section of film with a view to rating the skill level of either the individual or team on a one-to-ten scale (one is good, ten is poor). Do not talk to each other or share any thoughts until you have each declared your scores. It is likely the scores will differ. Now discuss why they differ. Try to identify where you differ and where you agree. Also try to determine the reasons you see different things. Is anyone prepared to alter their views having heard the others speak?

- Keep the same group of people. Identify someone in the group who is prepared to have a go at three-ball juggling (use three lawn tennis balls or juggling balls if available). Observe the person juggle for a couple of minutes. Firstly, try to describe their performance in qualitative terms (how co-ordinated, fluent, balanced, precise, etc.). Write down a few notes. Then, whatever their level of skill, attempt to provide some useful feedback (without being too cruel!). Give a few more minutes for practice and then write down again a few descriptive comments about the skill level. What differences did you note? What changes took place? How did improvement manifest itself? If there are no differences, try to explain why there was no improvement from one practice to the next.

- This task requires two people. Sit down and each take five minutes to make out a list of ten sports (e.g., curling) or skilled actions (e.g., back flip). Once the lists are complete exchange them. Now identify the place of each sport/action on each of the following continuums: open/closed, discrete/continuous, simple/complex, self-paced/externally-paced. Once this is complete, exchange sheets and examine whether or not you agree with your partner.

- Work in pairs and stand about ten feet apart. Take a lawn tennis ball and throw it underarm to your partner so it arrives about waist height. Exchange the ball a few times until you get a good feel for the task. Now, throw the ball again but this time, the catcher keeps their eyes closed! It is important to make a comment (such as "Now") to indicate when you release the ball and also, to make the flight of the ball the same every time. Provide your partner with feedback such as "Late" or "Early". Repeat this several times. You should find that with practice, it is possible to catch the ball even though it has not been seen. This goes to demonstrate the importance of anticipation in skilled performance as well as the value of feedback in learning.

REVIEW QUESTIONS

How you answer these questions depends on your experience and whether you have any experience working as a coach or teacher. There are no specified correct answers to each question. These questions can be answered alone or, better still, in pairs or small groups. Comparisons can then be made in order to see the kinds of ideas other people bring forward. Don't forget that learning is a social activity. There is much scope for learning by listening to other people and taking their ideas on board.

• Identify a sport or skilled movement that involves a strong emphasise on perception and decision making. In contrast, identify a sport or skilled movement that places greater emphasis on technique and movement execution.

• Take a particular sport and identify some elements that should be learned before others. What are those elements? If the order of introduction does not matter, indicate why not.

• What methods are available for getting across the idea of the elements identified in the last question, without employing actual physical practice?

• What objective procedures (e.g., tests) could you employ to verify skill improvement?

• Take a particular technique from one of the sports/skills chosen in the first question. Describe clearly the difference seen when comparing the action performed correctly and performed incorrectly? In other words, what kinds of errors might you observe?

• Are there any elements of this sport/skill that the learner concentrates on initially but later goes unnoticed?

• If you have some coaching experience, give an example where the skill of your players/performers is limited by their age, gender or lack of strength.

• As a performer, have you ever felt that a limitation to your skill level was a physical weakness? What was it?

• It is sometimes said that a person who has reached a high level of personal performance in their sport does not necessarily make a good coach! It is reasoned that the expert may forget the problems and issues relevant to early learning and attempt to impose high level technique and concepts on the learner too early. Comment on this argument from your own perspective. Have you ever seen this happen? Have you been a culprit? Have you ever been on the receiving end of such coaching?

• Take another sport or skill and identify the sources of external information the performer needs in order to carry out the action successfully.

• State where on the open/closed skill continuum the following skills lie – hockey penalty flick, basketball dribble, receiving a serve in lawn tennis, uprighting a capsized kayak, triple jump.

• Why is difficult to classify skills accurately? Indicate one skill that can change depending on circumstances.

References

Alderson, G.J.K., Sully, D.J. and Sully, H.G. (1974). An operational analysis of a one-handed catching task using high speed photography. *Journal of Motor Behaviour,* 6, 217-226.

Archontides, C., Fazey, J., Smith, N. and Crisfield, P. (1994). *Understanding and improving skill* (Coach resource pack). Leeds: National Coaching Foundation.

Davis, B., Bull, S., Roscoe, P. and Roscoe, D. (2000). *Physical education and the study of sport.* London: Harcourt Publishers Limited.

Foxon, F. (1999). *Improving practices and skill.* Leeds: The National Coaching Foundation.

Magill, R. (1993). *Motor learning: concepts and applications.* Dubuque, Iowa: Brown and Benchmark.

Martens, R. (1997). *Successful coaching* (2nd Edition). Champaign, Illinois: Human Kinetics.

Matheson, H. and Mace, R. (2001). *Skill in sport.* Droitwich: Sport in Mind.

McCarthy, J. (1990). *Journal of the Canadian Association for Health, Physical Education and Recreation,* 56, 3, 34-35.

Mind over matter (Video, 1986). Leeds: National Coaching Foundation.

Saunders, N. (2003). *Personal communication*. 1st September, 2003.

Shedden, J. Quotations from Sharp, R.H. (1986). *Acquiring skill* (Coaching education module 1). Edinburgh: Scottish Sports Council.

Schmidt, R.A. and Wrisberg, C. (1999). *Motor learning and performance* (2nd Edition). Champaign, Illinois: Human Kinetics.

Scully, D. (1996). *Skill acquisition*. In P. Beashel and J. Taylor (Eds.). *Advanced studies in physical education and sport*. Walton-on-Thames: Thomas Nelson and Sons Ltd.

Williams, M.H. (1998). *The ergogenics edge*. Champaign, Illinois: Human Kinetics.

CHAPTER 2 – THEORY INTO PRACTICE

"... there is no single theory of learning that would explain learning or the lack of it in all situations, and therefore, there can be no single approach to instruction. Each theory of learning is used to support an approach to instruction. Each has but a piece of a very complex phenomenon we call learning."

Rink (1999)

WHAT ARE THEORIES?

A chapter devoted to theories is almost guaranteed to turn away readers! Please don't – much invaluable information is contained in the next few pages. There is a common view that theories are not relevant to practice, they are difficult to understand and very remote from the real world, especially the very practical world of teaching and coaching. This view has some

 **KEY QUOTE**

"Boxing got me started on philosophy. You bash them, they bash you and you think, what's it all for?"
Arthur Mullard

validity. Indeed, how often do we hear the cliché 'it's OK in theory, but it rarely works in practice'. The author asks readers to be patient and read on. There is much in this chapter that will confirm the thoughts and practice of many people and enlighten others on how they may develop their teaching and coaching approaches.

Let's begin by examining how theories develop. We'll take a couple of examples from the sporting world. Suppose two coaches are working with similar-ability gymnasts and that one group learns a lot faster than the other does. A third coach who observes this also notes the better group are coached by someone who seems to have a much better relationship with his athletes - he takes more time with individuals, he offers very informative advice and is more understanding, etc. Add to this another situation, this time skiing, and suppose that an aspirant skier is having extreme difficulty progressing beyond, say, the snow plough stage. After years of practice she is getting no closer to skiing parallel than when she first began. She then decides to take a course with a professional instructor who videos her performance and, all of a sudden, things improve – she begins to un-weight at the correct time, her skis are closer together and her body posture is better.

What do these two scenarios suggest? Well, they seem to indicate that feedback information – of a certain kind – is crucial to success. In the first example it is what the coach says and in the second example it is what the learner sees. Suppose we explored this idea and found that it held well in many other situations with different sports and different people. All of these observations would lead to some kind of statement/s about the value of feedback in the learning process. For example, it might be concluded that 'long term improvements take place only if the learner receives continuous feedback about their performance'. This statement could be the starting point for a new theory about skill learning; it is a generalisation about how something works.

A theory is a general statement (or set of such statements) based on observations, experiences and perhaps formal research which accounts for and summarises numerous observations.

KEY QUOTE

"Like maps in general, models and theories should not be regarded as exact copies of the processes they attempt to explain. Theories, like maps, are tools that are devised for a particular purpose. Hence a map of the London Underground system is very well adapted to helping you travel by underground train across London, but incorporates distortions of scale and direction that would be quite misleading as a guide to driving by car across London."
Baddely (1997)

Theories are rather like educated guesses that describe or explain how/why things occur. Well known theories include Einstein's *Theory of Relativity* and Newton's *Laws of Motion*. The latter has particular application in the world of sport because it predicts very accurately the movement of players and objects such as the flight of a football as it is kicked from one player to another. Theories of learning attempt to explain why people learn and also describe the conditions for learning to take place. It is important to recognise that theories are tentative. Because they only describe current observations and cannot verify what might hold true in the future, they must always be treated with some suspicion. Indeed, it is just this uncertainty which stimulates researchers to examine them further. They do this by using the theory to generate or predict other phenomena to test.

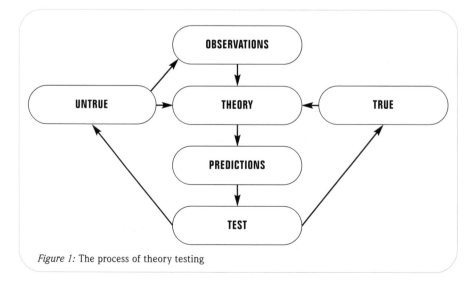

Figure 1: The process of theory testing

If the predictions hold good then the theory is strengthened (and in time may become a law) but if not, then the theory is weakened and consequently modified or rejected (see *Figure 1*). In the gymnastics/feedback example above, it would be possible to make many predictions. For example, if feedback was initially given to a learner – say a gymnast practicing a new floor routine – and then withheld as she continued practice, performance would be expected to increase and then plateau. This could be tested (although it might not be ethical to do it for real – a laboratory equivalent might be constructed) and the results would let us know if the theory was robust or not. Out of interest, the reader may wish to guess the outcome of such an experiment.

Theories then, are more than single observations, they are generalisations and they may not always be correct. As Robson (1993) says:

"A theory is a general statement that summarises and organises knowledge by proposing a general relationship between events - if it is a good one, it will cover a large number of events and predict events that have not yet occurred or been observed."

So what is their value to the practicing teacher or coach? Quite simply, they give direction and structure to ones thinking, planning and practice. They provide a reliable and sound framework within which to work. Rather than trying things out in a piecemeal fashion – 'off the top of your head' – theories allow the teacher and coach to cash in on principles and ideas that have been shown to work or stand a good chance of working.

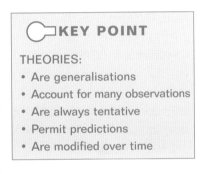

KEY POINT

THEORIES:
• Are generalisations
• Account for many observations
• Are always tentative
• Permit predictions
• Are modified over time

The wise person may have at their disposal a variety of theoretical ideas and principles that can be used when appropriate and when circumstances demand. This would be called a pragmatic approach. What they will find is that theories do not always work nor do they always work consistently. For example, a well known (and very simple) theory is that feedback should always accompany practice. However, presenting some learners with too much feedback may have the opposite effect to improving their skill level. Theories do not always work or work the same for all individuals.

Effective teaching is therefore the timely application of theoretical principles together with ideas and approaches acquired through experience. In time and with much practice, the wise teacher or coach probably develops a personal theory about how people learn best – an internal model constructed from recognised learning theories together with principles derived from effective practice. And of course the good teacher will be prepared to modify ideas and change approaches as experience grows and develops and as theoretical knowledge also changes. Indeed, some theories stand the test of time (particularly those in the physical world such as Newton's *Laws of Motion*), whilst those which attempt to explain human behaviour are less robust. As Key (2003) says:

"History brings with it changes in the way we see the world, shifts in perspective that completely alter our fundamental beliefs and the consequential ways we live our lives"

It is also worth clarifying at this stage the value of research to the practicing coach or teacher. Research provides the 'raw data' for theory construction (called the 'inductive' process). Because it is often carried out under meticulous and well controlled circumstances, there is a tendency to think that research provides clear answers and stable ground plans for action. The view expressed in this book is that research, just like experience and theories, provides nothing more than food for thought and information that the coach can use or discard at his will. Magill (1990) is of the view that research can be an invaluable aid to developing teaching guidelines and Whiting (1982) underlines this point when he says that:

"... research does not tell people what to do, but only provides some of the information on which judgements might be based as to the value of one procedure rather than another."

Readers may care to note that this book is based on the author's study of theory, research findings and the observation of teachers/coaches in practice. It is also founded on his own learning and practical experience in sport over many years, together with a lifetime of teaching in sport and outdoor education. The point here is to express the view that whilst theoretical knowledge and understanding is vital to becoming an effective practitioner, it is only one contribution from a wide set of data sources.

UNDERSTANDING SKILL – HISTORICAL LANDMARKS

Before taking a detailed look at some of the key theories relevant to skill acquisition, we will step back in time and note some of the historical landmarks that have helped shape current understanding about skill learning and performance. The investigation of skill learning goes back many decades and this section takes a cursory look at some of the critical ideas and research landmarks that have led to our present stage of understanding. Sometimes, understanding the present is clearer and easier when it is seen in perspective against historical developments. The past always gives direction for future thinking and ideas for new research. And, of course, theories are based on historical information.

One of the most often quoted landmarks is the work of 18th century astronomers at the Greenwich Observatory near London. They noted differences in each other's observations when viewing stars through the telescope. In noting the time of a star's travel some observers consistently underestimated the period of travel compared to others. In addition, these times depended upon how bright was the star and how unexpected it's appearance. What the astronomers were actually noting was the difference in reaction time between people. Reaction time is important in some sports especially those where reflex-like actions are required, e.g., sprint starts or goal keeping.

A century later, Bryan and Harter carried out what is now recognised as the first formal study of skill acquisition when they examined how people learn morse telegraphy (one of the early forms of electrical communication). Morse telegraphy is a complex task that requires the acquisition of a new language, perceptual skill in identifying transmitted messages as well as motor skill essential to sending messages. Bryan and Harter noted two important things. Firstly, that learning is discontinuous in nature. People seem to proceed fairly quickly but then reach a 'plateau' where there is no apparent improvement. After a while they continue to improve once more. Secondly, learners acquire the ability to execute small units of work (e.g., learning how to type single letters) which are later combined into larger units (e.g., typing whole words). We shall examine the validity of so called plateaus later on. The second point, which has been called 'hierarchical learning', is still very much a current topic and has credibility 90 years after it was first conceived. We'll return to this point in the chapter devoted to practice.

During the early part of the last century many psychologists set about to examine how and why people learn. Two competing philosophies emerged, namely the Behaviourist and Cognitive approaches. We shall come back to these topics later in this chapter, but it is important to note here that despite Bryan and Harter's important earlier work, the efforts of the early psychologists did little to further the systematic study of skilled motor performance for the next 30 years. It was during the 1930's that interest in skill learning accelerated through the efforts of researchers in physical education. Investigators, especially in North America, devised practical tests to measure sporting skill and also attempted to identify individual characteristics (human abilities) which predispose people to excellence in sport. During this period, 'time and motion' experts began to look at skill in industrial settings. For example, they assessed how quickly workers carry out tasks (e.g., lathe operations) and what are the factors affecting their speed of working. This work has its modern counterpart in the field of ergonomics. Sports ergonomics is a recent area and is concerned with sports problems such as the design of equipment, the composition of playing surfaces and the manufacture of 'tailor made' running shoes. These matters will be addressed in more detail when we look at guidance.

During the 1940's, research into motor skills accelerated dramatically. The Second World War gave rise to rapid and dramatic technical developments in radar, vehicle control, high speed aircraft, etc., which in turn focused interest on the operational/skill problems this kind of technology presented to the user. The result was an explosion of research – especially by English and North American psychologists – designed to understand the factors that created these difficulties. Investigators looked at problems such as methods of controlling equipment (e.g., use of levers/steering wheels, size of controls), the relationship between displays and controls, etc., etc. Several prominent investigators developed ideas and theories during this time which subsequently spawned a generation of research and which still have currency today. The English psychologist Kenneth Craik was the stimulus for the development of many modern ideas. For example, he raised attention to the importance of timing and anticipation in skilled performance and he laid the foundations for the comparison that is often made between man and computers. Frederick Bartlett was another Cambridge psychologist who, based partly on his personal interests in playing cricket, emphasised many important notions of skill acquisition. For example, he viewed feedback as critical to learning and he also believed that complex skills evolved from much simpler skills – a similar notion to that of Bryan and Harter's.

The '50s and '60s saw further advances in research and changes in philosophy. This period saw the development of 'Information-Processing Theory' and with it the view that man and computers communicate and operate in much the same way. The idea that people take in information from the environment, decide what to do about it and then plan and effect a motor program still has credence and is discussed later. Other people who reached prominence during this time included the American psychologist Paul Fitts who was responsible for, amongst many other things, specifying the stages that people pass through when learning new skills. His three-level theory (cognitive, associative, autonomous stages) was based on comprehensive discussions with teachers, coaches and many others concerned with instructing people. Today, it still stands as a sound description of the learning process. In the 1970s, Jack Adams and Richard Schmidt in North America and David Lees in Scotland spearheaded research on how people control their movements, focusing on the importance of

There isn't a quick fix to gaining wisdom. Wisdom is based on experience. Both of these contribute to the development of theory.

environmental information and different kinds of feedback in the control/learning process. Notions of motor programming, motor schema and the role of errors in learning, which all stem from their work will be discussed throughout this book. The 1970's also saw much attention to short term memory of motor skills and comparisons were made between the way in which people remember words, pictures and physical skills. Research on motor memory has diminished in importance in recent years and overall, the emphasis today centres much more on cognitive processes in skill learning (Baddeley, 1997). Through the 1990's research in skill acquisition has continued in many traditional areas such as practice regimes, attention and motor control. Information processing theory has continued as a major theoretical framework, although the 'dynamical systems theory' approach is beginning to provide an alternative view. Publications such as the Journal of Motor Behavior and the Research Quarterly for Exercise and Sport are the focus for much of the research in skill acquisition at the present time.

Currently, the field of skill acquisition is one that attracts people from many and varied backgrounds, e.g., physical educationalists, sports coaches, sports scientists, child psychologists, ergonomists, physiologists, and so on. Universities offer courses and employ lecturers in the subject, professional organisations mount conferences and many publications focus on skill learning and skilled performance. In Great Britain, skill acquisition is studied in schools as a formal part of the examinable physical education programme and is a core area in the work of 'Sports Coach UK'.

The subject of skill acquisition is well researched and its content and focus continually changes. But, unlike the 'hard', human sciences such as anatomy, physiology and kinesiology which benefit from an abundance of concrete, scientific evidence, much of what we know about how and why people learn stems from practical application and educated reasoning. In physiology there are precise and objective techniques for monitoring the inner workings of the body. In contrast, skill psychology has to base its knowledge largely on behavioural evidence and sound reasoning. As Holding (1989) says:

"Theoretical research soon becomes sterile in the absence of the reinvigoration provoked by practical issues."

The construction and testing of theories is therefore very much an integral part of this subject. With this as a backcloth, it follows that the present text cannot be a tight, prescriptive treatise that describes neat facts all fitting well together. The intention is to raise issues and provoke discussion, helped with examples from the coaching world, and in so doing lead the reader to think more deeply about how people learn.

We will continue with an examination of key principles of the major theories of learning and skill acquisition.

ASSOCIATION OR BEHAVIOURIST THEORIES

Firstly let us take a look at some of the important findings from early psychological research on learning. This work was not aimed specifically at motor skills and much was based on animal research. However, many findings are relevant today and are especially appropriate to sport. Research and thinking in the first half of the twentieth century led to a clear dichotomy between Association (stimulus-response) and Cognitive theories. The difference is fundamental and the implications are quite marked. Association or S-R theories consider that learning is dictated largely by stimuli within the learner's environment and that what is learned is the connection or association between these stimuli and the learner's movements. Connections are strengthened through repetition and reinforcement of correct S-R associations. Internal processes such as perception, thinking and anticipation have little importance within the S-R scheme of things because they are impossible to quantify in the same way stimuli and responses can be accurately measured. Let us examine some of the important principles of Association Theories.

Conditioning – classical and operant – is the fundamental process of learning. Classical conditioning occurs when a previously established stimulus-response connection is replaced by a new connection in which the response remains the same but the stimulus differs. One experiment often cited is of the dog which salivates (the response) when presented with food (the stimulus). There follows a period when a bell is rung at the same time as the food is presented, after which the dog salivates when it hears the bell alone. In

> **⊂]KEY POINT**
>
> ASSOCIATION THEORY
> * Is all about the establishment of links between stimuli and responses
> * Supports the practice of parts: the whole equals the sum of the parts
> * Highlights the value of practice and reinforcement (feedback)

this example, the dog has learned a new relationship, viz., bell-salivation. In humans this kind of learning (sometimes called stimulus generalisation) can occur quite unconsciously, often with negative results. For example, a child who suffers an accident in say rugby football and consequently stops playing, may transfer the dislike to other sports which appear to be dangerous. Positive generalisations may also occur as when someone is rewarded for success in one sport (say they achieve their first proficiency award in swimming) and then develop newly found interests in other sports. What is happening in these examples is some kind of transfer – dislike or enthusiasm. This notion of transfer was not accepted by all of the association theorists. Guthrie viewed that skill comprises a large collection of highly specific associations and that transferring a skill to a new situation only occurs if there has been practice in that situation. Today, we do not accept this very rigid stance, although the principle of skill specificity that was central to Guthrie's theory does have a place in modern thinking as will be examined in a later chapter. We shall also return to the

Before leaving the topic of classical conditioning it is important to stress that there are many examples of stimulus-response learning in teaching which are quite appropriate. For example, when trying to encourage a beginner trampolinist to open from a somersault at the correct time the instructor might shout 'Now'. On hearing this command the learner knows when to open and prepares for landing. The learner may not have the experience to 'feel' the correctness of this action, but it does have the desired effect in producing good timing. With further practice, the learner can take over and begin to control the action because she/he learns to associate the internal feelings accompanying the command. At this point the sound becomes redundant. The use of well-timed commands to stimulate action is a very powerful technique and is applied to many sports. This principle will be returned to later when we discuss the topic of attention.

Operant conditioning is quite different. It is not concerned with associations between stimuli and responses, but the association between responses and their consequences. Take the sport of artistic gymnastics and the case of a coach teaching an upstart on the high bar. Suppose the learner makes repeated attempts, but is only rewarded positively (e.g., praise from the coach) when the correct/nearly correct technique is employed and that poor attempts are not rewarded. In time, the correct technique predominates, i.e., the upstart occurs more often, because the learner strengthens the link between it and its successful outcome. It follows from this that movements which are reinforced are strengthened, whilst those which are not reinforced are weakened. One of the important features of this theory is that reinforcement must be immediate and occur before the learner has had a further chance to act. A corollary to this theory is the idea of behaviour shaping. Shaping is the process of developing complex forms of behaviour in small steps. In the example just given it was assumed the learner would at some point, actually emit the correct technique. However, this is highly unlikely especially with complicated or dangerous skills. Adopting a shaping regime the coach would simplify the overall action and reinforce each small step. Through the reinforcement of closer approximations to the correct technique the overall movement is gradually developed. A related idea is that of part learning. One of the S-R theorists, Skinner, viewed that difficult tasks must be broken into smaller parts each of which grows out of previous learning. Each part must be reinforced separately and in this way the whole skill is gradually built up. Thorndike was also a supporter of operant conditioning and he derived several 'laws of learning' which he believed applied equally well to man and to animals. Thorndike gave great weight to the outcome of learned movements. He felt that satisfying and gratifying outcomes are more likely to lead to repetition of movements than negative outcomes – hence his *Law of Effect*. He also emphasised the importance of practice and repetition – the *Law of Exercise*. Repetition strengthens the association between stimuli and responses whilst lack of practice weakens the association. Thorndike was keen to point out however, that practice alone is not enough - reinforcement must also take place. This idea is still pertinent today and is evident in the statement 'practice, with feedback, makes perfect'. Thorndike's third 'Law of Readiness' was concerned with development of the nervous system and the notion that learning only takes place when the nervous system is sufficiently mature (see chapter on differentiation).

COGNITIVE THEORIES

The cognitive or 'Gestalt' learning theories rose to prominence in the 1920's in opposition to the S-R theories. In contrast to S-R theories, cognitive theories attenuate the importance of stimuli and responses and focus on thought processes, the learner's 'mind' and their understanding of how things relate to one another. The individual's perception which is determined by a multitude of factors including environmental stimuli as well as internal thoughts, expectations and needs, is the driving force in learning. Understanding, meaningfulness and the individual nature of learning are all critical features.

Within Cognitive Theory, the importance of the individual's feelings and motives is recognised

Some proponents of the Cognitive school of thinking viewed insight or intuition as the mechanism of learning. Intuition stems from a problem solving approach. In their experiments with animals they demonstrated that learning is preceded by a period of 'trial and error' learning – although they referred to this period as one of 'purposeful experimentation' – followed by an immediate and permanent improvement. This latter stage was seen as demonstrating the animal's ability to restructure or re-organise all the elements in the display to create an instant solution – the 'Eureka' phenomenon. A good example in gymnastics would be an upstart where the learner who, having already tried unsuccessfully, was then given say an explanation of the mechanics involved and suddenly achieved success – because she now understands how her actions produce correct technique.

The 'Gestalt' theorists who proposed the notion of insightful learning adhered to the principle of 'whole' learning ('the whole is greater than the sum of the parts'). Here, learning is not a matter of connecting particular stimuli with associated responses; rather, the learner uses past experience and current knowledge to plan or predict solutions that involve whole and perhaps lengthy patterns of behaviour.

For the Gestalt theorists, part learning is inefficient because it does not present to the learner all of the information necessary for complete understanding. They would argue that in swimming for example, the stroke should not be broken down into its constituent parts (arm action, breathing, etc.), but be taught as a whole skill. This idea is consistent with the recent emphasis on the 'Games for understanding' approach to teaching activities. As a reflection of this Maynard (1991) suggests that teaching/coaching should permit the learner to make decisions about the tactics to be used in a game situation. He goes on to state that:

"... most teaching is accomplished by creating conditioning or adapting games rather than perfecting in isolation the techniques required in the definitive version of the activity."

This philosophy fits in well with the Gestalt approach because it focuses on learner understanding and the 'wholeness' of activities.

One of the Cognitive school, Tolman put great weight on the importance of goal direction in learning as well as expectation and planning. For Tolman, behaviour was purposeful. Learners consciously strive to achieve particular goals. People learn to recognise cues (e.g., the manner in which a volleyball player prepares his service) and how these cues relate to the solution of specific goals (e.g., how to prepare for and respond to the expected kind of service). Tolman suggested that people acquire cognitive 'maps' or sets of relationships between events – they don't learn movements per se – which can be employed on future occasions to solve related problems. Here, he was stressing the importance of past experience in learning as well as the importance of transfer of learning.

Finally, it is important to mention the significance of individual differences within the cognitive theory of learning. Because learning is based on the individual's perception of problems, their expectations, motivations and needs then, almost by definition, people will inevitably learn in different ways with varying rates of progress. Lewin especially, stressed the importance of individual traits; the learner's motivations and goals, their knowledge and understanding and 'philosophy' on life. Close to this idea is that of 'self concept'. Self concept is the individual's perception of themselves and is based on a number of things such as the person's physical nature, age, experience, values and needs. By and large, people behave in a way that preserves and/or enhances their self concept. This suggests that the manner in which they learn and the content of what they wish to learn is dictated by their self concept. Behaviour therefore is ultimately the result of how things 'appear' to the individual. There are important implications here for teaching which include for example, the need for the teacher/coach to be sensitive to individual needs and competencies. We shall return to this and other issues stemming from the cognitive approach to learning in later chapters. Wade and Tavris (1998) give a comprehensive summary of traditional learning theories and their applications.

HUMANIST THEORY

The Humanist theory of learning emerged as a backlash to behaviourist approaches. It focused on the uniqueness of the individual acknowledging that a person's core personality is their positive drive to fulfilment. Carl Rogers and Abraham Maslow were leading exponents of this theory and looked at the individual as

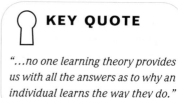

KEY QUOTE

"...no one learning theory provides us with all the answers as to why an individual learns the way they do."
Grant (2002)

having free will and free choice. They postulated that everyone has an ultimate drive towards personal growth and learning. This theory takes an holistic overview of an individual's total personality matrix – their background, upbringing, childhood, life experiences, aspirations, hopes and desires, cultures, ethnicity, gender and religious background. They suggested that a person's total personality and life journey dictates how best they learn rather than a measure of intelligence or social background alone. This view of human learning provides good support for approaches to learning which consider the importance of the individual and their involvement (choice, self analysis and so on) in the learning process, as well as there preferred 'style' of learning (Honey and Mumford, 1992). This latter topic will be elaborated on later in the book.

The approaches to learning we have summarised are quite different and demonstrate a number of divergent views on how human learning occurs. History has shown that people (teachers, researchers, and theorists) have often 'taken sides'. There are a number of possible reasons. For example, researchers often set tasks that tended to demonstrate the kind of learning advocated. In addition, experiments were designed largely to lend support for a particular theory and not to test it. Also, methods of teaching were never a focus of attention. Had they been, then there might have been greater integration and understanding of the various approaches.

Some authors do not see different approaches as being independent, but rather as different points along a continuum. This more pragmatic view is adopted by many teachers and coaches who employ principles from different schools of thinking as well as ideas from current models of learning, which work in practice.

FITTS'S THEORY OF SKILL ACQUISITION

The cognitive and association theorists were not directly interested in motor skill acquisition. Paul Fitts, an American psychologist (Fitts and Posner, 1967) was one of the first people to take a systematic look at skill acquisition per se. He based his ideas on laboratory observations of people learning and upon extensive interviews with sports coaches, physical education teachers and instructors in skills other than sporting ones. He asked them questions such as "what is the most difficult thing for beginners?" and "how long must a beginner practice before he knows the skill?". His theory has stood the test of time and is a very plausible description of the learning

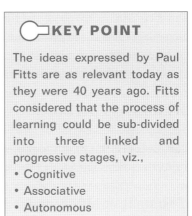

process. Fitts reckoned there are three phases involved in the acquisition of skill, although he did recognise that the distinction between them was rather arbitrary.

The early or cognitive phase

The initial stages are concerned with trying to understand what the task or skill is all about. This is a stage where events and cues which demand much attention early on, later go unnoticed. The beginner has difficulty deciding what to attend to and has particular problems in processing information concerning his/her own limbs – hence the aspirant basketball player must watch the ball as it is dribbled and the would-be dancer watches his/her own feet. Early learning is characterised by many and often gross errors and may look like a 'patchwork of old habits' put together into new patterns supplemented by a few new ones. The implications for the coach or teacher at this stage of learning are numerous. Attention must be directed to individual learning styles and methods must reflect the different ways people learn. Demonstrations, instructions and physical guidance are all suitable methods. Cues which are relevant and meaningful to the learner must be selected for emphasis. Practices must be simple but still convey the essence of the sport or skill being learned. Information must be kept to a minimum and potential distractions eliminated. Success is important and teachers should recognise the value in providing praise that, occasionally, is not commensurate with performance levels.

Fitts used the then emerging jargon of computer technology (early '60s) and likened the early phase to one where the learner begins to acquire an 'executive program' for an activity.

The intermediate or associative phase

The intermediate phase is so called because it marks a period when old habits previously learned are tried out and are either consolidated if successful or else discarded. Gross errors are gradually eliminated. Actions are better timed and smoother movement patterns ('sub-routines' to use the jargon again) emerge. The appearance of new movements depends in part on the amount of transfer from previous learning. During this phase, the learner begins to use increasingly more complex or subtle cues and there is an overall change in feedback control from visual/verbal to internal/kinesthetic. It is a period of consolidation of correct or near-correct responses which lasts for varying periods of time depending on the complexity of the skill and the extent to which it calls for new sub-routines and new integrations. A number of key issues concern the coach during this period, viz., the length of practice sessions, the breakdown of complex skills into smaller parts, specificity of feedback, etc.

The final or autonomous phase

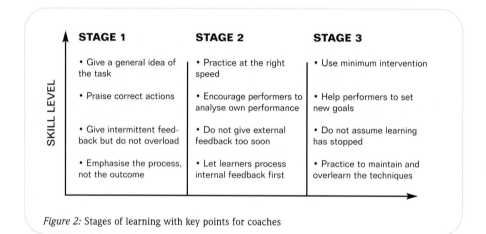

Figure 2: Stages of learning with key points for coaches

During the final stage of learning, skilled movements become increasingly autonomous, less subject to conscious control by the individual and less subject to interference from other, ongoing activities and environmental distractions. Skills require less processing, i.e., they can be carried out whilst new learning is in progress or while the performer is engaged in other activities. The speed, efficiency and consistency of performance increases, although at a slower rate than previously. Individuals are more able to analyse their own performance and progress does not depend on external feedback or rewards. As far as coaching is concerned, attention can focus on the fine detail of technique or strategy and performers can be encouraged to contribute more and more to their own learning – through self analysis, mental practice and personal motivation. Foxon (1999) highlights the value of Fitts's thinking and presents some of the key ideas in schematic form as shown in *Figure 2* above.

Adams's closed-loop theory

Adams's ideas on skill learning stemmed from a weakness in S-R theory (see *Figure 3* adapted from Scully, 1996). He took issue with the notion of reinforcement. In par-

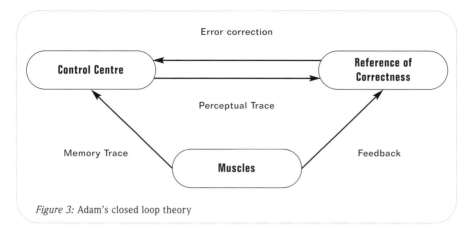

Figure 3: Adam's closed loop theory

ticular, he considered that whilst S-R theories can demonstrate relationships between particular types of reinforcement (e.g., saying "well done") and particular actions (e.g., learning a forward roll), they do not explain why these come about. Adams sought to provide an answer here. In his theory, movements are initiated by what he calls a 'memory trace' and subsequently controlled by another one known as the 'perceptual trace' (see *Figure 3*). The memory trace is developed through experience and based on external knowledge of results about earlier attempts at a movement. Skill learning per se involves the acquisition of the perceptual trace which is used as a reference to compare feedback from current movements. The perceptual trace is developed as a result of exposure to various sources of feedback; muscular, auditory, visual, etc. Through practice the perceptual trace and feedback are continuously matched. If the match is perfect, the learner proceeds confidently with the movement, but if there is a mismatch the learner's confidence in the correctness of the action is reduced and he moves to eliminate the error. The learning process is one of continuous error-nulling throughout the course of making a movement.

Whilst Adams's theory underpins what is undoubtedly an essential ingredient in skill learning, i.e., feedback and knowledge of results, it has a number of weaknesses. One criticism is that for every movement, there is assumed to be a separate memory trace. Given the infinite number of movements that can be performed, this assumption poses a very great burden on the individual's memory capacity. This and other weaknesses are addressed by Schmidt in his schema theory.

Schmidt's schema theory

Like Adams, Schmidt sought to answer the criticisms of previous theories. He also made an attempt to take the strong parts of existing theories, adding and modifying so as to answer the existing criticisms. Schmidt drew attention to the storage problem of Adams's theory and also the so called 'novelty' problem. Schmidt reasoned that every movement we execute is different. Even similar movements carried out in the same environment (e.g., a tennis serve) are slightly different in some way. He posed

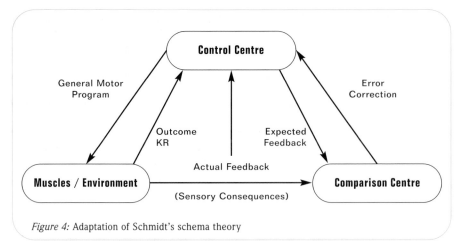

Figure 4: Adaptation of Schmidt's schema theory

the question that if this is the case, then where does the 'reference' for initiating actions (the 'memory trace' in Adams theory) come from?

To counter this and other problems Schmidt proposed a 'schema' model of learning (see *Figure 4* adapted from Scully, 1996). His theory does not rely on fixed memory traces but assumes a generative process developed through experience, feedback and error correction. People store in memory not specific copies of movements for later replication but ideas of relationships (schema) that can be used to produce different but related movements. Each time a movement is performed the individual stores in memory four items, viz.,

• The initial state of the muscles and environment prior to a movement (e.g., what is the batsman's starting position at the wicket?)

• A specification of the movement to be produced. This is called a motor program (e.g., how fast does the bat move and in what direction?)

• The sensory consequences (feedback) of the movement (e.g., did the swing feel as if the ball hit the bat's 'sweet spot'?)

• The outcome of the movement in terms of its success or otherwise in relation to the expected outcome (e.g., was the ball caught or did it reach the boundary?)

Through practice, the learner abstracts relationships between these various sources of information. In time, although the learner forgets the individual movements, they remember the general movement 'rules' (or schema). These can be used on future occasions to predict and implement actions for particular circumstances. In Schmidt's theory, it follows that the strength or utility of schema is directly related to the variability of prior experience. Increasing the amount and variability of the learner's experience leads to the development of increasingly strong schema. This idea has implications of course for the manner in which practice is organised and will be discussed in the Chapter 5. This section has touched on Schmidt's ideas only briefly. A more thorough description can be found in Schmidt and Wrisberg (2000).

Information processing theory

The author's own theoretical position leans heavily in the direction of information processing theory. It has served him well for over 30 years in various contexts – as a performer, learner, teacher and researcher. Many of the premises and concepts central to information processing permeate this book. For this reason, greater attention will be given to this theory than others.

The information processing approach has dominated theories of skill acquisition for very many years. The view of man as a processor of information has been a focus of attention for several decades and still has credibility today (Davis, Bull, Roscoe and Roscoe, 2000; Schmidt and Wrisberg, 2000). Information processing theory likens the individual to a computer or communications system, in which information is stored, manipulated, sometimes distorted and finally output. It attempts to explain behaviour in terms of stages of central nervous system activity rather than as a series of actions made towards reaching some goal. The brain is viewed as a hierarchical control system where the mind represents and communicates information (see *Figure 5*).

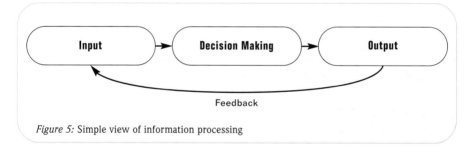

Figure 5: Simple view of information processing

Theorists describe the mechanisms of information processing usually in terms of a two-dimensional model. In the first edition of this book, the particular model described by Martenuik (1975) was used as a basis for elaboration. In the present case the model developed by Schmidt is used. Schmidt's model has evolved over many years and represents current thinking in the area. *Figure 6*, over, is adapted from Schmidt and Wrisberg (2000). How does it work? The 'Input' box represents the input or sensing of all kinds of sensory information (hearing, seeing, feeling, etc.). 'Stimulus identification' is the stage at which information from the display is received and is recognised. It is concerned essentially with detecting sensory information and interpreting what has been received as in judging the speed of an approaching ball, the relative position of opponent players or the height of knee/leg lift in sprint hurdling. The senses are initially responsible for providing the raw data (e.g., sound of the starter's gun, feel of a cricket bat in the hands, sight of an approaching ball).

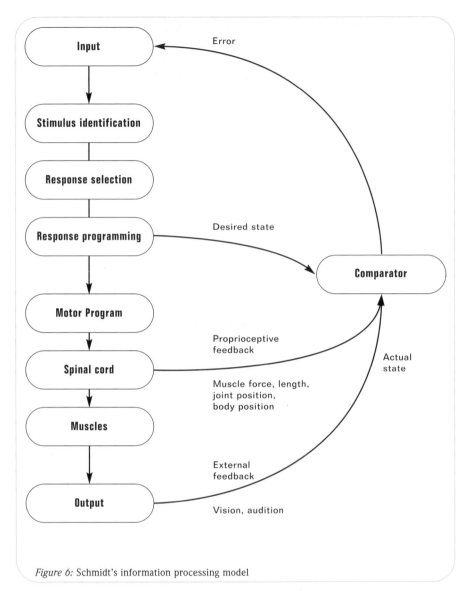

Figure 6: Schmidt's information processing model

As a consequence, the stage of 'Response Selection' is provided with a description of the environment. 'Response Selection' is the stage where the individual makes a decision about how to respond in regard to current objectives. Thus, a defending player may choose to move to their left in order to intercept the attacking player with the ball. 'Response Programming' is the stage where the individual initiates a set of movements to put into effect the decision to respond. In the example, this results in a set of co-ordinated movements of the arms, legs and body in both space and time that result (hopefully) in a successful interception. Schmidt refers to the three processes of stimulus identification, response selection and response programming as the Executive Process. A key element in the model is the 'Comparator'. When a decision is made to respond, a 'desired state' of how the action/s should appear in terms of its sensory qualities (sight, hearing, feeling, etc.) is generated and a copy is sent to the Comparator. Commands for achieving the desired state are then passed on to the next stage resulting in the selection of an appropriate 'motor program' which specifies the required actions. Lower centres of the nervous system are then activated involving the transmission of signals via the spinal cord and muscles and movements take place. Once movements begin, feedback is generated in the form of exteroceptive sources (sight, sounds) and propreoceptive sources (muscular tensions, limb articulation) and this is compared with the stored desired state in the Comparator to indicate whether or not the

Information processing: this young girl has to judge the distance between adjacent poles, decide how far/fast to step between them, and then effect movements to meet those requirements

action was appropriate or in error. If an error signal is generated then a correction takes place as that error is processed through the system as just described.

It is vital to note that the model predicts the manner in which many activities in daily life are organised and executed, not simply sporting actions. However, there are many classes of activity, particularly those which are executed very quickly, that do not involve the operation of all processes. There are numerous movements required in both sport and daily life that have to be executed so quickly there is insufficient time for the various feedback processes to operate. Kicking and striking actions in ball games, serial movements in gymnastic routines and defensive reactions (e.g., removing a hand from a hot plate) must occur without the Comparator being involved. In these cases, control has to rely on the effectiveness of the motor programs meeting their intended objectives without recourse to feedback evaluation and error correction. This kind of activity is called open-loop control. We will return to the notions of open and closed loop control in the chapter on feedback.

Serial and parallel processing

Having described Schmidt's basic model let us elaborate on some principles not identified in the diagram which are relevant to future discussions. Firstly, the distinction between serial and parallel processing. There is a lot of evidence to suggest that in the early stages of the information-processing, events take place in parallel (Schmidt and Wrisberg, 2000). In other words a number of streams of information such as the colour, sound and position of objects in the display are all processed simultaneously. It makes sense for sensory information to undergo parallel processing. From a survival point of view, it is important for the individual to recognise what is happening in the environment immediately without having to wait for things to be sensed in a serial manner one at a time. As information proceeds through the various stages it is thought that processing takes on a more serial character. Thus, when items compete for attention (e.g., when a football player has to decide whether to pass the ball or not, who to, how to negotiate an approaching defender, etc.) the delays and possible errors that result, occur because of interference in selecting a response.

A key distinction is that between controlled and automatic processing. Consider a beginner learning to swim whilst their coach offers advice and feedback about their actions. In situations like this where the individual is required to carry out two tasks simultaneously it is considered that such activities are governed through controlled processing. Controlled processing is effortful and relatively slow in nature; information overload results in performance decrement. In contrast, automatic processing is less tedious and characterises highly skilled performance. In this case, there is little conscious thought given to an action; it takes place automatically and with little active involvement from the performer. Take the example of a mogul skier. The performer might make a conscious effort to start a run, but then complete a rapid sequence of technically and physically difficult moves by paying attention only to perhaps certain elements of style and flow. There is little demand on the performer's attention as multiple actions are executed simultaneously and almost involuntarily. In summary, controlled processing tends to be slow, attention demanding and voluntary. In contrast, automatic processing tends to be fast, not attention demanding and involuntary. The transition from beginner to expert reflects, in part, a shift from controlled to automatic processing.

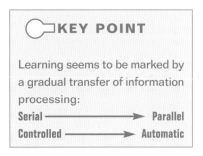

KEY POINT

Learning seems to be marked by a gradual transfer of information processing:

Serial ⟶ Parallel
Controlled ⟶ Automatic

Attention

Attention is central to information processing and is a subject with which most people are well aware. Attention tends to be aligned with our consciousness. We talk about not being able to attend to something because of a distraction in the background. We also say it is very difficult to attend to more than one thing at a time. It seems that we have a limited attention capacity as well as a limitation in being able to attend and deal with several things that happen simultaneously. A wealth of research has examined this topic which is central to both a theoretical understanding of motor control and teaching and learning. Research has examined how able people are to perform a skill whilst also being required to complete a secondary or competing task. The general finding is that performance of the secondary task diminishes, as the attentional demands of the primary task increases. This finding is taken as support for an attentional mechanism that has a limited capacity. The locus of this limitation seems to be, as noted above, in later stages of information processing (response programming and response selection) where a 'queuing' effect occurs. Sometimes, when a performer is required to respond to two events which happen close together in time (e.g., an attacking player moves to the left to pass a defender, but then fakes and quickly turns to the right), he responds much more slowly to the second event than the first. This happens because there is a need to complete processing of the first stimulus before the next one can be dealt with. In a fast ball game situation, the extra delay (called the psychological refractory period) can have devastating consequences for the individual in terms of their speed of response and consequent inability to react successfully.

The fact that attention is always 'to something' gives rise to the expression 'selective attention'. We focus our attention selectively either voluntarily (e.g., when we choose to read a book or watch a television programme) or involuntarily as when something unexpected or interesting catches our attention (such as a fast moving vehicle that appears in peripheral vision). A vast literature has examined this topic.

A general finding is that people attend to things that are unexpected, pertinent or interesting. With practice, learning is reflected in the relegation of items that were initially the focus of conscious attention, to lower levels of consciousness (automaticity). The expert has the capacity to attend unconsciously which permits them to make decisions rapidly, react quickly and effect fluent movements with precision and accuracy. Integral to this process is the ability to identify and attend to those cues in the environment that are most essential to successful performance.

Memory

Our ability to 'filter' out information that is not relevant to performance is based on the way information is stored in our memory. The information-processing model depicted before does not include a memory component. One reason is that memory is all-pervasive and linked to almost every component of the model. The currently accepted view is that we have three broad memory systems – sensory memory, short-term memory and long-term memory. Baddeley (1997) says:

> *"The briefest memory stores last for only a fraction of a second. Such sensory memories are perhaps best considered as an integral part of the process of perceiving. Both vision and hearing then appear to have a later but temporary storage stage that might perhaps be termed short-term auditory and visual memory, leaving a trace that lasts for a few seconds. In addition to these, we clearly also have long-term memory for sights and sounds. We can remember what a sunset looks like, could probably recognise a photograph of Albert*

*Einstein or Joseph Stalin, or identify the voice of a close friend, or the sound of
a creaking door. All these indicate some form of long-term sensory storage."*

This way of viewing memory is shown in *Figure 7*. It is best to think of the elements
within the model as processes rather than distinct physical capacities. In the model,
information that we sense (hear, feel, touch, see, etc.) enters a very high capacity,
but short-lived (about 1 second) sensory store. In fact, it is thought that we have a
sensory store dedicated to each sense. The purpose of these stores is to ensure that
everything in the environment is noted. This provides the individual with a complete
basis for later processing. If we did not have stores like these, we would never know
what was, or was not important in the environment – including objects that could be
life threatening. This stage of processing is automatic and involuntary. There is obviously a reference to some kind of long-term memory in order that information can
be identified and recognised. Sensory short-term memory provides a 'picture' of the
environment.

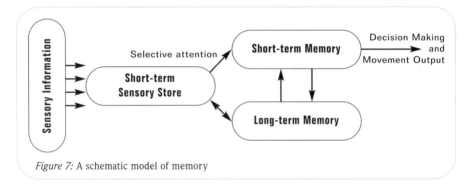

Figure 7: A schematic model of memory

From sensory memory, information is selected and passed to short-term memory. The
transfer process is dictated by what the individual deems to be pertinent or relevant
to task in hand. This is the process of selective attention mentioned previously. Short-
term memory is also short-lived (around 1 minute) but can retain information if it is
actively rehearsed by the individual. This may take the form of some kind of imagery
process or verbal repetition. Short-term memory is often called working memory. In
one sense, it can be likened to one's current state of consciousness. If information is
rehearsed well enough and long enough it stands a good chance of being transferred
to long-term memory. Long-term memory is considered to have an unlimited capacity.
The nature of what is stored in long-term memory is thought to be connected to what
is meaningful to the individual. The schemas discussed previously certainly reside in
long-term memory. One school of thought argues that long-term memory contains
virtually everything that we sense in life. The reason why we seem to forget things
is not that they disappear from storage; rather, we lack the capacity to retrieve the
information. To retrieve items from long-term memory requires making correct
associations. For example, when trying to think of the name of a person you know, it
often helps to think of aspects of their behaviour or looks. The problem of memory

then appears to be a retrieval issue. In the chapter devoted to practice, we will look at some of the techniques used to facilitate memory.

Reaction time

There are a number of stages in the model and each one takes time for information to be processed. The overall delay in processing information is known as reaction time, and it can seriously limit the way we perform. It is seen, for example, in race starts when sprinters move from the blocks a fraction of a second after the pistol has sounded. Reaction time has a number of components; the time to detect

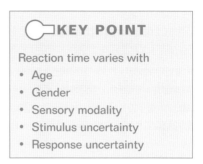

KEY POINT

Reaction time varies with
• Age
• Gender
• Sensory modality
• Stimulus uncertainty
• Response uncertainty

and recognise environmental information, the time to energise muscles before they move, and the time to make decisions. The latter typically generates the largest time delay. Reaction time varies with many things including age (we all begin to slow down after about 20 years), gender (males are faster than females) sensory modality (reaction time to sound is faster than that to light) and uncertainty (a goalkeeper is likely to react faster if there is one approaching attacker rather than two or three). The need to make decisions and respond quickly is important in almost every sport – particularly those involving open skills. Goalkeepers need to move rapidly to intercept a penalty kick and tennis players must move quickly to receive a quickly returned service. In both of these examples, skill hinges on reacting not only to when the ball arrives (temporal uncertainty) but also to where it goes (spatial uncertainty). Fast reactions are critical not only in ball games but other sports such as judo, fencing, skiing, kayaking and water polo. A key question for the performer is how to avoid reaction time delay or at least minimise its effect? The single most important technique is to reduce the degree of uncertainty present; the less the uncertainty the faster the reaction time. The way to do this is through anticipation. Anticipation involves 'looking ahead' to detect important cues and, on the basis of advance information, plan a response before it is required. Thus, a goalkeeper should decide which way the ball will go by watching the run up of the penalty taker and other subtle information that might provide a clue about the ball's direction, weighting and trajectory. If he is good at doing this, then he can initiate his response in time to intercept the ball. Batsmen in cricket try to do the same. In fact, it is calculated that when a fast bowler delivers the ball, the time of flight is less than a reaction time. This means the batsman has to work out every detail of his movement and begin its initiation even before the ball has left the bowler's hand!

Skill at the highest level involves finely tuned anticipation developed over many years. It involves a thorough knowledge of the game and skills involved as well as a keen awareness of the cues (often centred on how players move) that permit accurate predictions to be made. Interestingly, whilst accurate anticipation is the goal of the skilled player, an equally important goal for an opponent is to confuse things to make anticipation difficult. One way to do this is by concealing intended actions to mask the anticipatory cues (as when a bowler in cricket or pitcher in baseball hides his wrist action) or by varying the style of play to increase the number of movement permutations.

Practical applications of information processing theory

The importance in viewing people as processors of information is that it permits the break down of a very complicated problem into manageable proportions. Researchers are interested in verifying the logic of such models and describing the capacities and limitations of each stage. For the teacher or coach however, the advantages are much more practical. Firstly, the information processing model provides a logical way of examining the important ingredients comprising skilled action. Describing movements in this way makes sure that nothing important is missed out. For example, before teaching say a snow plough turn to a novice skier, the instructor would assess what are the perceptual, decision making, movement and feedback aspects. They would decide which aspects are relevant and which could be delayed until later. Hence, they might decide that it was vital to concentrate on developing anticipation or memory or judgement. Such an approach would at least guard against an emphasis on technique alone – a common problem in many sports. The second benefit concerns error identification. Given that learning is largely a matter of solving problems and minimising error there is a need on the part of the teacher or coach to assess the reasons why learners make errors. Through questioning whether the reason is a perceptual, decision making or technical one, the teacher has a systematic and comprehensive tool for eliminating most possible sources.

KEY POINT

INFORMATION PROCESSING THEORY
• Permits an understanding of human performance by breaking down complex problems into logical parts
• Provides a logical basis for understanding the reasons for performance breakdown

The information processing model therefore provides a clear structure to facilitate teaching. However, it is not a panacea and some authors argue whether it is the correct approach. Handford, Davids, Bennet and Button (1997) question whether the brain really functions like an engineering control system. They suggest that the brain does not work like a computer and that researchers have tended to idealise the mind (as a computer) rather than studying it within a biological framework. They also point to a number of methodological weaknesses in the research that has supported the information-processing model. For example, they suggest that many of the laboratory tasks used to investigate information processing theory (reaction time, linear positioning) are not representative of the complex actions that are central to sporting activities. They provide evidence in support of these concerns and also proffer an alternative 'dynamical systems' model.

Dynamical systems theory

The past 10/15 years has seen a number of concerns expressed regarding the robust-ness of information processing theory in explaining skill acquisition and human performance. Recent research and thinking has adopted an 'ecological' approach to help understand the ways in which people learn and respond to the environmental (Handford et al, 1997). One particular approach has focused on 'dynamical systems'. The dynamical perspective has arisen mainly as a critique of the motor program concept and stems largely from the work of the Russian physiologist Bernstein (Bernstein, 1967). Dynamical systems theory argues that patterns of movement (skilled sporting actions as well as other movements) are not the end result of a chain (in both time and structure) of information processes. Rather, they result from the interaction between the individual and their environment. Walter, Lee and Sternad (1998) note that:

"... the dynamical systems approach assumes control is autonomous (i.e., human movement evolves as a function of current state rather than as a result of a pre-organised time series."

Specifically, movement patterns are responses to the person's physical characteristics (their height, weight, etc.), the environment (such as other players and equipment) and parameters set by the task in hand (such as the individual's perception of the rules of a game). Movements are not based on a selection of stored responses, but generated in regard to these three sets of 'constraints' (Magill, 1998).

Supporters of dynamical theory predict that movements are not represented through motor programs, but emerge naturally as a result of complex interactions between the various physical elements. Thus, for example, as an individual sits down in a chair, the movements which eventually result in a position of posture are dependent on the initial will to sit down, the physical characteristics of the individual (leg length, hip mobility, weight, speed of movement, etc.) as well as features of the environment such as the type of chair, its springiness, cushioning, seat height and so on. All of these factors interact to produce a unique set of movements to meet the goal of sitting down. Every time the individual sits down, the same variables interact, but using different parameter values to produce the desired movement. Evidence to support the dynamical systems approach arises from biomechanical research into the action of simple limb move-ments. For example, it has been shown that the precise movement patterns of walk-ing/running can be explained through the simple mechanical properties of the mus-cles as they react to gravity. This evidence indicates that motor control is more a fea-ture of the physical/dynamical properties of the human/environment situation, rather than a direct consequence of stored motor programs held centrally by the individual.

Schmidt and Wrisberg (2000) provide the following analogy to illustrate the dynamical systems approach. They refer to the manner in which water heated in a pot transforms from a static state to a moving (boiling) one; the change is one of spontaneous organisation. The same follows when water moving in a river changes course as it falls over ledges and swirls behind boulders. In these examples there is an order in the movements that obeys well-defined

physical laws. The movements are never the same twice because the parameters are always different (amount of water in the pot, size of the pot, etc.), but there is order and co-ordination by virtue of the interaction of the many variables. Because of this, proponents of dynamical systems theory propose there is no need to think of motor programs controlling actions; they are superfluous. Schmidt and Wrisberg (2000) regard the dynamical perspective as one which is useful to scientific debate, but they add that the best explanation of movement control may involve a combination of the various perspectives (information processing and dynamical systems). They advocate that the information-processing approach to the study of human performance and learning is a highly practical and tested approach that has stood the test of time.

The pragmatic approach

Many teachers and coaches with years of experience who have worked with different kinds of learners will say that they know what works; they do not need to resort to theory, read books or be told what to do. This statement does not imply that theories are useless or that practitioners fail to recognise the value of theoretical knowledge. It is likely that experienced practitioners gain

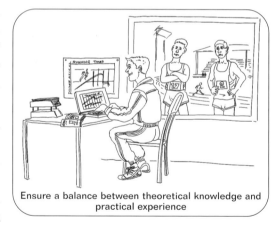

Ensure a balance between theoretical knowledge and practical experience

knowledge about what works best from many different sources; learners, other teachers, theoretical knowledge, printed material, personal experience and so on. This point is well made by Matheson and Mace (2001):

"... there are a number of different approaches to studying skill in sport. Most sport scientists have adapted an eclectic approach, i.e., we pinch a bit from every approach in order to explain how learning takes place. This enables teachers and coaches to help athletes speed up the learning process and ulti-

mately achieve higher levels of performance."

The pragmatic approach founded on eclectic experience often leads individuals to establish a set of principles and methods that prove valuable in many situations. Cooper (1998) lists a number of ingredients that he believes are central to learning. His ideas are based on personal experience as a teacher and instructor in the field of outdoor education. He suggests that teachers should be mindful of a number of ingredients central to learning. He advocates that people learn well when:

- There is a problem to solve
- Learning is shared
- The learner is involved in doing
- Learning is related to the learner's own life
- There is a challenge
- There is time to reflect
- Learning is enjoyable.

Foxon (1999) adopts a similar stance. Speaking from the world of sports coaching he lists a number of principles that facilitate learning. He suggests that people learn best when:

- They are actively involved in taking part, i.e., doing
- They are able to recognise the relevance and application of techniques
- Given the opportunity to build new learning from previous experiences
- They are interested and motivated to learn
- Provided with positive praise for successes.

There is clearly an overlap between the views of Foxon and Cooper. Many of the principles identified here will be reinforced as we go through this book.

SUMMARY OF THE KEY POINTS

- Theories are generalisations about how things work and why things take place. They are based on observations and research and allow predictions of how things take place. Theories are not exhaustive nor are they complete or necessarily correct explanations of the phenomena they represent.

- Theoretical knowledge is useful for a number of reasons, viz., it gives direction and structure to ones thinking and provides practical ideas based on sound, well tested principles. Effective teaching and coaching is founded on the interplay between theoretical knowledge and practical experience.
- The history of skill acquisition is punctuated by a number of landmarks, viz., the observation and measurement of reaction time by early astronomers, the 'discovery'

of plateaus and hierarchical learning by Bryan & Harter; the development of motor skills tests in the first half of the century; the emphasis on man-machine relationships through the advent of World War II; the efforts of particular researchers, e.g., Craik, Bartlett and Fitts which led to an increased interest in skill acquisition and a focus on topics such as: anticipation, feedback, motor programming; research on motor memory; the information processing approach to the study of skilled performance.

• Traditional theories of learning are split into Associative and Cognitive approaches. Association theories emphasise:

  • *Stimulus-response learning* where development is a matter of linking specific stimuli with particular responses through repetition and reinforcement.

  • *Conditioning.* Classical conditioning is the process whereby the learner links a new stimulus to a previous stimulus-response connection. Operant conditioning occurs when a response occurs more often through successive reinforcement. Behaviour shaping is the gradual refinement of a movement through reinforcement.

  • *Reinforcement.* Immediate reinforcement is essential to the strengthening of responses.

  • *Repetition.* Movements are more likely to be learned if they are satisfying to the learner. Repeated practice is important, but only if there is positive reinforcement. Learning can only be expected if the person is physiologically and psychologically 'ready' to learn.

  • *Part learning.* Complex problems are best broken down into smaller parts to yield short learning steps that can be linked together.

• Cognitive theories emphasise:

  • Importance of perception. Learning is based not only on cues in the display, but also the individual's perception of those cues. This in turn depends on the learner's self-concept, his motivations, experience and expectations.

  • Problem-solving. The learner plays an active role in the learning process; searching and trying to understand how the cues and stimuli in the environment relate to the problem's solution. Insight, where the learner 'suddenly' finds a solution, marks an immediate and permanent stage in learning.

  • Whole learning. Cognitive theories advocate that understanding and insight are only possible if the learner is confronted with the whole problem.

- Individual differences. Due acknowledgement is given to the individual nature of learning. The individual's 'self-concept' not only determines the course/manner of learning, but also is itself altered through the learning process.

- Effective teaching takes advantage of principles from both approaches to learning and combines them with ideas from practical experience.

- Fitts's theory of skill learning divides the learning process into three broad areas, viz., the cognitive, intermediate and autonomous stages.

- Adam's closed-loop theory focuses on the importance of feedback in the learning process. Feedback and knowledge of results is used to compare with the 'perceptual trace' as a way of identifying whether performance is successful.

- Schmidt's schema theory takes the view that people learn sets of 'rules' or schema that are used to organise movements. The theory has important implications for the manner in which practice is planned.

- Information processing theory views the individual as a processor of information. Information enters from the outside world, or from within the individual, and passes through a series of stages such as perception and decision making, before movements occur.

- In general terms, information which enters the system first is dealt with quickly, in a parallel manner. As it is processed further, serial processing takes place that leads to longer delays. Learning seems to be mirrored by a change from serial to parallel processing. This also reflects the learner's attentional capacity. In early learning attention is limited and focused, whilst in later learning attention seems to increase and several competing tasks can be dealt with simultaneously.

- Memory can be thought of in three stages. Sensory short term memory is highly transient with a large capacity. It quickly looses information (within a second or two). Information retained passes to short term memory whose capacity is limited to those items which receive attention. Information retained beyond short term memory goes to long term memory which has a very large capacity. The characteristics of long term memory seem to depend on the meaning it has to the individual.

- Reaction time is defined as the delay between a stimulus appearing and the individual's response to that stimulus. The exact delay depends on many variables including the sense involved, the intensity of the stimulus and the level of the individual's attention. Most important, it depends on the uncertainty associated with the appearance of the stimulus and the associated response.

• Information processing theory has two particular merits. It permits an understanding of human performance by breaking down complex problems into logical parts and it provides a logical basis for understanding the reasons for performance breakdown.

• The dynamical perspective to understanding skill acquisition and human performance has arisen mainly as a critique of the motor program concept. Dynamical systems theory argues that patterns of movement are not the end result of a chain of information processes; rather, they result from the interaction between the individual and their environment. Specifically, movement patterns are responses to the person's physical characteristics, the environment and parameters set by the task in hand.

PRACTICAL TASKS

• To gain an understanding of reaction time and the limitation it presents you can measure it reasonably accurately in the following manner. Obtain a one metre wooden ruler. Work in pairs – one person is the tester and the other the subject. The tester holds the ruler vertically so that the bottom end is about five feet off the ground. The subject stands with their preferred hand open just below the bottom of the ruler. The task is for the subject to grasp the ruler as quickly as possible when released (vertically) by the tester. The tester alerts the subject with a word such as "ready" and then releases it within a period of 3 seconds. Once the ruler is grasped, the distance in mms (d) it has dropped is noted. The following formula is used to calculate reaction time:

$$t^2 = d/490$$

t is the measure of reaction time and should be in the order of 250 msec. The degree of uncertainty can be adjusted by changing the waiting period. Try making it zero seconds (drop on the command "ready"), three seconds or ten seconds. Reaction time should increase the longer the delay. Theoretically, it should be zero when dropped on the command "ready" since then there is no uncertainty.

• Work in pairs. One person writes down a sport. The other person is required to state whether or not reaction time is important and if so, why/where it is important. For example, if the sport is 'sprint hurdling' the answer would be 'the start'. The person asking the question now has to describe how reaction time can be reduced. In the example, the answer might be 'the hurdler has to tense their leg muscles and watch very closely the hand of the starter to see when he pulls the trigger'.

• A good way to examine the effect of uncertainty on reaction time is to measure how long it takes to sort a pack of cards into piles (by colour or suits). Work in pairs again. Take a pack of playing cards. One person is required to sort the cards firstly into two piles based on colour (hearts and diamonds into one pile and clubs and spades into another). They should do this as quickly and accurately as possible. The second person records with a stopwatch how long this takes. Secondly, the same person now sorts the cards into four piles (by suit) and their time is recorded again. This can be repeated a few times to gain an average time. A comparison of the two sets of times should reveal faster sorting for colour (2 piles) compared to suit (4 piles). This arises because the uncertainty, about which pile a card goes into, is greater with suits than colours.

• Here is a workshop to examine short-term memory. Work in pairs. One person makes out a list of five, three letter words and types it on a sheet of paper (e.g., now, cat, and, hit, all). The words should not be connected as a sentence. Show the list for 10 seconds to the other person who is then required to write down the same five words. If they recall every word correctly in the correct order, give them a score of 1. If they make a mistake, show the words again. If they recall successfully this time award a score of 2. Repeat this until they achieve perfect success. Now make another list of five, three letter words, but this time the words should be nonsense (e.g., wxp, dhw, oft, lpf, wqs). Repeat the task with the new list. You should find a much higher score with the nonsense list compared to the first list. This shows that things are better retained in short-term memory if they are meaningful.

• Short-term motor memory can be tested as follows. Work in pairs. One person is required to draw (blindfold) a straight line approximately 25 cms long on a piece of A4 paper. Upon completion, they attempt to draw the same line by overwriting the first one (blindfold again). Measure the distance in length between both lines. Repeat this but add a delay of 10 seconds between the first and second movements. The error this time should be greater than in the first trial. Repeat again with a delay of 60 secs. You should find an even larger error.

• Playing 'Kim's Game' can also test short-term memory. Locate 15 everyday items on a tray and show it to a partner for 15 secs. Remove it from view and ask the partner to recall as many items as possible. Without adopting any strategy, the person should be able to recall about 7 ± 2 items.

• In groups of two or three, watch a slow motion replay of a sporting action (say catching or hitting). Observe repeatedly for about five minutes. During observation, write down words to describe what you see in terms of input information, decisions made, output or actions. At the end compare notes to judge if you all agree. What you are doing here is analysing skill using the information processing model.

REVIEW QUESTIONS

• It is said the fundamental role of the brain is to control movement. Think of two contrasting examples where information held in memory manifests itself in physical movements (e.g., smiling at a joke, speaking to a friend).

• Consider a simple action such as a basketball chest pass and describe those factors other than the technique (such as the flight characteristics) which the teacher or coach must consider in order to produce an effective practice situation.

• Think of a well known theory that you may have learned about at school (e.g., Newton's first law of motion) and show how it applies in the real world.

• Researchers during the last war considered anticipation to be critical to skilled motor performance. Can you think of examples in your sport where anticipation takes place? Furthermore, can you identify a situation where, as a player, you attempt to make it difficult for your opponent to anticipate?

• Have you ever experienced a 'plateau' in your own learning before your performance subsequently improved? If so, what do you think was happening to you during this period?

• Isolate two clear examples from sport where success demands the timely execution of a movement response in reply to a given stimulus.

• In what way would you interpret the skill of a rock climber as a matter of problem solving?

• Take a specific situation in sport (say, a long pass in football) and examine the types of feedback the player receives. Consider both internal and external forms.

• Consider Schmidt's schema theory and the learning of rules. What kinds of rules would need to be acquired in activities such as orienteering and snooker?

• What items does the tennis server need to perceive just before he serves the ball to his partner? One would be the position of his/her body in relation to the net. Name some others.

• How would you characterise skilled performance? What are the criteria that define skill?

• How could you try to improve the reaction time of say a sprinter or goalkeeper? What would you tell them to do?

• Have you ever felt your coach or teacher was giving you too much information to remember before you practice? If so, what stage of memory is being overloaded? How many things should you give a learner to think about before they practice?

• Memory can be assisted through using analogies or metaphors. For example, the detail required to describe a table tennis shot could be translated into an instruction such as "imagine throwing a frisbee". Can you think of other phrases or words to help you remember an action?

References

Archontides, C., Fazey, J. and Smith, N. (1994). *Understanding and improving skill* (Pre-course workbook). Leeds: National Coaching Foundation.

Baddeley, A. (1997). *Human memory. Theory and practice* (3rd Edition). Hove, Sussex: Psychology Press.

Bernstein, N.I. (1967). *The co-ordination and regulation of movement.* Oxford: Pergamon Press.

Cooper, G. (1998). *Outdoors with young people.* Lyme Regis: Russell House Publishing Ltd.

Davis, B., Bull, S., Roscoe and Roscoe, D. (2000). *Physical education and the study of sport.* London: Harcourt Publishers Limited.

Fitts, P.M. and Posner, M.I. (1967). *Human performance.* Belmont, California: Brooks/Cole.

Foxon, F. (1999). *Improving practices and skill.* Leeds: The National Coaching Foundation.

Grant, F. (2002). *Learners and learning.* Horizons (Journal of the Institute for Outdoor Learning), 18, 27-29.

Handford, C., Davids, K., Bennet, S. and Button, C. (1997). Skills acquisition in sport: some applications of an evolving practice ecology. *Journal of Sports Science,* 15, 621 - 640.

Holding, D.H. (Ed.) (1989). *Human Skills* (2nd edition). Chichester: John Wiles.

Honey, P. and Mumford, A. (1992). *The manual of learning styles.* Maidenhead: Peter Honey.

Key, D. (2003). *An act of prayer.* The Great Outdoors, April, 37 - 38.

Magill, R.A. (1990). Motor learning is meaningful for physical educators. *QUEST,* 42, 126 - 133.

Magill, R. (1998). Knowledge is more than we can talk about: implicit learning in motor skill acquisition. *Research Quarterly for Exercise and Sport,* 69, 2, 104 - 110.

Martenuik, J.G. (1975). *Information processing, channel capacity, learning stages and the acquisition of motor skill.* In H. T. A. Whiting (Ed.), *Readings in human performance.* London: Lepus Books.

Matheson, H. and Mace, R. (2001). *Skill in sport.* Droitwich: Sport in Mind.

Maynard, I. (1991). An understanding approach to the teaching of Rugby Union. *British Journal of Physical Education,* 22, 1, 11 - 17.

Rink, J. (1999). *Instruction from a learning perspective.* In C. A. Hardy and M. Mawers (Eds.). *Learning and teaching in physical education.* London: Falmer Press.

Robson, C. (1993). *Real world research.* Oxford: Blackwell.

Schmidt, R.A. and Wrisberg, C. (2000). *Motor learning and performance* (2nd Edition). Champaign, Illinois: Human Kinetics.

Scully, D. (1996). *Skill acquisition.* In P. Beashel and J. Taylor (Eds.). *Advanced studies in physical education and sport.* Walton-on-Thames: Thomas Nelson and Sons Ltd.

Wade. C., and Tavris, C. (1998). *Psychology* (5th Edition). Harlow: Longman.

Walter, C., Lee, T.D. and Sternad, D. (1998). The dynamic systems approach to motor control and learning: promises, potential limitations and future directions. *Research Quarterly for Exercise and Sport,* 69, 4, 316 - 318.

Whiting, H.T.A. *Skill in sport - a descriptive and prescriptive appraisal.* In J. H. Salmela, J. T. Partington and T. Orlick (Eds.), *New paths to sport learning.* Ottawa: The Coaching Association of Canada, 1982.

CHAPTER 3 – PROVIDING INFORMATION TO LEARNERS

"If the teacher is to provide the learner with information on how to do a skill, the presentation skills of the teacher are important components of effective teaching. In the development of skill the teacher is going to have the ability to clearly communicate the essential aspects of performance."

Rink (1999)

INTRODUCTION

When you wish someone to try a new skill or practice part of a new skill what do you tell them? Indeed, do you need to say anything? Perhaps it is sufficient to provide a demonstration of the skill without any accompanying instructions. And is there any value in physically helping a learner to practice a new skill by, for example, manipulating their limbs in the desired manner for them? This chapter focuses on that part of the teaching/learning process concerned with the provision of information to learners to guide them to practice effectively.

It is useful to start by distinguishing between practice and training. For the purposes of the present discussion, physical activity that takes place with help from an outside source such as a coach or teacher is known as training. In contrast, practice involves physical activity without any kind of outside assistance. Both situations have a part to play in skill learning for there are times when the learner needs advice from the coach and other times when either it is unavailable or simply not required. Let us look at practice for a moment. There are a number of disadvantages associated with practice. In the first place, learning can be a trial and error affair. Without input from the coach learners only have their own model of skill to use as a basis for error correction – and the model may be inaccurate or wrong. As a result, errors may build up which, if unnoticed or uncorrected, may give rise to the learning and consolidation of bad habits. An additional problem is that as soon as the habits are recognised, practice time and effort is required not only to learn the correct movements, but also to 'unlearn' the faulty ones. The boxing coach Hickey (1986) raises these points:

"Uncoached practice is bad. Not just because of the time wasted and perhaps the high risk of injury, but also what's going to happen is that bad habits will be formed. So with uncoached practice what will happen is that the technique will be grooved which is perhaps mechanically unsound, which may not cause problems

in the early stages but once the boxer goes into competition at the higher echelons he will certainly have problems simply because he was allowed too much free time. Coaching should be structured. Practices must be pointed and precise and there should be no question of a boxer doing his own thing literally."

A second problem of practice alone is that whilst it encourages success very quickly, it often leads to movements that are technically unsound. As a result, skill level remains mediocre and potential goes unrealised. Coupled with the absence of outside praise and corrective advice, the scene is set for little or no progress, frustration and possible dropout by the learner from the sport. These are rather negative features but it would be wrong to think that practice has no place. Many people are happy to practice alone or with their friends in the complete knowledge they will improve very little; the social or therapeutic element is often much more important than skill improvement per se. And of course many top athletes work alone improving their skill and levels of fitness. However, there is a very big difference with experienced performers. They are better able to make adjustments to their performance because they have an internal model of skill that is much more likely to be correct. Also, they are able to interpret their own feedback and self analyse more precisely. This is based in large part on the accumulation of advice and guidance from other people. Let us now look at the methods of guidance available to teachers and coaches.

METHODS OF GUIDANCE

A useful way of categorising methods of guidance is to examine the various ways we receive information. We possess a number of senses and some are more important (from a learning perspective) than others. The obvious ones are seeing (vision), hearing (audition), feeling (kinesthesis) and touch (tactile). It seems unlikely that the coach would take advantage of the remaining senses of smell and taste. There are a number of interesting things about the way in which our senses are structured and function. One feature is that whilst they are physiologically different and respond to distinctly

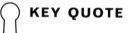

> ### KEY QUOTE
>
> *"Designing instructions to both give students the ability to execute a motor response as well as to use motor responses appropriately in meaningful and often complex activity environments would seem to be ... a challenge that is likely to involve the need for a variety of instructional processes."*
> **Rink** (1999)

different kinds of energy (e.g., the eyes respond to light energy whilst the ears respond to mechanical energy) they can present to the brain the same information. To give a rather dramatic example of this, imagine a pig walked into your living room! You could recognise that it was a pig by using any single sense. Thus you would be able to see that it was a pig. You would smell that it was a pig. You could tell from the noises it made that it was a pig. By moving your hands over its body contours (with your eyes closed) you would feel that it was a pig and perhaps if you were to take a bite then you would also identify the characteristic taste of a pig. The implication of this for learning is that it makes it possible to present the same things to people in different ways. This is useful because people seem to have preferred ways of picking up information, i.e., some prefer to see a demonstration whilst others may prefer a detailed verbal account. We will look at individual differences like this in much more detail in Chapter 8 which focuses on learning 'styles'.

Another important thing about the senses is the manner in which they interact with one another. The brain seems to process information from the various senses not separately but in a co-ordinated, interactive manner. The observation that taste seems to go when you have a cold, points to the fact that taste is based on both taste and smell. Similarly, if watching television and there is a fault in transmission such that either sound or vision is lost, then the viewer is often left extremely frustrated and misses vital information. It follows that complete perception is only possible if both vision and audition are present together. And in the same way, the pleasure in reading a book or newspaper can be a function of the paper quality (how it feels) and not just the content of the printed matter. 'Sensory integration' has important implications for learning. It allows teachers and coaches to use a variety of presentation techniques in combination to transmit ideas and information to learners. Thus, if a learner fails to understand a particular learning point (how to deliver bottom spin to a table tennis serve) through watching a demonstration and listening to a brief explanation, she may benefit from say a longer description coupled with some form of manual assistance. Another person may learn best by just watching a video of an expert performer and feeling the movements through guidance from the coach. Sensory integration permits the 'mix and match' of a variety of methods to appeal to individual people.

Visual guidance

Harrison and Blakemore (1989) have estimated that about 83% of all learning occurs through showing people what to do, 11% through hearing and 6% through other senses. Although it is debatable whether these kinds of figures are really accurate they do support a common belief that the visual sense is probably the most dominant way ('visual dominance') we communicate with the outside world. Schmidt and Wrisberg (2000) suggest that vision is so dominant it has the power to unavoidably capture the attention of people when

Some sports are dominated by visual information

their attention should be focused on information from other sources. They cite the example of sailing where the richness of visual information provided by sails and their movement caused by wind action, can mask the importance of sound as the boat makes it way through the water and the feel of forces exerted by the water on the tiller. Given the dominance of vision, it is not surprising that one of the most common techniques used in teaching and coaching is visual guidance. Shedden (1986) underlines this point in the following comments:

> *"One of the most important forms of information is visual information and this is especially true of children. But even for adults, to have an impression of what the movements look like in motion, very often from a totally different viewpoint than the demonstrator would give if he were standing with the group is important. This can be given by film or by videotape presentation. Videotape is also very good for allowing performers to see themselves and therefore match their own visual impression of themselves with the ideal visual model. The most common means of communicating to a beginner in skiing what to do is the use of a demonstration – the ski instructor or coach demonstrates to the beginner. As the beginner gets more expert, the use of demonstration becomes more and more limited and information from other sources is more desirable."*

Methods of visual guidance can be categorised in the following way:

- Demonstrations
- Use of visual materials (e.g., wall charts, video)
- Re-structuring of the visual display

Let us take each one in turn.

Demonstrations

Observational learning takes place when people watch the behaviour of others and then adapt their own behaviour as a result of that experience. The use of demonstrations by the teacher or coach is a simple example of observational learning. The aim of a demonstration is to present to the learner a visual model which they can then copy. Demonstrations take advantage of a very powerful principle in learning, viz., learning by imitation. There is a rich body of literature which shows that people

 **KEY QUOTE**

"When Tiger was six months old, he would sit in our garage, watching me hit balls into the net. He had been assimilating his golf swing. When he got out of the high chair, he had a golf swing."
Earl Woods
(Father of Tiger Woods)

do learn by imitating others. Almost everyone can think of examples where this has happened. Young children are especially good at picking things up very speedily although, as many teachers and parents will know, they are equally adept at learning things they shouldn't!

Demonstrations have a number of highly positive characteristics. They are very efficient in terms of time. They offer an immediate picture and also save the coach the problem of expressing the task in words, which could confuse the learner. The saying "a picture paints a thousand words" is especially true when it comes to describing complex movements. Williams, Davids and Williams, (1999) make this point when they say:

"A significant aspect of modelling is that learning time is reduced because a great deal of what is to be learned can be accomplished in a single exposure to the model's action."

Demonstrations have a place at all stages of learning. A demonstration gives the novice a general idea of what is required and is intuitively more appealing than, say, a lengthy talk. The fact that it takes place in real time and in the immediate vicinity of the learner adds to its general impact and value in motivating the beginner. A demonstration for the expert is useful in highlighting specific points – say the manner in which the bowler moves his hand when imparting spin to the ball – which could not be examined in any other practical way. Demonstrations also allow advantage to be taken of other peoples' skills and expertise. For example, if the coach or

Demonstrations can be very powerful if the learner is allowed immediate practice

teacher cannot perform then it may be possible for someone else – perhaps one of the learners – to show others in the group how the movement is carried out. The coach is in a particularly advantageous position here because attention can be drawn to specific points in the demonstration that would be impossible if they were per-forming themselves.

Demonstrations by learners with particular weaknesses are also a useful technique if handled carefully and can be used to highlight differences between good and bad techniques. Indeed, Rink (1999) notes:

"Most research has assumed that the demonstration should be accurate, and in the case of new and complex skills should be performed more than once. More recent research has questioned that assumption and has suggested that a 'learning'

demonstrator, meaning a student who is also learning the skill who may not be proficient at the skill, might be equally effective as an accurate demonstrator."

It seems this only works if learners have a clear cognitive understanding of what the skill is all about. Those who have little understanding of what they are trying to do are unlikely to benefit by watching someone perform a skill inaccurately.

These are some of the advantages, but demonstrations are not always the panacea they are assumed to be. Social learning theory (e.g., Bandura, 1969) indicates that 'observational learning' only occurs if the learner:

- Attends to the demonstration
- Remembers the information conveyed by the demonstration
- Possesses the ability to reproduce the movements
- Has the motivation to practice.

With these considerations in mind, it should not be assumed that demonstrations work automatically. Careful thought must be given to the timing, nature and emphasis of a demonstration. For example, the learner has to make a 'transformation' from what their eyes tell them to what their muscles must do. It doesn't follow that learners can convert visual images automatically into physical movements. It has been shown that the value of demonstrations depends on a number of criteria.

- The demonstration must be relevant to the needs of the learner and must be pitched at the correct level. An example from the building industry makes this point very well. A bricklayer has three different kinds of demonstration – a fast one, a slow one and one for the benefit of apprentices. The same also holds true in sport where the coach or teacher should tailor the precision and intention of demonstrations to suit the aspiration and skill level of those in their charge. For example, a demonstration that uses a star performer may display technical detail which is not only unattainable but which

KEY QUOTE

"If you are demonstrating a particular technique, make sure the demonstration is basic enough to be repeated by your participants. There is little point in serving like a top professional tennis player if you are trying to show a service that will get the game started for a beginner."

McQuade (2003)

also discourages the learner from trying. Newell, Morris and Scully (1985) suggest further that demonstrations in early learning only have temporary value because practice and feedback provide much more important sources of information.

- Demonstrations must, generally, be accurate and emphasise the required point. It is always possible that demonstrations given by the coach reveal personal errors they are unaware of and also present too much information. In contrast, a demonstration given by another person allows the coach to monitor possible faults as well as focus on the relevant points. Demonstrations also depend on the level of learning. Jameson (1986) highlights this in relation to dinghy sailing. He says:

"Demonstration takes place at two levels. In teaching beginners the instructor actually gets into the boat and demonstrates movements before handing the helm over to the beginner. In race training, its not possible to do this because the relationship and the movements between helm and crew are very fine and the only way that demonstrations can be done here is by using members of a particular squad or possibly bringing in a sailor from a higher level to come in and demonstrate."

• A vital point is that learners should be left to watch demonstrations without having to listen simultaneously to someone else. In the knowledge that people can only attend fully to one thing at a time (particularly beginners), it is good practice for the coach to talk through the movement and highlight the points to observe in advance of the demonstration, then allow unhindered observation afterwards. For example, in coaching a forward somersault on the trampoline, the coach might talk about the need to move the hips behind the vertical and then tell the learner to watch the hips during the demonstration. This should direct the learner's attention away from irrelevant aspects of the movement and allow concentration during the demonstration to key aspects of the technique alone. It is also vital to repeat demonstrations to make sure everyone has seen and to confirm that important information has been understood. Research shows that repeated demonstrations help reinforce ideas.

• The exact nature of the model upon which a demonstration is based should be considered. Is the model appropriate for the learners in question? Is it pitched at the right level? A model for teaching a javelin throw to beginners will be quite different to that for assisting international competitors. Anyone giving demonstrations must recognise that models on which they are based change over time. They are not fixed but alter with the individual learner, the stage of learning as well as changes to equipment, technology and tech-

Learners must be positioned correctly to gain most from a demonstration

nique efficiency. For example, recent radical changes to ski design (carving skis) have impacted on the type of demonstrations given by ski instructors. The good teacher recognises the need to adapt with regard to changes in the sport and differences between individual learners. This aspect is discussed again in Chapter 6.

• A fourth aspect concerns positioning of the learner in relation to the demonstration. To take the trampoline example cited before, it would be pointless standing people around the perimeter of the trampoline because those standing to the front and rear of the performer would not see any hip movement. Only those positioned laterally would observe the point being made by the coach. The same goes for demonstrations of asymmetrical movements. For example, in showing a golf swing or how to tie a climbing knot, the person demonstrating should consider whether it is best to face the learner so revealing a mirror image of the movement, or turn around to present the

 **KEY QUOTE**

"When you speak to your athletes, be sure to organise them so they can see and hear you. If they are milling around or crowding together, it will be much harder for you to keep their attention. Be certain that the background behind you is free from distractions and that athletes are not facing the sun. Try also to select a practice area with minimum noise so that athletes can hear you."
Martens (1997)

movement proper – albeit slightly obscured. Therefore, precise positioning on the part of the demonstrator is important. Other related considerations are distance the learner is from the demonstration (consider the ski instructor mentioned before who runs the risk of moving away very quickly from his group) and background obstructions such as lighting and texture which could render observation very poor.

• Finally, demonstrations provide a good basis for discussion. The coach should encourage question and answer as a way of solving uncertainties in the learner's mind. It is insufficient to provide a demonstration followed by practice without first ascertaining whether learners have fully understood and know what to do next. And lastly, it is vital the coach does not spend too much time on personal demonstrations – after all, it is the learner who is there to improve and not the coach! The importance of involving learners pro-actively in assessing their own learning is developed more fully in later chapters.

Visual materials

Wall charts, colour slides, posters, three-dimensional models, etc. are initially attractive and may serve to enhance the learning environment but their static nature soon renders them redundant (think of a living room clock whose constant tick soon disappears from attention). From a practical viewpoint it follows that static displays convey little or no information about the movements (timing, speed, co-ordination, etc.) to be performed. They may help focus attention on positional information but, by and large, their value is very limited. Dynamic media such as film loops, CD ROMs and especially video of experts or learners are much more beneficial. Video is useful if the coach/teacher cannot give a competent demonstration and slow motion capability reveals precise form that might be missed in a real time demonstration. With regard to the latter however, Scully (1988) has shown that slow motion replays of movement can be a very limited source of information. They may indicate 'relative' movement between body segments, but they provide nothing about absolute movement.

Let us focus on the use of video for a moment. Video is commonly used by coaches as a medium for demonstration and to provide learners with feedback information. However, it is well established that video is effective only if certain conditions are met. Firstly, the learner's attention must be directed to selected points in the demonstration. It is no good allowing people to watch a video without any kind of intervention or analysis by the coach/teacher. The risk is that it becomes just an opportunity for enjoyment alone – or possibly sleep on the part of those watching! Secondly, the learner must be given an opportunity to practice before their memory of the points made in the video has faded. This at least suggests the showing must be brief. Thirdly, the learner must possess the ability to reproduce the desired action shown in the demonstration – the point about relevance was made at the beginning of this chapter. If the object is to present a model to be copied then the model must be attainable. Fourthly, repetitive use of the video is necessary for there to be any significant performance gains. This may involve alternate use of practice and observation to ensure the learner has fully appreciated what is required. And lastly, the learner must be motivated to reproduce the action. They must possess a level of interest to understand and learn new things. Teachers or coaches may have the best will in the world but if they fail to set attainable goals and establish a purposeful atmosphere then learners may not wish to follow advice. These issues and others related to goal setting and motivation are elaborated in Chapter 7. It is also worth drawing attention once more to the slow motion/freeze frame facility that video offers. Some research has shown that slowing down certain actions (those that are especially complex or fast) aids learning because it facilitates the perceptual process. However, showing actions that are slowed down should be supported by real time actions in order to give a true picture of what is to be done.

Display changes

One of the difficulties often experienced by learners is that there is simply too much information; too much too see, listen to, think about, decisions to make, etc. The problem for learners and coaches is to contain the overload of information that produces such a confusing picture. Information overload is a particular threat to effective learning when providing guidance. One way around this is to highlight or enhance important cues by changing the display in some way. If done well, this has the effect of 'forcing' the learner to focus their attention on important features whilst ignoring distracting ones. This principle is applied in sports such as table tennis, cricket and lawn tennis where sightscreens make it easier for the player to spot the ball against what might otherwise be a confusing background. It is also used in football and some other ball games where coloured balls help players see the ball better in bad light situations. The same technique can be used to help learners concentrate on particular aspects in the display. For example, the use of fluorescent volley-balls or tennis balls makes it easier to spot the ball's position and speed in flight. In gymnastics the drawing of chalk marks on the floor helps to direct hand placement and direction during a floor sequence. And in lawn tennis it helps the would-be server to aim the ball accurately when the floor has been chalked or marked in a way to provide a clear target. In a similar way, the actual playing area can be manipulated to encourage certain techniques. For

The square on the backboard provides a very useful visual reference

example, a soccer pitch can be reduced in length to encourage passing skills; a badminton court can be reduced in width to focus attention on particular shots such as lobs and clears. Digital video (see Chapter 9) can be used to display movements overlaid with graphics to highlight key actions.

In many sports the coach/teacher can help the learner by emphasising the use of existing visual points of reference in the display. For example, the black square on the basketball backboard can be used as a target when shooting. In the front crawl, the black line which finishes in a 'T' just before the wall can be used as a reference for beginning a tumble turn. In kayaking, the use of paddles coloured on one side only assists visual reference when attempting to roll. And in rock climbing, the presence of chalk left by climbers on the rock can be used to focus beginners on where to locate their hands and feet.

Methods such as these are potentially very useful and can be applied to most sports, but their use demands some imagination and initiative on the part of the coach or teacher. They seem to have particular benefit in 'one-off' situations when assisting particular learners to overcome a difficult problem.

Verbal guidance

"My team talk was very simple. I said: 'Let's just have an old-fashioned match. Get the right result and go out for a few drinks afterwards.' It seemed to work

better than all the tactical crap."

Ron Atkinson (former football manager)

Team talks by football managers today are likely to be much more considered and informative. But the quotation by Atkinson does underline the value of talking to people. And British Telecom has even used the slogan 'It's good to talk' as a marketing tool. It cannot be denied that talking to both performers and learners alike can help in numerous ways – to motivate, provide feedback, help organise and provide useful information. But what is the exact purpose of verbal guidance? From a technical point of view, verbal instructions can:

• Describe an action – what it looks like, what it feels like to perform and what the objectives are. A coach may explain for example, what a volley pass looks like, the flight path described and when it would be used.

• Explain how a movement can be executed. The coach could describe what the learner must do to volley the ball in terms of the required body position, arm action, when to jump, and so on.

The first point is all about describing movements. In the main, coaches and teachers are very good at doing this. As long as they have an accurate model it is relatively easy to express movements in words – although it might be a rather lengthy description. The second point is concerned with explanation and is arguably more complex since to do so often requires an in-depth knowledge of the action and its constituent parts. An example from trampolining illustrates these points very well. It is quite easy to describe a seat drop and a front drop in terms of their spatial requirements – perhaps a demonstration or video would enhance a description to the learner. But it is more difficult to isolate important cues and actions and express them in a way that allows the learner to link the two movements together and carry out the action successfully.

In this example, one way to make the link is to tell the learner to "move their head to their toes" as they leave the bed from the seat drop. It is important to note that comments such as these may not relate directly to the required action or describe the action itself. In large part, instructions that tell people how to do something are based on the coach's personal knowledge and intuition and their experience of trying different methods with learners. This kind of experience is vital to good coaching because the 'how' to execute a skilled action is much more important than just stating what it looks like. And this is especially

Don't go overboard with too much verbal information!

important when teaching hazardous or complicated movements (e.g., canoe rolling, somersaults).

Another distinction can be made between direct and indirect verbal guidance. Direct verbal guidance specifies something clear about the task in hand, e.g., "angle your chest to the side wall" or "point your toes". Indirect verbal guidance or 'hinting' as it is sometimes known is a technique for achieving a particular movement without exactly specifying it. For example, to encourage a novice skier to rotate their body towards the fall line the instructor might tell the skier to imagine placing one hand in the opposite pocket. This has the effect of rotating the learner's trunk in the appropriate direction. In swimming, learners are told to imagine moving through a narrow tube. This helps to avoid exaggerated movements sideways and also inclining the body (see *Figure 1* below). In teaching a support stroke in canoeing it useful to tell the learner to pull the blade under the canoe – even though this never actually happens. Similarly, to develop correct hip movement in a trampoline somersault the learner could be told to push their hips through the ceiling window! Comments such as these can be fruitful because they make it easier for the coach to describe complicated movements and also easier for the learner to identify with the coach's requirements. In the same way it is useful to provide learners with rules or principles which help explain what they are

KEY POINT

HINTING

In climbing, novices are told to "climb with their eyes". This is not a literal instruction but helps focus attention on decisions about correct handholds.

In many ball games, learners are told to "keep their eyes on the ball". This not only provides useful flight information, but also helps angle their body to the approaching ball in the correct manner.

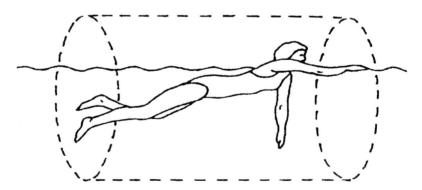

Figure 1: Diagram showing how a learner might visualise swimming within a constraining tube

doing and which may apply across a number of different sports (e.g., moving off the ball, anticipation, wide base of support, angular momentum). Research and anecdotal evidence suggests that if people understand more fully what they are doing then they remember better. However, the teaching of strategic or mechanical principles needs to have regard to the learner's ability to understand the points involved. In summary, hinting is a technique that can be applied with very good effect, but demands from the teacher/coach a degree of imagination and certainly experience to discover what works best. We'll come back to 'hinting' in a later chapter.

An additional facet of verbal guidance is what Ormond (1992) calls 'prompting'. Ormond talks about giving learners brief cues during performance (cues which may take the form of a single word or even a gesture) which are timed and designed to maximise the learners attempt to perform correctly. For example, whilst watching a beginner tackle a front somersault on the trampoline, the teacher may say "now" or "hips" to coincide with the moment the learner opens from the tuck position. Thus, rather than simply instructing and waiting for the learner to complete a movement, which may turn out incorrect, the teacher/coach prompts during the movement to shape it more quickly. This is a procedure that many good teachers adopt automatically and is useful in helping learners understand more fully the importance of timing and cue relevance.

Verbal guidance has been shown to be particularly beneficial where discrimination, decision-making and perceptual judgements are critical (the 'Cognitive' dimension – see Chapter 1). Often, it is simpler to talk about the intricacies of tactical and strategic play (probably backed up with demonstrations) – at least initially – than just demonstrating them without a verbal description. For this reason it seems that 'open' skills benefit more from verbal guidance than 'closed' skills. This makes sense when con-

Do you provide too much information to learners?

sidering the varied nature of open skill situations. It is also suggested that verbal instruction has more meaning at higher levels of skill; the more experienced a person, the greater their skill vocabulary and hence the greater their ability to understand and benefit from technical descriptions. To illustrate, the experienced badminton player will know what it means to "shorten or lengthen their backswing" or "keep a wide base and flexed knees," whereas the novice might be lost. It should not be concluded that verbal guidance does not help learners. But, there is a need to acknowledge that learners typically do not have the same kind of attention span as experts and certainly lack the knowledge base required to understanding technical jargon. Research has shown that too much talk can have a detrimental effect on learners and anecdotal evidence also supports this conclusion.

It should also be realised that with any kind of guidance, learners have to translate the information given to them into a physical movement. However, with a verbal description the transition is less direct than say a visual demonstration. It also requires greater attention and imposes an extra memory load on the learner. And it should be borne in mind that learners are usually eager to practice. Hence, an over-lengthy description may bore or frustrate the learner and even create unnecessary feelings of uncertainty about what to do.

There is another important feature of verbal guidance that should be noted. It relates to research on 'attentional focus'. The question has been posed about what exactly should learners concentrate on when practicing a motor skill? Normally, the attention of learners is directed to aspects of their movements such as the manner in which arms and legs co-ordinate with each other (e.g., "your backhand smash is taking place when your legs are incorrectly positioned" or, in climbing, "your arms are too stretched to see the rock face"). Comments like this that are designed to focus 'awareness' are common practice, but their effectiveness has recently been called into question. It has been argued that since expert performers don't think about the details of their movements, it may be ineffective to force beginners to consciously think about their movements. Wulf and her colleagues have shown that instructing learners to focus on details of their movements during performance can be detrimental to both learning and performance. She has found it is more effective if a learner's attention is directed to the effect their movements have on the environment, rather than the nature of their movements. In one of her studies (Wulf et al, 2000) subjects were required to learn a golf swing. Those subjects instructed to focus on the movement of the club head showed greater accuracy in hitting the ball towards a target than those who were instructed to focus on their own arm movements. One explanation for this is that in the normal course of skilled movement, actions are planned and controlled according to their intended effects and not the precise movements (Prinz, 1997). As Wulf, McNevin, Fuchs, Ritter and Toole (2000) point out, people tend to 'know' how their body works, so attending to movements is relatively uninformative. What this research seems to suggest is that at some point during the learning process, it may be more important to draw the learner's attention away from their own movements and instead, direct it to the effects of their movements. More research is required on this subject; especially deciding at what point the transitions should be made.

Finally, there are a number of practical considerations relevant to verbal guidance. The acoustics of the working area can play a big part in how well messages are conveyed to people. Swimming pools are notoriously poor and outdoor playing areas can present competing noises (e.g., road traffic, aircraft, building works). In all of these cases, it is vital to bring participants close in and keep instructions to a minimum. When working with groups of people, instructions should always be directed to the furthest person and checks should be made to see if they have heard/understood. The coach/teacher should be positioned so that all can see/hear and the group should be positioned to minimise any noise/visual distractions. The use of simple commands (prompts) such as "stop" or "hold it" combined with manual gestures to direct people's attention all aid effective verbal communication. Miles (2003) discusses some of these practical teaching strategies.

Manual guidance

Having focused on vision and hearing it remains to examine the physical or kinesthetic sense and the importance of internal sensations in learning. Boyce (1991) has suggested that teachers should spend less time on 'show and tell' procedures and more time on those that encourage the feel of movement. The feel of movement is very much associated with the kinesthetic sense that has for many years been of great scientific and practical interest to sports scientists, physical educationalists and

Subtle manual guidance helps this learner maintain balance prior to rolling the kayak

coaches. In some ways it is the least understood of all the senses. Questions surrounding its exact nature – which nerve receptors serve kinesthesis and whether kinesthesis also includes our perception of touch and balance – permeate the academic literature. Investigators have examined kinesthetic short-term memory, the effect of movement-generated feedback on levels of arousal (does chewing gum keep you alert?) and the relative importance it plays in maintaining balance. One thing is clear. The kinesthetic sense provides a rich source of information feedback for learners and a channel through which teachers and coaches can communicate.

Specifically, manual guidance involves some kind of physical contact between the learner and coach or between the learner and another device (e.g., a swimming float). As well as providing information about 'how to do it', a major function of manual guidance is to control movements made by the learner. Specifically, the aim is to minimise or eliminate completely any kind of movement error. There are two kinds of guidance, viz., physical restriction and forced response. With physical restriction, the learner's movements are restricted either by another person or by an external object. Typical examples would be the use of a float in swimming or physical assistance from a canoe coach to help a learner upright a capsized canoe. Here, the coach or device acts in a guiding capacity whilst the learner applies the effort to produce the action. Another example would be the use of a hinged plastic device that attaches to the tips of downhill skis. This device is used with physically disabled skiers who may have difficulty controlling their actions. The device is sufficiently flexible to provide 'give' when the skier is moving and will snap into two sections if the skier falls. With forced response methods, a second person/s physically transports the learner through the movement with little or no effort from the learner. An example would be the coach moving a player's arm through a tennis serve action. Another would be a gymnastics coach transporting a young child through a forward roll. These techniques reduce errors on the part of the learner and dramatically reduce the elements of fear and danger. In this way they aid confidence and encourage learners into situations where they would otherwise not venture (e.g., deep water). They also offer potential for learners to progress beyond previous levels. For these reasons manual guidance is especially useful with very young children, anyone with low confidence and those with special learning difficulties.

Despite the obvious advantages of manual guidance (e.g., consider the widespread use of swimming aids) the research is somewhat guarded on the benefits. It is recognised that manual techniques assist in giving the learner ideas about the gross spatial patterns involved in movements (e.g., an up-side-down position in a somersault or a horizontal posture in water). They do not always help in the discovery of critical cues, timing, co-ordination or the forces involved in actions. The essential problem with manual guidance is that the feeling of movement which it creates is not the same as the individual's own kinesthetic perception – the kinesthetic sense responds differently. Thus if the coach moves a learner's arm through a serving action it will not result in the same 'feeling' as if the learner had initiated the movement. The pay-off is that the guided action is technically correct. It follows that physical restriction produces a more realistic picture than forced response, but the weakness remains that the learner does not receive exactly the correct kind of feedback and may even be encouraged to depend on the support given. It should be mentioned that current theories of learning emphasise the critical nature of active participation by learners. This is negated by the use of manual techniques. This particular topic is discussed in the next section as well as in Chapter 4.

THE LEARNING GRADIENT

"When I hear, I forget;
When I see, I remember;
When I do, I understand"
Confucious.

We have looked at a variety of ways in which teachers and coaches can provide information to learners – hearing, seeing, touch, feeling and so on. Some of these ideas and principles have been used by Priest and Hammerman (1989) to formulate what they call the learning gradient. They identify four distinct approaches to teaching an activity, viz.,

- Speaking to the learner   (INSTRUCTION)
- Demonstrating the activity   (DEMONSTRATION)
- Ensuring the learner practices the activity   (APPLICATION)
- Questioning the learner about the activity   (CONFIRMATION)

They suggest that each of these can be located on a continuum in regard to the 'amount that is learned' (see *Figure 2*). It is worth noting the points they make about

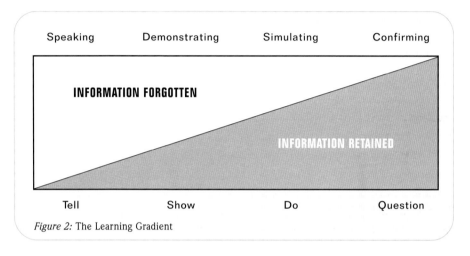

Figure 2: The Learning Gradient

each one as many confirm much of what has already been said in this chapter. Verbal instruction aims to convey to the learner what a skill is all about, what are the aims and how it should be executed. The dangers of verbal instruction are that too much information may be given, the learner may be confused through new terminology. Further, it may not be very easy for the learner to convert what they hear into actual movements. Unless verbal instruction is brief, relevant and simple to understand it may be forgotten very easily. Demonstrations involve showing the learner what to do ('a picture paints a thousand words'). They are extremely valuable but must be well planned in order to convey the relevant points. They do not need to be technically perfect, as long as they convey the right kind of information. Practice or application is essential to learning as long as due consideration is given to the exact conditions of practice – how long, how frequent, what should be practiced – and so on. The adage 'learning by doing' is extremely valid and applies to learners at all stages of their development. Confirmation focuses on the feedback or review stage. Priest and Hammerman suggest it is a stage that is typically omitted by many teachers and coaches.

A strong body of evidence shows that when learners (and experts alike) are given the oppor-

> ### KEY QUOTE
>
> *"Good coaches try to empower their participants and encourage them to analyse their own performance. By using effective questions to aid this self-assessment and reflection, coaches can guide participants in finding their own solutions to improving their performance."*
> **McQuade** (2003)

tunity to analysis and appraisal their own learning there are a number of benefits that enrich the learning process. Generally speaking, self analysis leads to a better understanding what the learner is doing which in turn, enhances motivation and improves the ability to set appropriate goals. It also leads to greater memory retention. For these reasons, whilst each of the four steps have their strengths and characteristics, Priest and Hammerman place great store in the fourth of component. They advocate that all good coaches and teachers should find ways to move along the learning/teaching continuum to encompass the confirmation stage.

LEARN-LOOK-DO OR DO-LOOK-LEARN?

The author once had a friend who was a medically qualified doctor. The doctor explained in simple terms how he had been trained. He used the expression "see one, do one, teach one." Whilst this was a gross simplification, it did reveal something about the kind of teaching philosophy adopted by his medical school and the sequence of operations deemed to be important in the learning process. Koziey (1987) focuses on the importance of sequencing. He contrasts two ways in which people can learn. The Learn-Look-Do approach he says is that which is commonly used by teachers and coaches. The 'Learn' phase is characterised by some kind of formal, direct input – reading or listening to the teacher/coach. Learners then 'Look' at someone demonstrating the skill (the teacher of another learner) and this is followed by physical practice to effect what has been heard and seen – the 'Do' phase. This sequence of operations is effective for many individuals. Koziey contrasts this with another approach which is a reversal of the sequence of processes. With the Do-Look-Learn approach, learners firstly engage in a discovery-based period where, with little guidance, they practice the to-be-learned skill. During the 'Look' phase learners reflect on their practice by observing others, including a demonstration of the correct actions by the teacher or other learner. Koziey suggests this phase is critical in that it provides the learner with an opportunity to determine what they did, how it happened and what factors are important to success. From this experience, the 'Learn' phase involves the learner internalising their observations and experiences, which subsequently allows them to apply their newly acquired skills to new situation. It is easy to see the similarity between Koziey's two views on learning and the part/whole practice dichotomy discussed in a previous chapter. The Learn-Look-Do approach lends itself to a part practice approach whereas the Do-Look-Learn approach is very much a holistic and all-encompassing approach to learning. Furthermore, it should be noted that the Learn-Look-Do approach is one that is supported by Behaviourist learning theory, whilst the Do-Look-Learn approach is supported by Cognitive theory.

Koziey's views on learning point to two very different ways in which people can and may prefer to learn. They also imply two different teaching/coaching strategies.

To appeal to people preferring to learn via the Learn-Look-Do approach requires a traditional, teacher directed style of teaching whereas the other approach requires a more experiential-based approach. We will look more closely at teaching styles in Chapter 8.

SUMMARY OF THE KEY POINTS

• Guidance is information provided by the coach before the learner makes an attempt at the movement.

• Practice is the act of going through a movement without any guidance whilst training is the process of learning with guidance.

• Practice is potentially limited in a number of ways:

  • Trial and error practice may result in the formation of bad habits
  • Extra time is required to eradicate bad habits
  • The learner's performance level remains low
  • Risk of dropout from the sport is increased.

• Guidance is provided through the three senses – vision, audition and kinesthesis.

• The separate senses can each provide the same information and they interact to give the learner a total picture of the movement or task.

• Visual guidance can be one of three kinds, viz., demonstrations provided by the coach, expert or learner; visual materials such as film loops or wallcharts; changes to the display such as the addition of a sight screen or colouring important pieces of apparatus to cue on.

• Demonstrations rely on learning by imitation; they are intuitively appealing; they are immediate and practical to employ; they avoid lengthy verbal descriptions; they should be used with caution, i.e., they should be relevant, accurate and repeated. The position of the learner must be considered and the time spent on demonstrations should be balanced against total practice time.

• Visual aids that are static in nature are of questionable value.

• Video film of experts/learners has a number of advantages. It is intuitively appealing, offers immediate feedback and replay/slow motion facility.

• Video is effective only if certain conditions are met. The learner's attention must be directed to specific points. Practice must be allowed immediately following replay and the learner must have the potential to copy the points made on the video. Repeated viewing is vital to success and the learner must be motivated to succeed.

• Rearranging apparatus or highlighting features by colouring/texturing is a useful way of emphasising important cues.

• Verbal instructions serve two purposes, viz., to describe what an action looks like and to explain how it may be executed.

• Direct verbal guidance expresses something concrete about an action or task, whereas indirect instruction hints at the action or indicates another action which if attempted results in the desired one.

• Verbal guidance seems to be particularly useful for advanced learners and with skills that have an important 'perceptual' element, e.g., tactical/strategic play in soccer.

• Verbal guidance is limited in a number of ways. The learner may not understand. The learner is required to 'cross the bridge' between words and action. The learner may be bored by lengthy talks and there exists the difficulty of explaining some movements in words.

• Manual guidance takes two forms:

  • Physical restriction where a second person or other device is used to guide the learner through a movement
  • Forced response where a second person physically transports the learner through a movement.

• Manual guidance is valuable in:

  • Reducing the fear element in difficult/dangerous activities
  • Reducing the element of danger
  • Highlighting spatial elements in a movement
  • Illustrating an action that would be difficult to express in words
  • Use with special groups, e.g., young children, old people, those wit low skill levels.

• Manual guidance is limited because it provides different feedback from normal performance and reduces the learner's degree of active participation.

• The 'Learning Gradient' suggests that people learn best when they are involved in questioning their own learning. Speaking to learners, demonstrations, practice and questioning are increasingly richer learning experiences.

• Evidence shows that when learners are given the opportunity to analysise and appraise their own learning there are a number of benefits that enrich the learning process. Self analysis leads to a better understanding of what the learner is doing which in turn, enhances motivation and improves the ability to set appropriate goals

PRACTICAL TASKS

• This task looks at the relative advantages of three methods of guidance. The task is to teach someone to draw an accurate picture of the 'plough' constellation. First, obtain a copy of the constellation and draw/copy it to a sheet of A4 using a bold black pen. Now identify three willing learners. The first will be taught using verbal guidance. The learner sits down at a table with a sheet of white A4 paper and a pen/pencil. Tell them to locate the pen in the top left hand corner. Now talk them through the action with commands like, "draw a line 10 cms long in a direction of 120 degrees, then stop. Now draw a second line etc." Repeat this two or three times then ask the learner to draw the plough without any guidance. The second learner is given visual guidance. Place the picture on the table and ask the learner to copy it on their own sheet. They repeat this two or three times before drawing it without any help. The third person is given manual guidance. Ask the learner to hold the pen firmly in their hand whilst you physically guide it through the desired pattern. The learner must close their eyes and not resist the movements made by their/your hands. Repeat this two or three times. Finally, the learner draws the pattern with out any help, but they can keep their eyes open. A comparison of the three patterns should reveal the superiority of the visual method.

• To demonstrate the importance of tactile 'feel' when carrying out a skill, try the following. Obtain a variety of balls (basketball, lawn tennis ball, table tennis ball, volley ball). Also obtain a number of different types of gloves of varying thickness and materials (gardening gloves, plastic washing up gloves, leather gloves, woollen gloves). Now attempt to bounce each ball repeatedly on the ground or throw and catch each ball in turn using the different gloves. You should find each of these tasks much easier with thinner gloves. What this demonstrates is that performance is aided with more sensitive information input. Can you also think of other reasons why each of the ball handling tasks is easier with thinner gloves? (Hint: think ergonomics)

• To demonstrate the critical importance of visual guidance try a basketball free shot under the following two conditions. In the first case, try to sink the basketball with your eyes open. Have a couple of familiarity shots then try to score as many out of 10. A partner can keep score. Next, try to shoot 10 baskets but this time close your eyes for 10 seconds just before you shoot. You should find performance is worse under these circumstances. This reveals not only the value of visual guidance in performing a skill correctly, but also the serious limitations of short term memory (see Chapter 2).

• This task is a critical analysis of demonstrations. It requires someone to think of a skill (e.g., golf swing) and simply demonstrate it to a group of friends. The demonstration should take about 2/3 minutes and also include some verbal comment as appropriate. Those watching/listening to the demonstration should make a few written comments as soon as the demonstration is complete. The aim is to be as critical as possible (Was it a good demonstration? Did it last too long? Was to much information conveyed? Could everyone see? Was the demonstrator positioned effectively?). Following this, everyone can engage in discussion and debate with a view to identify some of the key features of a good demonstration.

REVIEW QUESTIONS

• What are your views about novices practicing by themselves? For example, do you think it is good for the novice to make errors during learning?

• Can you think of an example in your sport where once a bad habit has formed it is difficult to eliminate?

• Why does the habit appear in the first place?

• Examine a situation in your sport where you could communicate the idea of a skill using different senses.

• Is it likely that you would use different senses to get across the message?

• Have you ever examined whether your own personal demonstrations (as a teacher or coach) are correct?

• How useful is it to strike a balance between your own demonstrations and those of say a team member?

• At what stage/s in the learner's progress do you think demonstrations are most important?

• In your sport is it important to consider how people are positioned with respect to a demonstration?

• Comment on the view that the practical difficulties in using video (e.g., cost, operational skills) outweigh the benefits.

• If you have used video in your sport state the circumstances in which it has been most valuable.

- Are there instances in your sport where visual cues are highlighted in some way to make it easier for the learner or expert performer? If so, state what they are.

- In your coaching or teaching are you aware of the important distinction between describing and explaining skill?

- Consider an activity or movement in your sport and write down the instructions you would use to express HOW to do it.

- How do you know whether people have understood your instructions?

- At what stage/s of learning do you think that 'chat' is most beneficial?

- Can you provide examples of manual guidance as used in your sport?

- Are there particular instances when manual guidance is of special value in your sport?

- What are the major problems with manual guidance?

- Can you think of situations where you actively involve your learners in assessing their performance or learning problems? In other words, do you let them speak out about their difficulties or strengths? Do you let them try to work out where problems lie? Do you permit different learners in a group to assess the performance of one another?

References

Bandura, A. (1969). *Principles of behaviour modification.* New York: Holt, Rienhart & Winston.

Boyce, B.A. (1991). Beyond show and tell – teaching the feel of the movement. *The Journal of Physical Education, Recreation and Dance,* 62, 1, 18 - 20.

Harrison, J.M., and Blakemore, C. (1989). *Instructional Strategies for Physical Education.* Dubuque, Iowa: W. C. Brown.

Hickey, K. (1986). Quotation from Sharp, R.H. *Acquiring skill – Coach Education Modules.* Edinburgh: The Scottish Sports Council.

Jameson, J. (1986). Quotation from Sharp, R.H. *Acquiring skill.* (Coach education modules). Edinburgh: The Scottish Sports Council.

Koziey, P.W. (1997). Experiencing mutuality. *Journal of Experiential Education,* 10, 3, 20 - 22.

Martens, R. (1997). *Successful coaching* (2nd Edition). Champaign, Illinois.: Human Kinetics.

McQuade, S. (2003). *How to coach sports effectively.* Leeds: Coachwise Solutions.

Miles, A. (2003). *What is sports coaching?* Leeds: Coachwise Solutions.

Newell, K.M., Morris, L.R. and Scully, D.M. (1985). *Augmented information and the acquisition of skill in physical activity.* In R.L. Terjung (Ed.), Exercise and Sport Sciences Review (Vol. 13). New York: Macmillan.

Ormond, T.C. (1992). The prompt/feedback package in physical education. *Journal of Physical Education, Recreation and Dance,* 63, 1, 64 - 67.

Priest, S. and Hammerman, D. (1989). *Teaching outdoor adventure skills.* Adventure Education, 6, 4, 16 - 18.

Prinz, W. (1997). Perception and action planning. *European Journal of Cognitive Psychology,* 9, 129 - 154.

Rink, J. (1999). *Instruction from a learning perspective.* In Hardy, C. A. and Mawer, M. (Eds.). *Learning and teaching in physical education.* London: Falmer Press.

Schmidt. R.A. and Wrisberg, C.A. (2000). *Motor learning and performance – a problem-based learning approach.* Champaign, Illinois: Human Kinetics.

Scully, D.M. (1988). Visual perception of human movement: the use of demonstrations in teaching motor skills. *British Journal of Physical Education (Research Supplement),* 19, 6.

Shedden, J. (1986). Quotation from Sharp, R.H. *Acquiring skill.* (Coach education modules). Edinburgh: The Scottish Sports Council.

Williams, A.M., Davids, K., and Williams, J.G. (1999). *Visual perception and action in sport.* London: E & F.N. Spon.

Wulf, G., McNevin, N.H., Fuchs, T., Ritter, F., and Toole, T. (2000). Attentional focus in complex skill learning. *Research Quarterly in Exercise and Sport,* 71, 3, 229 - 239.

"To develop skill, performers need relevant, corrective and positive feedback. Feedback involves the performer in collecting and interpreting information about performance from both internal and external sources."

Foxon (1999)

INTRODUCTION

Feedback is considered by many people to be the single most important variable in the learning process. The word 'feedback' is used to express many things such as reinforcement, reward and knowledge of results. It is taken to mean information that occurs as a result of executing a movement. In this sense it is quite different from the word 'guidance' dealt with in the previous chapter. Guidance is the information the performer receives before movement, whilst feedback is the information received after movement.

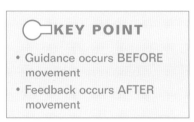

KEY POINT

• Guidance occurs BEFORE movement

• Feedback occurs AFTER movement

The word feedback is borrowed from disciplines quite different from the world of coaching and teaching. The word comes from the field of control engineering. It refers specifically to the flow of information within a control system to inform the system what it is doing and what effect the constituent parts are having on one another. An example of a control system which contains a feedback device (sometimes called a servomechanism) is a home refrigerator. A refrigerator aims to keep its contents cool to a prescribed temperature. If the temperature goes lower than that set by the owner, the fridge switches itself off and consequently proceeds to warm up. When the

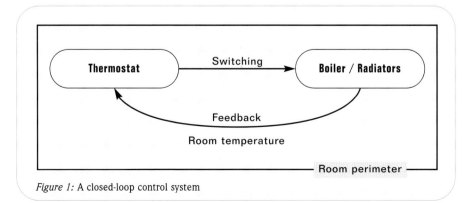

Figure 1: A closed-loop control system

preset temperature is exceeded the fridge is switched on again to begin the process of cooling once more. The feedback in this example is the present air temperature within the refrigerator. *Figure 1* illustrates this schematically in relation to a domestic central heating system. It will be recognised that for feedback information to be of any use the fridge or heating system must have a means of sensing the information. The sensing device in both cases is the thermostat, which opens and closes an electrical circuit as appropriate. Any system, which uses feedback, must have a sensing element. In the case of humans, the sensing element is the senses (vision, touch, etc.).

It is relevant to point out that there are two basic kinds of control systems. A control system, which monitors the effects of its operation, is called a 'closed loop' system. Refrigerators and central heating systems operate like this. In contrast, an 'open loop' system does not have a feedback device. An example is an ordinary electrical bar fire. A bar fire when switched on will continue to heat the room regardless of its effect. *Figure 2* shows these two systems in schematic form.

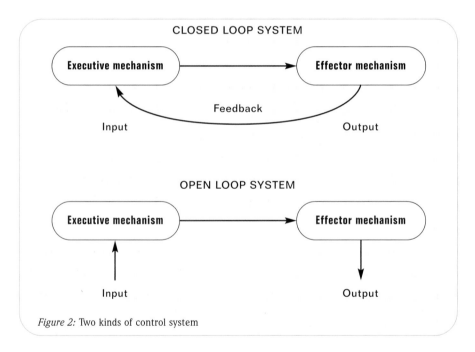

Figure 2: Two kinds of control system

The Executive Mechanism is that component which issues the commands, (e.g., the switch on the bar fire), whilst the Effector Mechanism actually carries out the commands (e.g., the heating element). There are many systems in everyday life that can be examined in this manner. Take, for example, a small industrial company or retail outlet. Consider the workforce as management and workers and take two distinct modes of operation. Management could take an autocratic stance and not listen to its workers (open loop) or they could adopt a democratic stance by listening to the workers and making changes based on information received a (closed loop). These are extreme situations; in reality, both approaches probably occur from time to time. Another example would be the reader's own coaching or teaching style. Sometimes it might be appropriate to make decisions about content and method without consulting the individual learner whilst on other occasions (perhaps most frequently) it is better to listen to learners so that coaching becomes a two-way affair. Which style is best? It is likely that in both these examples, sometimes an open loop approach is best whilst at other times a closed loop approach is preferable. We will return to the matter of coaching styles in Chapter 8.

Systems that employ feedback are more sophisticated and adaptable than those which do not. For this reason, the use of feedback as an information giving tool is central to good coaching and teaching. From the learner's point of view, in order to move skilfully and adapt to an ever-changing world there is a need to constantly observe actions, their effect and react accordingly. Feedback is critical to learning and to successful performance. A simple demonstration of the importance of feedback is seen in the act of picking up a cup from a table.

An initial command from the brain results in the arm extending in the cup's direction. As the arm moves closer, the eyes make an accurate assessment of distance between cup and hand (use of visual feedback) which allows the hand to move more precisely for the fine grasping action. Visual feedback may be used once or twice in such a task. To prove the value of visual feedback in this example, try picking up the cup but close your eyes just after starting to move your arm. The results will be obvious; you may fumble to make contact or may even knock over the cup.

The examples given before illustrate a number of features about feedback which are critical to skill acquisition. Firstly, for feedback information to be of any value there must be some kind of model or reference against which it is compared. In the fridge example the reference is the preset temperature. If there is no model then feedback information has no value because there is no point of reference to judge whether or not the system is working optimally. Secondly, the system must be able to detect the error between the reference and the feedback and consequently do something useful about it. That is, the system must be able to effect corrective action to minimise the error. Thirdly, it must be noted that feedback is, in effect, information which tells the system about errors produced, i.e., how far away from the intended performance is actual performance. Feedback information derives from the difference between desired and actual performance. From the point of view of the learner and the coach/ teacher this poses a potential problem; it would be de-motivating to continually tell the learner they are making errors. Feedback (error) information must be presented in a manner that has a positive influence on learning. As we all know, it is very easy to find fault and criticise – even naive observers are sometimes good at spotting performance errors. The real skill is in turning such information into positive assistance so that it is used to encourage people to improve and try harder. We shall pick up these issues later following a broader look at what feedback means for human learning and performance and what effect it has on the individual. To place this discussion into the correct context, it's useful to note the views of Crisfield (1986):

"Feedback is absolutely vital. Lacrosse is a very complex game because there are 24 people on the field of play. Consequently, decision making has to involve almost all those people. Therefore it's very difficult to evaluate your own role without some kind of external feedback. I try to give them two forms of feedback – objective feedback from game analysis as well as subjective feedback from my own perceptions. I try to give players feedback on a personal basis, face to face, and if that's not possible, which sometimes in a large team game it isn't, I'm forced to give them feedback on paper. I try and give feedback as soon as possible after the game but this depends on the individual and what has happened in the game."

IMPORTANCE OF FEEDBACK

Let us now look at some of the evidence that supports this kind of thinking.

Homeostatic systems

It appears that we use feedback of different kinds constantly, simply to regulate and control moment to moment activity. This is particularly so with physiological systems such as breathing and bodily temperature which are maintained at an adequate level despite a constantly changing environment (the process of homeostasis). Posture is controlled in the same manner; as the body leans forwards, receptors in the calf muscles stretch. As a consequence, signals are returned to the same muscles, which causes them to contract in a manner that returns the body to a balanced position. This cycle continues – quite unconsciously – to maintain the individual in a postural state. There are many closed-loop feedback systems in the body like this (pupil diameter, respiration rate, blood pressure and so on) which ensure that vital bodily systems take care of all these themselves quite automatically.

Feedback studies

The value of feedback in controlling physical activity is demonstrated by studies that artificially remove or distort feedback. In one study, squash players were asked to play a game whilst wearing headphones through which was played 'white' noise. The noise was chosen to mask any sound of contact between ball, racquet and the walls. In many cases players found it very difficult to time their strokes effectively and were very surprised at their failure. They were still able to make contact with the ball, but their timing accuracy deteriorated markedly. In another study, people were asked to balance standing on a narrow lathe of wood whilst the (artificial) room was physically swayed a minute amount backwards and forwards. Invariably, people found it more difficult to balance when the room moved compared to when it was stationary. And there have been studies that have delayed the auditory feedback people receive when they speak. In these studies, subjects have been required to read from a written text whilst listening to their recorded voice through headphones. If the recording is heard immediately, then subjects have no difficulty reading. If, however, their voice is delayed by a second or two, there comes a point when it is almost impossible to speak. It seems that the delay disturbs the normal pattern of information feedback essential to optimal performance. Other studies have removed sensory feedback to examine the consequences on performance. In one study subjects were required to execute a manual tapping task whilst kinesthetic feedback was blocked using a tourniquet arrangement. Subjects were still able to make the required movements but aspects of timing and co-ordination were lost. There are numerous situations in life that rely on visual feedback. This is verified when such feedback is removed. Try writing your signature a few times with your eyes closed. Also try typing on a computer keyboard without vision. In both of these cases, it is very likely that performance will be less successful than with the eyes open.

What do these studies reveal? They demonstrate the critical importance of feedback to successful performance/behaviour. They also indicate that feedback control can occur quite automatically without any conscious awareness of the information being used to control behaviour. The squash players were not aware they used auditory cues and the subjects in the balance experiment were not conscious of using visual cues to assist their balance. The studies also indicate that different sources of feedback (i.e., auditory and visual) are used in controlling physical activity. Linked to this finding is the observation that through learning the nature of feedback control changes. It is recognised that as people improve with practice they change from predominantly visual/verbal form of feedback control to one where they rely more on internal or kinesthetic feedback. This point was made in Chapter 2 when discussing Fitts's theory of skill learning. The squash and balance studies show further that experts do not just rely solely on internal feedback, but use a number of different kinds of information – which may depend on the kind of task in hand. Thus, it may be that whilst performers at all levels of skill use the same kinds of feedback mechanisms, the relative importance of each may change with practice and through learning.

EFFECTS OF FEEDBACK

Let us now examine some of the major principles of feedback, which are relevant to the study of skill learning. These principles stem from a number of sources – the experience of coaches and teachers, research findings, as well as theoretical principles. Firstly, let us consider the particular effect that feedback has on learning. It is agreed that although feedback provides information about performance it may serve four different purposes – to motivate learners, to change their performance, to reinforce learning and to create dependency.

Motivational feedback

In its role as a motivator, feedback tells the learner that errors are reducing and consequently that skill level is increasing. In this respect feedback acts rather like a reward. It is well known that people are motivated to improve if suitably rewarded and are stimulated to greater efforts if they succeed; the so called 'law of effect' was described in the first chapter. Feedback as a motivator works particularly well with tasks that are repetitive, boring or take a long time to perform. It is also known that if feedback is withheld or given infrequently, motivation tends to weaken. There is a potential problem here. As noted earlier, caution must be expressed when telling people about their errors and mistakes. Coaches and teachers need to be careful because with some learners, error information ("your legs are both bent and your head is not tucked at all," to a learner gymnast) may inhibit learning as the comment is construed as criticism. The point was made before that feedback must be presented in a constructive manner if it is to have a positive effect. Coaches and teachers must therefore consider the manner in which they provide feedback, the timing as well as the kind and amount of feedback given. Sensitivity to the learner's personality, needs and goals and intellectual capacity should provide answers to these problems. It may help (as indicated in the previous chapter) to ask the learner what they believe to be their weaknesses. It may be easier for a learner to accept (and hence treat positively) information about their errors when it is self-generated rather than imposed by someone else. It is also worth noting that feedback can serve as a helpful source of motivation when learners are progressing very slowly. For example, a beginner kayaker may demonstrate improved forward paddling technique, although it is not reflected in overall improvement (they still capsize frequently). In cases like this, a comment such as "great – you're doing really well," which focuses on the actual improvements, can be highly motivating and spur people on to greater efforts.

Information feedback

The second and perhaps most common function of feedback is to provide information about performance. If a ski instructor tells the learner that his body weight is too far backwards, the learner uses this information to adjust their posture accordingly and performance improves. Information feedback like this only 'works' if the learner can interpret the feedback and judge it against a reference or model of what is correct. In the ski example the instructor might ask the learner to lean forwards and then backwards a few times to compare the correct and incorrect positions. This could be augmented through the instructor demonstrating the incorrect and correct positions for the learner to see themselves. Feedback might not always be so clearly interpreted however, especially in sports where visual feedback is absent. Take a front drop in trampolining where the lower legs cannot be seen. It is virtually impossible for the novice to gauge leg position because kinesthetic sensitivity of the knee joint is very crude. Therefore, telling the learner about incorrect leg position may be less informative than physically moving their legs into and out of the correct position several times. In its informative role, feedback narrows down the discrepancy between what the coach and learner are trying to achieve and what the learner is presently doing. This process hinges on correct error identification and the possession of a model of excellence by both coach and (gradually) the learner. In this regard, Schmidt and Wrisberg (2000) distinguish between descriptive and prescriptive feedback. Descriptive feedback states something about what the learner/performer did, such as "that was very fast", or "you are not aggressive enough when tackling". In contrast, prescriptive feedback goes a stage further and provides an explanation about what should be done to improve a movement. Thus, if a field hockey coach says "you keep loosing the ball because you dribble it too far ahead of the stick", this tells (prescribes to) the learner what he/she should do to remedy the situation. On balance, prescriptive feedback is more beneficial to learners than descriptive feedback.

Reinforcement feedback

Feedback also has a reinforcing function. It confirms to the learner that progress is being made in the right direction. In this sense, it increases the likelihood that the performance will be repeated in the same manner again. Coaches and teachers can provide reinforcing feedback both verbally or through gesture/facial expressions. Indeed, sometimes, a simple smile or nod can convey information more clearly and quickly than a lengthy verbal description. Confirming success may be just as desirable as providing new information to learners. Sometimes, coaches and teachers tend to ignore the value of confirmation/reinforcement because the assumption is made that when learners are performing as required, they know they are doing so. This can be a false assumption. Learners who lack experience of success and who do not have a clear idea of 'excellence' (particularly in activities where success is not easily quantifiable such as in football) may not always be in a good position to judge their own performance. Regular feedback in these cases is vital, even though it serves merely to confirm success.

Dependency feedback

Research shows that too much feedback can be given to learners. If feedback is given too frequently, people can depend on it to generate movements, rather than using and relying on intrinsic feedback. If learners fail to begin the process of internalising their learning and rely almost totally on external feedback, their performance deteriorates when the feedback is removed. There are several ways in which the dependency effect can be minimised, one of which is to adopt the technique of 'fading' where the frequency of feedback is gradually reduced with improvements in skill. A fading strategy would be marked by frequent feedback in initial practice; a learner may be given feedback following every attempt at a skill, followed by a gradual reduction until the learner was able to utilise internal sources alone. The speed of fading depends very much on the individual's rate of learning and their ability/motivation to process internal sources of feedback.

KEY POINT

Feedback can:
• Motivate learners
• Provide key information
• Reinforce good practice
• Create dependency

As a rule, all four aspects interact. Sometimes however, the coach may wish to direct feedback for a particular purpose as when willing a person to greater effort following say an injury or loss of confidence. In this case, their comments – which may not accurately reflect the learner's performance – are intended as a spur to effort, to enhance confidence and develop interest. The important thing is for those giving feedback to know why it is being given. Then, there is a good chance it will have the desired effect.

MODELS

The provision and utilisation of feedback assumes that the coach or teacher has a reference or standard by which to judge performance. Feedback cannot be evaluated without a definitive model for comparison that is technically appropriate. A clear example of this is seen in those sports where successful performance depends largely on conformity to a prescribed movement pattern, e.g., trampolining, high jumping, and ski jumping. A coach teaching the Fosbury flop say, must have a clear idea in their mind's eye about correct technique to be able to judge incorrect attempts at the movement. Such a model must be technically accurate but also flexible enough to allow for individual variations in body shape and levels of performance. Thus, the model for say a beginner (front somersault in trampolining or penalty kick in football) would be quite different for the

KEY QUOTE

"There is no substitute for knowing skills well in correcting learning errors. The better you understand a skill – not only how it is done correctly but what causes learning errors – the more helpful you will be in correcting mistakes. One of the most common coaching mistakes is to provide inaccurate feedback and advice on how to correct errors. If you are uncertain about the cause of the problem or how to correct it, continue to observe and analyse until you are more sure."
Martens (1997)

expert. The sensitive coach or teacher therefore assesses feedback in relationship to a flexible model that depends on factors associated with the individual and their stage of learning.

A further requirement of the coach is that they be able to detect differences between the model and the learner's performance. The ability to spot errors depends on an in-depth knowledge of the activity. This may arise from personal participation in the sport as well as experience of watching and coaching people at different skill levels. It may also arise from more sophisticated examinations based on video film or computerised notational analysis and it may include information about the physiological and biomechanical requirements of the activity. Armed with such knowledge, the coach will know that technical weaknesses are not always the result of learning problems per se. Poor technique may lie in a fitness deficiency or possibly a weakness caused by injury. In swimming for example, a common problem is that learners tend to sink their hips too low. This happens because the head is held too high out of the water. The actual problem however, may result because the learner has not developed correct breathing or they lack the appropriate body tension. In this case, the coach would take the swimmer back to basic confidence work and help them swim with face submerged, or attend to their fitness weaknesses.

Error spotting is often difficult because performance is too rapid for considered appraisal. This is an area where video replay comes into its own. This is seen increasingly in fast moving sports such as rugby and cricket where the umpire or referee requests a video replay to confirm a given action/decision. In addition to error identification, a related skill is the need for the coach to rectify the errors once spotted. Feedback is therefore only the start of a complex process in which the coach compares a learner's skill with an ideal model, evaluates feedback and then guides the learner through some kind of corrective practice. This process is viewed schematically in *Figure 3*.

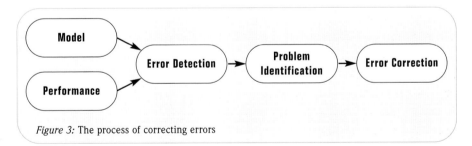

Figure 3: The process of correcting errors

It may be worth highlighting at this point the important difference between knowledge of results (KR) and knowledge of performance (KP). If the coach provides the learner with information pertaining to the outcome of a performance (e.g., the ball landed in the rough, or the time taken was 12 seconds) – this is known as KR. If the coach discusses details of the movement itself (e.g., the gymnastic routine was clumsy, or knee rise in the sprint was too low), this is known as KP. Thus, KP is concerned with feedback about the actual movement whilst KR is concerned with feedback about the effects of that performance. It seems logical that feedback in the form of KR is more appropriate to open skills (because success is measured largely by outcomes) and KP more appropriate in closed skills (where success is monitored largely through movement execution). However, this distinction does over-simplify matters. For example, closed activities such as diving or sports acrobatics involve more than the execution of a well co-ordinated sequence of movements. Similarly, skill in sports which are predominantly open in nature such as football, embody more than the capacity to reach tangible targets such as score goals. A good way of assessing the kinds of feedback is to adopt a 'systems approach'.

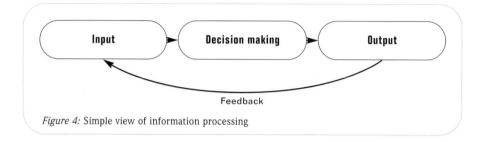

Figure 4: Simple view of information processing

Figure 4 is the same one as shown in Chapter 2. This approach focuses attention firstly on Input (perception) and questions whether the learner has a perceptual problem, which requires examination. For example, do they understand the task, are they looking in the correct direction, are they moving too early. It then proceeds with Decision Making by looking at how well the learner links the input of information with their actions. Finally, the actual movement (Output) is examined to see if there are problems with technique, timing, co-ordination, force, etc. In this way, the chances of spotting errors and providing the right kind of feedback are maximised.

Before leaving the subject of models it should be underlined that learners too, should develop a model or 'motor plan' of what is required. As indicated previously, it makes sense that the learner should play an active role in their learning as this helps make feedback more meaningful. One problem is that because the learner's model is internal in nature, there is little way of knowing if they are formulating an accurate model or even attempting to do so. Ways of examining both of these problems are looked at in the next chapter.

FORMS OF FEEDBACK

Feedback can take on a number of forms. For example, feedback can occur as a natural consequence of the activity (e.g., sight of the ball hitting the cross bar following an attempt at goal) or it may be augmented information such as the coach's remarks or a press photograph. Feedback can also be categorised with regard to the various senses. It may be visual, auditory or kinesthetic in nature. Magill (1993) presents a simple

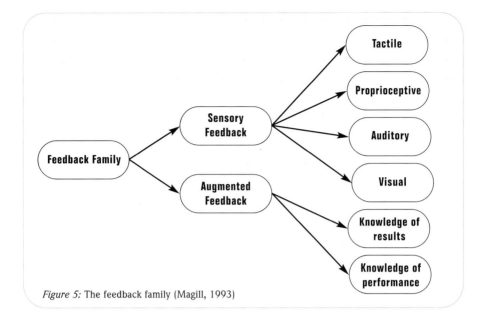

Figure 5: The feedback family (Magill, 1993)

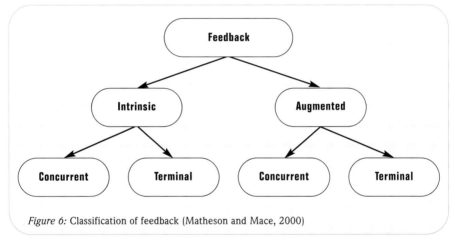

Figure 6: Classification of feedback (Matheson and Mace, 2000)

hierarchical family tree to illustrate the various kinds of feedback (*Figure 5*). Another way of classifying feedback is provided by Matheson and Mace (2000) (*Figure 6*).

In this model, intrinsic feedback which is generated internally is a natural consequence of the activity (e.g., feeling and seeing that a penalty shot was wide of the posts). Augmented feedback is supplementary or additional to the movement such as that provided by a coach or video film (e.g., hearing the crowd shout when the penalty was missed). Concurrent feedback occurs at the same time as the movement takes place (e.g., feeling pain in the legs or hearing the crowd cheer whilst running). Terminal feedback occurs at the end of a performance/movement and summarises the activity in some way (e.g., noting the distance jumped in a triple jump event or watching a video replay of a trampolining performance). Knowledge of results is information that describes the end product of a performance (e.g., the final score in a football match).

Knowledge of performance is information about the actual activity or performance (e.g., being told by the football coach that the team's performance was slow, lacked spirit and variety).

Research suggests that people use different kinds of feedback at different times and in different situations. Coaches and teachers should therefore consider how these various categories may be used. Some individuals are able to self-analyse and require minimal prompting whilst those less confident may benefit from constant encouragement and advice. Magill (1993) suggests the use of augmented feedback depends very much upon both the individual and the skill. There are some skills and situations where the learner does not need a great deal of feedback and additional feedback may even create a dependency on the part of the learner. Thus, when the learner has a clear idea of the skill they are trying to learn and they can access information themselves about their performance, then any additional feedback may be unnecessary. The sport or activity in question is also important. For example, in closed actions where consistency of movement is important the coach may wish to emphasise feedback, which directs the learner to their bodily positions and movements. Encouraging the learner to think about the 'feel' of a movement or employing manual guidance techniques may be important. In open skills where skill reflects how well the person reacts to a constantly changing environment (as in badminton or ice hockey), feedback which relates the players' actions to the consequences of those actions might be more important. In badminton, encouraging the learner to focus on the shuttle's direction in relation to the action which produced it, either at the time of playing or later on video might be most beneficial. With more skilled players it may not be necessary for the coach to provide augmented or supplementary feedback because the learner can assess internal feedback. A good coach would expect to develop in their athletes the ability to analyse their own performances.

Stage of learning may also be important in dictating the most relevant kind of feedback. A lot of research evidence shows that beginners tend to rely heavily on visual/verbal sources of input and only later in learning utilise internal or kinesthetic information. With this in mind then in early learning, talking about problems and illustrating them through video should be effective. Later in learning, when the learner has established a skill model and 'ironed out' most errors it would make sense to encourage them to introspect on performance and develop sensitivity to the 'feel' of movement. However, a word of caution at this point for it would be unwise to think this sequence (visual/verbal to internal) always applies. It is also clear

> ## ⊂⊐KEY POINT
>
> Feedback is generated from one of two sources:
> • Self-generated, internal or intrinsic feedback, such as how a movement feels, or sight of a successful penalty kick.
> • Augmented feedback from an external source – the crowd applauding a successful penalty kick, or a coach commenting on a poor gymnastic vault.

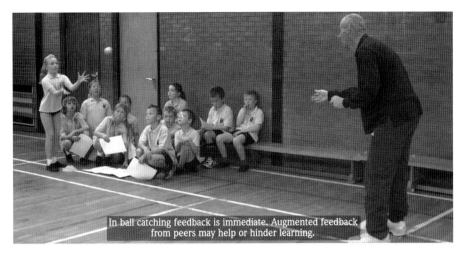
In ball catching feedback is immediate. Augmented feedback from peers may help or hinder learning.

from research that individuals choose to select information, which most appeals to them (see Chapter 8). There is no reason therefore to assume that, say, video feedback or kinesthetic feedback aren't useful at all levels of learning – but only for some people. The point is made once more that all feedback mechanisms operate but the relative weighting of each may depend on the individual and their level of expertise.

It is worth dwelling on the subject of augmented feedback. Research has revealed some interesting features. Firstly, the content of any augmented feedback is critical. It should certainly be relevant to the skill being learned. There is evidence that video film is of value only if used to focus the learner's attention on elements such as performance that are easily quantified and relatively objective. Learners also have to be relatively practiced in using such information. Focusing on 'qualitative' elements such as rhythm, co-ordination and elegance seems to have less effect. In other words, augmented feedback tends to be more useful if it is quantitative rather than qualitative in nature. Secondly, skilled performers need more precise feedback than novices do. Thirdly, the scheduling of feedback is important. Young and Schmidt (1992) showed that, in terms of long term learning, it is better for a teacher or coach not to provide feedback following every attempt at a skill by the learner, but to provide feedback following observation of several attempts. Fourthly, whilst it is recognised that learners need to understand errors in their learning, there is evidence that coaches should focus a learner's attention on their strengths as well as their weaknesses. This goes some way to engendering motivation and enthusiasm. It is worth restating this point because too often, the successes of learners are often overlooked and go unrewarded because everyone (both learner and teacher) concentrate too much on errors.

Finally, it should be noted that video is not the only way for a teacher or coach to provide augmented feedback. Recent technological advances in notational analysis (see Hughes and Franks, 1997) have made it possible for learners (as well as top class players) to receive objective and comprehensive feedback using computerised systems. This particular topic is discussed at length in Chapter 9.

TIMING AND FREQUENCY OF FEEDBACK

Let's now examine some of the temporal aspects of feedback. Intrinsic feedback (see *Figure 6* above) is ever present and is a natural consequence of movement (e.g., when a cyclist feels the pain in his legs during an uphill sprint); there is no obvious delay in receiving intrinsic feedback. Terminal feedback (e.g., when the basketball player sees the ball enter the ring) occurs at a point in time after the movement. A good example is seen in golf when a few seconds passes before the golfer sees what has happened to the ball. From a tech-

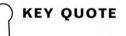

> **KEY QUOTE**
>
> *"...performers should receive extrinsic feedback soon after the event, particularly if it contains information about performance. However, if performers receive the extrinsic feedback too early, they will not have had sufficient time to analyse their own intrinsic feedback."*
> **Foxon** (1999)

nical point of view terminal feedback always arrives a brief moment after movement; movement has to take place first before feedback information is generated and becomes available. A key factor is the delay between movement and feedback. Feedback delay is seen most clearly in closed loop mechanical systems such as turbo systems in motor car engines, central heating thermostats and heating elements on a cooker. In each of these systems there is always a time delay before the command from the executive mechanism results in action from the effector mechanism (see *Figure 2*).

The same follows in human behaviour. For example, a rugby player who slices a penalty kick may have to wait a split second to see if the ball travels successfully between the posts. Similarly, a sprinter may have to wait several seconds for photographic evidence to show who won the race. And a pole vaulter may have to wait until they have actually landed to see whether or not the bar was clipped. The matter of delay, however, is most crucial with augmented feedback. An important question asks when should the coach provide feedback? Research seems to indicate that the sooner feedback is given following performance the more effective it is. This is because it is less likely the learner will forget what the feedback pertains to and consequently, the less likely they will practice incorrect movements. Marshall (1986) expresses this very well:

> *"When a skill is being performed it is important to give feedback at certain points, firstly because people don't know when the faults are coming in and secondly because you can perhaps encourage them to correct faults by giving them the right instruction. At the end of the performance try to give the feed-back what you've just done because if you wait even a minute the performer will lose the feeling of what he has been doing and it will be more difficult to relate to what the coach is saying."*

Immediate feedback therefore seems to be the ideal approach. However, unlike the example just given this may not always be practical (e.g., when a coach is on the side-

Observe a performance several times before giving feedback.

line during a match). Also, it may not be desirable. It could be confusing to a learner to comment on her performance (say an attempt at a new gymnastic vault) the very moment she finishes. She should be given a few seconds to recover from and reflect on the performance – perhaps to evaluate internal feedback first – before the coach offers advice. A general guide is 'count to ten' before giving feedback.

Further evidence from the research shows that as well as delay of feedback, the time interval lapsing before the learner has a new attempt at the skill is also critical. If practice following the coach's advice is delayed (or perhaps not allowed) then the learner forgets the advice and is unable to relate it to a renewed attempt at the skill. The exact time interval between practices depends on many practical factors (e.g., how fatigued the person is or how many other people are involved in the practice) but it should certainly not exceed a matter of minutes. The boxing coach Hickey (1986) discusses the matter of feedback delay and suggests that a critical issue is whether the individual is receptive to feedback:

"In training it is important to give the feedback immediately and to make it as positive as possible. Depending upon the complexity of the skill being learned it would then be up to the coach to decide how the individual should be approached in terms of his own personality and his own requirements, but also the type of fault that was appearing. When it comes to competition there is another factor, which is the actual ability of the individual boxer to be receptive to comments made. To try to give the feedback too close to the contest may be pointless. When, you give feedback to a boxer after a contest is important. To give a general indication in terms of how well he's done is sufficient when his mind may be in turmoil – he's on a high if he's won or a low if he's lost. If one went into too positive an analysis of his performance then it would not be well received. The balance of the emotional feelings of the boxer should determine to the coach by experience at what point the feedback would be received and applied to future performance."

Another time related question is, how often should feedback be given? Early theorists (see Behaviorist Theory in Chapter 2) viewed that stimulus-response bonds were strengthened only if feedback followed the response every time and very quickly. This view has now been overturned. Both anecdotal and research evidence suggests that giving information following every attempt does not necessarily produce the best learning effect (note comment on fading raised before). Studies have shown that learners who receive feedback intermittently often learn as well as those who receive feedback following every attempt at a skill. Furthermore, there is evidence that intermittent feedback can lead to enhanced retention compared to constant feedback. One explanation is that when learners are not given external feedback they are able to devote more time to internal sources; an activity that has long term benefits. As a general rule, a fading strategy has been shown to be effective. As mentioned before, this is when learners are given feedback constantly in the beginning stages of learning a new skill, but the frequency is gradually reduced over time. One particular advantage of fading is that by giving the coach or teacher an opportunity to observe the learner several times, it enhances the reliability of error detection and provides a greater focus on what are the key weaknesses.

One exception to the fading strategy occurs when the task being learned is highly complex. Research carried out by Wulf and her associates (e.g., Wulf, Shea and Matschiner, 1998) shows that in learning complicated perceptual motor skills, learning is most effective if feedback is given on a constant, trial-by-trial basis. The withdrawal of feedback should also recognise the complexity of the skill in question. And this in turn may also depend on the learner; some may find a skill more difficult than others, in which case fading should take place much later.

> **KEY QUOTE**
>
> *"...when individuals don't receive feedback, they engage in different kinds of information-processing activities than when they do. In addition, it is likely that, when learners are not given feedback on a frequent basis, they are less likely to become dependent on feedback. The result is more effective learning and better retention of the movement."*
> **Schmidt and Wrisberg** (2000)

Amount of feedback

By and large, coaches and teachers alike, perhaps because of their vast fund of technical knowledge are apt to give too much information to learners. They watch a performance, spot errors and then risk confusing the learner and overloading their memory by examining all the things that need to be corrected. This is a difficult situation for the coach. What they should do is weigh up the most important issues, select one or two and then present them in a simple and informative manner. It may well be that correcting one error has a knock-on effect in solving a number of others. For example, novice skiers often display a variety of problems – their skis lack co-ordination, they lack overall control, they keep falling over and they cannot turn very well. It transpires that a key problem with most people is weight distribution and body posture.

Correcting this often has an immediate and remarkable effect of the problems listed. Good instructors do not even need to draw the beginner's attention to their numerous problems because they are automatically solved through attention to a more fundamental one. As learners progress it makes sense for coaches and teachers to provide more information which is increasingly complex – whilst still monitoring the learner's capability to process that infor-

Don't bombard the learner with too much feedback!

mation. It is very important for coaches to know the relative ordering or priority of key cues so they can be introduced at the correct time and in the correct sequence. A useful method for reducing the amount of feedback is to watch the learner repeatedly and offer advice and comment only after several observations. Withholding information like this (related to fading as mentioned before) also facilitates the identity of the critical problems in a learner's performance as it gives time to assess practice over several trials. Providing summary feedback therefore reduces information load and increases the validity of the feedback eventually presented.

Sometimes there is a case for eliminating certain sources of feedback by physically excluding certain sources because they have a detrimental effect on the learner, e.g., negative comments from fellow learners. In such cases it would be appropriate to arrange practice in isolation from other people or control the unwanted feedback through strict control. Also, some kinds of feedback may divert attention away from more important sources of information. In putting (golf) for example, it has been known for learners to be blindfolded (close their eyes) to encourage attention to the physical movement and away from the actual outcome of the stroke. Similarly, novice skiers learning to snow-plough can be directed to close their eyes which helps them focus more on what the legs should be doing, viz., pushing the knees forwards and the heels outwards and less on what the skis are doing. And in canoeing, it sometimes helps when practising a ferry-glide to close the eyes, which helps concentration on the effect of paddling actions. Such techniques may appear a little dramatic, but (under the appropriate conditions) they add to the variety of the coach's repertoire and may allow them to solve infrequent, but perhaps persistent problems that other methods cannot tackle.

FEEDBACK PRECISION

Feedback precision concerns the degree to which feedback given to a performer accurately reflects the performance. For example, a novice long jumper might be told that their take off was much too early, or they might be told that it was 12cm too short. The latter statement is more precise because it contains more detailed information. The precision of feedback depends on a number of things. Firstly, if it doesn't matter how refined the skill needs to be, then feedback information doesn't need to be very precise. For example, a recreational golfer may be interested in improving their skill, but not to the level of a professional golfer. Therefore, a comment from a friend such as "your backswing is not high enough,"

may be all that is required; it would be pointless saying something like "your backswing is 6cm too low". Secondly, it depends on the stage of learning. Generally speaking, beginners make errors that are so gross that precise information is redundant. On the other hand, with more proficient learners, more precise information is required to enable them to reduce the error gap between actual and desired performance. Regardless of stage of learning, the coach must always check that feedback information has been understood. Good coaches not only provide clear, informative instructions, but also wait to observe whether their advice has been absorbed. One of the reasons for this is research evidence that questions the extent to which the learners can actually use detailed information to improve actions. The results of an experiment by Fazey and Ramsey (1988) serve to illustrate this point. In a simple, repetitive finger-tapping task, subjects were asked to keep time with a metronome set at a given rate. When the pace was altered by a small amount they were able to adjust their actions automatically even though the increase in pace was not perceived. When however, they were asked by the experimenter to adjust the pace to a higher/lower rate, the smallest increment they could manage was much larger. It seems that the 'grain of control' or precision which the individual can apply following the use of verbal information is far coarser than that of lower-level 'automatic' systems. This suggests that the learner may not be able to utilise information provided by the coach if it requires a very fine change in performance. Again, this reinforces a point made before about the value of verbal feedback in learning. It seems that verbal feedback is most useful in orienting behaviour at a time when gross improvements are being made. In other words, it plays an important guidance role early in learning or when skill has broken down. Later in learning however, when most actions are controlled automatically, verbal feedback is of lesser value than the individual's internal analysis and appraisal of what they are doing.

Many coaches and teachers adopt a 'bandwidth' strategy when giving feedback. As they observe the learner they spot various errors and decide whether or not to provide 'error' information. They may see two people making identical errors, but provide different feedback in each case. They make a decision about what information to provide based on their knowledge of the learner – their intrinsic abilities, motivation, potential, and so on. One learner may not have the interest or potential to improve in which case the coach's 'bandwidth' for giving information is wide. In contrast, for someone showing much promise and eager to progress, the coach may adopt a narrower 'bandwidth' for feedback.

It should not be forgotten that the nature of the feedback given must mirror the criteria that define the skill in question. Thus, feedback information may focus on magnitude (long jump take-off position), direction (in archery, left or right of the target), timing (in kayaking, applying a support stroke when entering an eddy), co-ordination (as in dance), and so on. Finally, if feedback is to be informative then comments should be more extensive than simply "good" or "well done". These may be motivating or reinforcing but tell the learner nothing about how they can modify or improve their movements.

CRITERIA FOR GIVING USEFUL FEEDBACK

To conclude this section let's summarise the features that make feedback useful. Marten's (1997) ideas are used as a basis for constructing the following list.

• It is vital to provide feedback. People do learn through sensing internal feedback, but their potential can only be achieved with additional external (augmented) feedback.

• Feedback is best given at the end of a performance. If given mid-way through a skill it may prove distracting and the learner will have a more difficult time remembering what it was.

• As a general rule, feedback should be given repeatedly and often. As learners progress they begin to rely more on internal sources and less on outside information. Some individuals may require much more feedback (for motivational reasons) than others.

• Feedback should focus on one aspect of performance at a time. Too much feedback simply serves to confuse and overload the learner. A decision must be made about which error or aspect of performance to highlight at any given time.

• Feedback from several individuals may be useful, if possible and practical. Different people see different things from their own perspective; they also express things in different ways. As long as those giving feedback are credible and knowledgeable (e.g., fellow learners or competitors) variety may be particularly helpful.

• Feedback information should reward good performance but also highlight errors. If learners fail to see what they are doing wrong, they stand little chance of realising their full potential and ultimate success. The key is to present 'negative' information in a positive manner.

• Feedback should be as informative and precise as possible. Comments such as "well done" or "great" carry little meaning unless the learner can relate them to precise performance details. It is far better to use words that describe performance (e.g., "your arm pull through the water is too fast") rather than the outcome of performance.

• Feedback may be visual or verbal in nature. Verbal feedback tends to tell people how they did something wrong and how to improve (prescriptive feedback) whereas visual feedback shows what they did wrong (descriptive feedback). Both kinds of feedback may be important for some learners.

• When providing feedback, it is important to be sensitive to the feelings of learners, particularly when in the presence of others. A comment intended to give precise information may upset a learner through embarrassment.

• A useful procedure to adopt when giving extrinsic feedback is to use the **PAT** principle (Foxon, 1999). **P**ause to give learners time to review and appraise their own intrinsic feedback. **A**sk learners questions to help them with this process. **T**ell them what you observed and what they should now do to practice further.

SUMMARY OF KEY POINTS

• Feedback is a source of information which arrives during or following a movement and which tells the person about the outcome of that movement.

• We may not always be aware that we are using feedback to adjust on-going activity.

• Feedback can arrive through different senses, e.g., vision, hearing.

• The type of feedback used may depend on the nature of the sport or activity as well as the stage of learning.

• For feedback to be of any value it must be compared against a reference or model (e.g., a person's previous performance).

• Feedback is error information (sometimes called negative feedback). Both the coach and learner must use such information so that it acts in a positive manner to aid the learner.

• Feedback can serve four purposes – to motivate, to change performance, to reinforce learning and to create a dependency.

• Feedback assumes the coach and learner have a model of what is correct.

- The coach must be skilled not only in detecting the differences between feedback and the model, but also in planning subsequent practices.

- It is important the coach is aware of how they manipulate the various kinds of feedback, viz., internal/external, visual/auditory/kinesthetic.

- Feedback is most effective when given shortly after performance. Subsequent practice must not be delayed or else the learner forgets what changes to make.

- The more precise the feedback the more beneficial its effect. The learner must be able to understand the feedback.

- Sometimes, a fading strategy of giving feedback (more frequent early on and less frequent later) is appropriate.

PRACTICAL TASKS

- Use an open area (e.g., gymnasium) about 15 metres long. Place three hoops (1 metre diameter) near the end of the room. Assign six people in three pairs to three Groups (A, B, C) and position them 10 metres from the hoops with their backs to the hoops. One person in each pair is given 10 beanbags and is required to throw them overhead to land in the hoop. After each attempt the partner in Group A gives the performer feedback about how close the beanbag landed to the hoop. With Group B the performer looks around after each attempt to see how accurate they were. With Group C, no feedback is given. It is clear that Group A receives immediate verbal feedback, whilst Group B receives immediate visual feedback and Group C no feedback. The overall performances should show Group B performs best, followed by Group A, then Group C.

- Sit at a table and place a sheet of white A4 paper with the centre at arm's reach. With a pencil or pen draw a circle about 1 cm in diameter in the centre of the sheet. Hold the pen in your preferred hand and locate the point on the table about 50cms away from the centre. As quickly and accurately as possible move the pen forward towards the circle to land the point of the pen in the circle. Repeat this quickly 10 times. You should find that most dots lie within the circle. Now draw a second circle alongside the first and repeat the task. But this time, close your eyes as soon as you move and keep them closed throughout the movement. You will find that the 'blind' set of trials are less accurate than the first. This happens because, as the pen moves closer to the circle, there is a point when you note the difference in position between the pen point and the circle and make a subconscious amendment to improve accuracy. If you cannot see at the time, then you cannot take advantage of visual feedback and consequently, make a less accurate movement.

• Sit at a table and place a blank sheet of paper in front of you. With a pen or pencil, sign your name five times one below the other. Now repeat this task by writing your name five times below the first five signatures, but this time, do it with your eyes closed. You will find that the second set of signatures are less 'refined' than the first set which reveals the absence of visual feedback. Try to explain why the errors made in the second set of signatures are different from the first set.

• This task examines the value of providing learners with feedback varying in precision. Use a gymnasium of large room. Locate a waste bin about 10 metres from a start line. The subject is required to stand on the start line and throw lawn tennis balls into the bin. The task has to be completed with eyes closed. Use two groups of subjects (say 3 in each group). Each group is provided with feedback from an onlooker. Group A is told only whether their attempt was "too short" or "too long," following each attempt. Group B is told how accurate their attempt was to the nearest half metre. The onlooker will have to make an educated guess rather than measure each performance with a tape measure. Each subject is given 20 trials with feedback. Following this, they then have 10 attempts without any kind of feedback. The number of successful shots is recorded. The average scores for each group should reveal higher performance with Group B.

REVIEW QUESTIONS

• How important is it to encourage learners to identify their own faults with perhaps just confirmation from the coach?

• When coaching do you adopt different 'standards' (models) for different people dependent on say how tall or muscular they are?

• Do you encounter problems in error spotting? If so state what are the problems and how you deal with them.

• Comment on the notion of allowing learners to make errors. Is this a desirable process?

• In your sport, state how you would use the three senses (vision, audition, and kinesthesis) to provide feedback.

• Do you agree with the research that through learning people change from using visual feedback to using internal feedback?

• How soon in the learning process do learners begin to feel what is correct without having to see or be told?

• Are you aware of how quickly you tell the learner what is wrong?

• Do you give learners time to think about their attempts before making a comment?

• Do you think that sometimes you confuse the learner with your advice? Do you talk too much? Do you know if you talk too much?!

• Do you adjust the detail/difficulty of feedback with regard to individual performers?

• Write down two examples of control systems found in everyday life, one of which is closed and the other open.

• In the closed system identified, is there a period of time before feedback has an effect in changing the system? If so, are there any disadvantages in this delay?

• Give an example of a bodily function that relies on feedback (e.g., breathing).

• In the last question state:

    • What dictates the 'normal' level of operation?
    • What exactly constitutes the feedback?
    • What changes actually take place, because of the feedback?

• Give an example of an everyday activity, e.g., sitting down, in which feedback is used.

• Can you think of a sporting skill, which doesn't apparently require feedback for it to be controlled?

• What techniques do you use to help learners acquire their own model or plan of action for a new skill?

• Imagine a situation where one of your players has made an error, e.g., landed on his back following an attempted gymnastic action. How you would translate this error into constructive, positive feedback?

References

Crisfield, P. Quotation from Sharp, R.H. *Acquiring skill.* (Coach Education Modules). Edinburgh: Scottish Sports Council, 1986.

Fazey, J. and Ramsey. Paper presented at the *Annual Conference of the British Association of Sports Sciences*, Exeter, September, 1988.

Foxon, F. (1999). *Improving practices and skill.* Leeds: National Coaching Foundation.

Hickey, K. Quotation from Sharp, R.H. *Acquiring skill.* Coach Education Modules. Edinburgh: Scottish Sports Council, 1986.

Hughes, M. and Franks, I. (1997). *Notational analysis of sport.* London: E & F Spon.

Magill, R. (1993). *Motor learning: Concepts and applications.* Dubuque, Iowa: Brown and Benchmark.

Martens, R. (1997). *Successful coaching* (2nd Edition). Champaign, Illinois: Human Kinetics.

Marshall, P. Quotation from Sharp, R.H. *Acquiring skill.* Coach Education Modules. Edinburgh: Scottish Sports Council, 1986.

Matheson, H. and Mace, R. (2001). *Skill in sport.* Droitwich: Sport in Mind.

Schmidt, R.A. and Wrisberg, C.A. (2000). *Motor learning and performance* (2nd Edition). Champaign, Illinois: Human Kinetics.

Wulf, G., Shea. C.H. and Matschiner, S. (1998). Frequent feedback enhances complex motor skill learning. *Journal of Motor Behaviour,* 30, 180-192.

Young, D.E. and Schmidt, R.A. (1992). *Augmented feedback for enhanced skill acquisition.* In, Tutorials in Motor Behaviour II, (Eds. G. E. Stelmach and J. Requin) Amsterdam: North Holland Publishing Co.

CHAPTER 5 – PRINCIPLES OF PRACTICE

"Should athletes simply be required to 'grind out' practice trials to develop movement skill, or are there strategies and procedures that teachers and coaches can implement to short circuit the long and arduous process of skill acquisition?"

Williams, Davids and Williams (1999)

The last two chapters examined guidance – how we give information to the learner before they practice, and feedback information that results from practice. Now we'll look at practice itself by examining a variety of critical topics such as the role of making errors in learning, how skills are broken down into smaller parts, how much time should be devoted to practice, imagery and the management of practice.

ENTRY AND TERMINAL BEHAVIOURS

Often, the most obvious or logical things go unnoticed. In planning a practice session it makes sense to look at what has been done before by the learner and to consider how they should change as a result of the session. The reader might question how often detailed questions like this are considered. Knowing what has happened in the past and what is expected in the future makes it much easier to plan practice. Psychologists refer to these end points as 'entry' and 'terminal' behaviours and this scheme of things is depicted in *Figure 1*. This general approach is known as a systems analysis – the process of breaking complicated problems down into logical, manageable sections. This model is cyclical in nature where assessment and feedback are used to modify/plan for practice the next time around. Entry behaviours underpin the skills and knowledge which the learner possesses before they engage in practice. If the coach or teacher knows what these are (and most of the time the coach should be

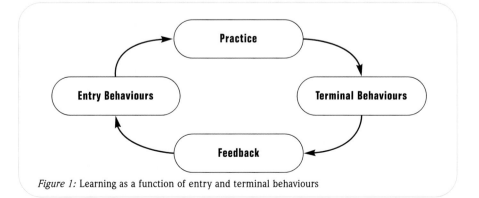

Figure 1: Learning as a function of entry and terminal behaviours

fully aware if working with the same people) then they are better able to plan events in a logical and smooth manner to ensure progression from the very start. The coach or teacher who doesn't bother or who hasn't checked the previous experience of a newcomer runs the risk of losing their confidence and interest. There is also the risk that potentials go unrealised. To provide an example of this, take say a ski instructor faced with a new group of students on their first day. The good instructor will check safety matters such as clothing and bindings, but will also examine the experience of each individual. If the instructor is very fortunate his students will all have the same ski experience so can be treated as a relatively homogeneous group. With this information to hand the day can be planned accordingly. The instructor may decide to stay low down on the hill where the terrain is relatively gentle or decide to treat the group as two different ability groups, and so on. At the very start the instructor is able to predict the likely outcome of the day in terms of skill progression, and plan and make decisions about what the group is likely to achieve (the terminal behaviours). Of course, experience of working with different groups will come in very handy. Thus, acquiring basic information about learners to begin with and then using experience to judge the amount and kind of learning possible, the coach or teacher can begin to plan specific practices in a meaningful manner.

STRUCTURING THE LEARNING/TEACHING PROCESS

Step	The Learner	The Teacher / Coach
1	Perceive and desire a goal/s	Provide a 'set to learn' and model of goal
2	Identify relevant stimuli	Provide teaching cues
3	Formulate a motor plan	Assist with motor plan formation
4	Execute a response	Provide opportunity to practice
5	Attend to results	Provide learning cues / assist interpretation
6	Revise motor plan	Adjust learner's performance
7	Practice	Provide opportunity to practice

Table 1: A simplified teaching/learning model (Pease, 1977)

The model described above can be applied to any sport or learning situation and is very general in nature. Pease (1977) describes another approach which also has a logical structure and is very practical in its application. Pease adopts the view that the teaching and learning should mirror one another, i.e., the stages involved in planning and organising practice should be based on the phases through which the learner passes as they become more proficient – see *Table 1*.

A learning model

The left side lists the sequential steps for the learner and the right side mirrors these stages for the teacher or coach. Let us focus on the learning stages firstly. Initially, learners must be motivated and possess an idea about what they want to achieve. It is well accepted that people learn best if they are interested and want to improve. However, understanding why a particular practice is important is not always obvious to the learner, especially if it doesn't appear to have a clear relationship to the final skill or activity in question. Inculcating a desire to learn is therefore the first thing the teacher or coach must do. Secondly, as learners practice they must have something on which to focus their attention and also understand the key points involved. For beginners, there are often a myriad things to deal with and this can be frustrating and confusing. Teachers and coaches have a responsibility to direct learners to those cues that are most appropriate at any given time. Next, learners must establish and formulate what is called a motor plan. A motor plan is an internal idea or image that describes the movement about to be executed. In a sense the motor plan is a kind of expectation about what to do and perhaps, what the consequences will be of carrying out a movement. Motor plans for beginners are likely to be very crude and not always accurate. The next stage is actual practice where learners attempt to put into practice the motor plan. Stage five describes the process where learners gather information about the movements executed and monitor the degree to which goals are achieved. Such information will be self-generated and will also come from the coach or teacher in the form of augmented feedback. The next stage involves learners establishing new motor plans, in light of feedback, in preparation for further practice. The new plan may be totally different or just a minor variation on the initial one. The seventh and final stage is practice once again. Stages five to seven are repeated until the learner has acquired the desired level of skill.

A teaching model

The right side of the table mirrors the left side and can also apply to any learning situation, sport or activity. The first step is all about motivating learners; learners must want to learn! The coach or teacher must do their best to facilitate interest and enthusiasm. This may or may not be necessary depending on how interested or motivated the learner already is. There are a variety of well-established ideas that can be used to encourage learners such as showing videos of experts in action, taking learners to displays or competitions, providing models through demonstrations, setting up practice – perhaps with little emphasis on scoring or competition. It is well accepted that when introducing activities to beginners, emphasis should be on enjoyment, the attainability of skills and understanding of some of the difficulties to be encountered. This first stage is all about getting the learner 'hooked' and interested, establishing rough motor plans and directing the learner's attention to the aims and purposes behind the sport or activity in question.

The second stage is one where the coach helps the learner identify those cues and events essential to attaining the goals. A number of approaches can be used such as manual and verbal guidance, demonstrations and hinting. These techniques were described in previous chapters. Skills may be broken down into smaller parts, modified or slowed down as appropriate. Teaching cues must not be too specific and must be relevant to the stage of learning. Detailed cues can be combined into larger units, e.g., in relation to the 'ready' position in tennis, separate points such as feet position, weight distribution, knee flexion, racket position, eye focus, etc. can be dealt with individually and gradually combined into a single event or cue, i.e., 'ready'.

In the third stage, the coach assists the learner's formation of a motor plan. This is not easy because, for one thing, it is impossible to gain direct access to the learner's thought processes. For this reason, this stage is often ignored. Techniques for overcoming this stage include discussing with learners what they plan to do (ask them to describe their intentions before they act), forcing concentration on the feel of movements – perhaps using manual guidance, use of imagery and ensuring that demonstrations which help to create a visual picture are clear and exact.

The next step is to provide the learner with an opportunity to practice. This involves structuring situations so that the learner can enact the internal model and concentrate on those cues which are especially relevant. With beginners especially, focus should be placed on safety, maximum participation, highlighting of relevant cues (using perhaps some of the visual techniques described in Chapter 3) and attention to the learner's performance (what went wrong and how can improvements be made) rather than its outcome (how successful was it).

The fifth step focuses on the use of feedback. As learners progress, they should be encouraged to evaluate their own performances and internal feelings and attempt to relate the motor plan to performance. If there are differences, it is important for the learner to try and identify what went wrong rather than be told by someone else. Feedback should be informative and immediate and take into account both internal feelings (kinesthetic feedback) as well as information about movement outcome (what it looked like, how successful it was).

Stage six is linked to the last one and is concerned with asking questions such as "what should the learner do next?" Discussion with learners should encourage them to revise their motor plan in the hope of better performance next time. The coach might, for example, question the learner about how their plan has changed, whether they understand any errors in performance and so on. The last stage involves practice once more and perhaps a rethink by the coach about the tasks set, equipment used, goals established or the manner in which the learner tackles the skill.

The learning/teaching model described by Pease highlights a number of important ideas. It is important for coaches and teachers to plan practice sessions within a wide framework that accounts for the learner's capabilities and overall time commitment (e.g., how many times each week is available and for how many months?). The learner's present skills and strengths should be monitored and goals set which are attainable and realistic. It is worth mentioning once again that if coaches know where they've started from and also know what they hope to achieve, there is a good chance of planning, in a logical and thorough manner, the various stages that will guarantee success! The model also highlights the benefits of learners playing an active and positive role in their own learning. It implies that learning should adopt experiential rather than didactic methods. Discussion between coach and learner about what to attempt, how things felt, why did things go wrong, etc., should take place constantly. Whilst this approach may not be the 'style' adopted by some coaches it certainly concurs with recent educational thinking on learner involvement and responsibility. It makes sense that if the learner is doing the learning then they should also be an active participant! Of course, this is not always possible or desirable. With beginners especially, it may be more appropriate and efficient for the coach to be prescriptive, particularly where safety or lack of confidence are key issues. We will examine more thoroughly the importance of learner involvement in a subsequent chapter. For the present, we will focus on some of the issues surrounding practice itself – what should be practised, how should skills be broken down, how long should learners practice for?

SKILL ANALYSIS

Before learners are presented with a task or asked to execute a particular movement, some thought on the part of the coach/teacher must go into deciding whether the task is safe. Consideration should also be given to whether the physical demands are appropriate and the task interesting, and whether the task highlights the relevant points and reflects the game or sport in question. At the very least, practice must be pertinent. In many cases, such questions are easily and automatically answered because there are accepted and traditional methods of doing some things. For example, if a novice swimmer has roughly mastered the breast stroke and can make progress without artificial support, but displays an asymmetrical leg kick, then it would make sense to isolate this

> **KEY POINT**
>
> Skill analysis is the process of breaking a skill into constituent parts in order to make both teaching/coaching and learning more manageable.

component so the swimmer can concentrate on it alone. The swimmer might be given a hand-held float and asked to repeat a push/glide with two good leg kicks. On the other hand, it may not be too obvious how to proceed. If the coach is new to the group or a different technique has been developed (as happens for example, in artistic gymnastics or ice skating) then existing methods may have little effect. In these situations there is a need to make decisions about practice – what to do, the sequence of progressions for a particular skill and how best to make the task relevant. A useful start can be made by carrying out what is called a task or skill analysis.

Task analysis is the systematic examination of a complex problem (such as a skill or game) to decide the constituent parts, how they are organised, which cues are relevant, what the objectives are, and so on. It is a procedure that is often carried out unconsciously. Many coaching texts provide comprehensive breakdowns of a skill's requirements (e.g., swimming practices commonly revolve around arm and leg actions together with breathing and co-ordination) although the 'cookbook' approach is not always the best. There are several approaches to task analysis. One method focuses on the nature of the activity under consideration. For example, is the skill open/closed, discrete/continuous or paced/unpaced? Analysing the skill like this allows one to make general decisions about the relative importance of certain features. For example, if the skill is a closed one (and hence by definition is not controlled by external information) then it would make sense to concentrate on the movement requirements for practice and expect little else to be very important. In gymnastics this would lead to an emphasis on movement technique per se. If the skill was paced and therefore controlled in part by the actions of others (as in badminton or basketball) then practice would need to take account of the element of uncertainty or unpredictability. Knowing the category of skill in question permits simple but important decisions to be made about practice.

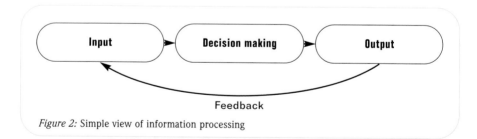

Figure 2: Simple view of information processing

Another approach is to use the information processing model discussed before (see Chapter 2). This is illustrated again in *Figure 2,* above. Here, the skill is examined in relation to each of four major components. In terms of the skill's input/perceptual requirements consideration would be given to the nature of stimuli which must be attended to (team members and opposition), the number of stimuli present (number of players, crowd, court markings) the speed of events in the display (variation in flight paths, movement of opposing players), the extent to which they conflict (background lighting and other distractions) and so on. With regard to decision making, an appraisal is made of the kinds of decisions required and the speed of decision making (in sprinting the only decision is when to move, whereas in basketball there may be a number: dribble or pass? If dribble, which direction? If pass, to whom? etc.). In terms of output/movement organisation an analysis would be made of the precision required, the number of small muscle groups, extent of limb co-ordination, cyclical or varying patterns of action, and so on. And finally, with

regard to feedback, the coach would examine the amount of feedback present (visual, auditory and movement cues may be available? do they confuse? which is more important?), the accuracy of feedback (is it satisfactory to say simply "good" or should a detailed explanation be given?) and also the intensity (is there a pain element involved or are there other people present who may comment/distract?). Answers to these broad questions together with knowledge of the learner's previous experience and present level of ability will give some clue as to what is important in practice and which parts should be introduced.

One particular merit of this approach is that it provides the coach or teacher with a balanced and complete view of skill. Too often, skill is viewed primarily in terms of movement execution alone and little regard is paid to other, equally important elements. If the model is adhered to then all potentially important components are given consideration and the chance of omitting key aspects from the analysis is minimised. In addition, the model provides a useful basis for error analysis. If a performer fails, then it is useful to examine each component in turn for possible causes. This approach avoids thinking once again that problems of learning are always movement ones. This point will be picked up again later when skill evaluation is discussed in Chapter 9.

WHOLE AND PART PRACTICE

A central problem in designing practice centres around whether relatively complex skills should be taught in their entirety or broken down into lesser, but constituent parts. Traditionally, teachers and coaches have used whole methods and part methods and also various combinations to good effect (e.g., whole-part-whole). Whole

KEY QUOTE

"Experience is a function of intensity, not duration."
Barnes Wallace (Inventor)

methods expose the learner to all elements of an activity. For example, a non-swimmer might try the breaststroke without any modification excepts perhaps with a buoyancy aid. A class of primary pupils playing football over their lunch break invariably play the whole game – perhaps with a few space and rule limitations which they have set themselves. In these examples, the important factor is that the skill or game in its complete form is the most important feature; direct learning of the constituent parts is less important. The whole approach is seen in modified games such as mini rugby and short tennis where rules and playing area are reduced, but which contain the essential ingredients. The whole method is often favoured by learners – they want to 'have a go'.

In contrast, part methods typically look at individual parts or elements of a skill before linking them together (sometimes called 'chaining' – Earle, 2003). For example, in football, learners are shown how to control the ball using different parts of their body and how to pass the ball in different ways before putting these skills into the game situation. Many coaches and teachers adopt a combination of whole and part approaches such as whole-part-

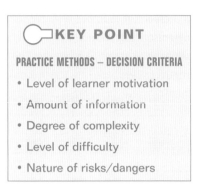

KEY POINT

PRACTICE METHODS – DECISION CRITERIA

• Level of learner motivation

• Amount of information

• Degree of complexity

• Level of difficulty

• Nature of risks/dangers

whole or a progressive part where elements are taught individually and gradually built up into the complete skill. In the progressive part method first one part is taught to a given level of skill, e.g., the approach run in triple jump. Then another part is taught, e.g., take off from the board. The two are then practiced together with an emphasis on co-ordinating the two parts. A third part is then taught before it is 'added' to the first two parts – and so on. Another technique known as the antecedent approach begins by showing learners the final part of a skill first and then working backwards. This is only possible where the skill has a clear sequential structure as in gymnastic or trampolining sequences. The philosophy behind this approach is that if the learner knows where they are going (the end point), it is easier to find their way there! It might also be more motivating to do this, because learners succeed immediately.

The nature of the skill provides some pointers as to whether skills should be broken down or left alone. Magill (2001) suggests skills that are best suited to the whole method of practice are those which are low in complexity and high in organisation. Complexity refers to the level of cognitive difficulty. For example, 3-ball juggling is a complex task for beginners, whereas 2-ball juggling is less complex. Organisation refers to the manner in which the component parts of

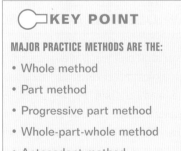

KEY POINT

MAJOR PRACTICE METHODS ARE THE:

• Whole method

• Part method

• Progressive part method

• Whole-part-whole method

• Antecedent method

the skill are phased or co-ordinated. Swimming is highly organised since leg action, breathing and arm actions invariably have to be phased in time with one another.

Cycling is less organised since movements of the arms (to control direction) have little to do with the peddling action. According to Magill then, swimming and cycling are best approached with the whole method. In contrast, Magill suggests that part practice is best suited for skills with high complexity and low organisation and skills that have an element of danger involved. Thus, a lay-up shot in basketball, which contains a series of actions that occur in sequence, is a good candidate for part practice. Part practice enables focus on key elements of the skill which can be learned in isolation. The potential drawback of the part method is that learners do not experience the timing qualities of the skill that may be central to creating the whole movement. With serial activities such as team games where elements are 'sequentially organised' and do not overlap in time (e.g., a chest pass in soccer precedes a dribble which in turn precedes a pass), then part practice of the more difficult elements should be expected to transfer positively to the game proper. With discrete activities which involve speedy movements taking less than a second to execute (e.g., a golf swing or corner kick), then the whole method is most appropriate. This ensures that the rhythm and fluidity of movement is not broken. With continuous tasks which may not have such well-defined end points as discrete ones, and where parts overlap in time and co-ordinate with one another (e.g., in the breast stroke, the arms and legs are synchronised in time), then research evidence points in favour of the whole approach.

A number of other factors are also important in the choice between whole and part-type practice. Assuming the beginner has the right set to learn and is motivated to 'play the game' or 'have a go' straight away, then even though the learner will not be fully skilled, an attempt should be made to present the whole skill as near as is practicable, simply to encourage interest, maintain enthusiasm and satisfy curiosity. Such an

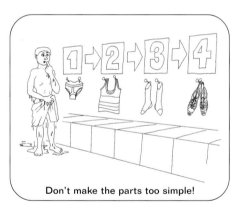

Don't make the parts too simple!

approach helps establish motor plans for action and also helps define the objectives of the skill in question. Mini-sport is one way to get beginners playing the game they want to play, whilst keeping rules, skills, fitness demands, etc., within acceptable boundaries. Once beginners have been introduced in this manner, they are in a position to accept more readily the need for specific part practices and drills. And it should be emphasised again that when parts are extracted from the whole for separate practice, they should be seen by the learner to be relevant and meaningful. If this is not obvious then the coach should make a conscious effort to justify part practice by perhaps talking about when the parts are required in the game or how the part is a necessary sub-component of a more difficult element. This point is very important. The learner must be kept informed and understand the 'why' of practice. They should accept more readily the need for practice, appreciate its contribution in the whole scheme of things, and the coach can consequently expect far greater transfer from part to whole.

Another consideration is the size of the task (be it whole or part). There is a need to balance the amount of information conveyed by the task, its physical requirements, level of meaning and challenge level. The task for the teacher or coach is selecting practices and designing learning experiences which promote challenge and involvement without putting the task out of reach of the learner. Two other points are also worthy of mention. People are individuals and different individuals learn in different ways. The point is made in Chapter 6 that some people prefer a lengthy account from their coach about the skill, whilst others pre-

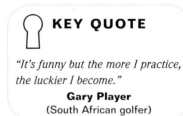
Part practice as a lead in to the game proper

fer to see demonstrations. Similarly, some learners prefer a progressive, part approach whilst others favour an attempt at the whole skill immediately. The literature talks about 'sequential' and 'holistic' learners. The coach or teacher should use this knowledge – it could prove a powerful force with some people. Finally, the coach's teaching style may suit one approach particularly; it would be unwise to discard proven methods without careful consideration of alternative ones. This point is also discussed at greater length in Chapter 8.

Merits and limitations

There are advantages, weaknesses and particular applications with all methods of practice. Part practice methods are supported by the Association school of learning theory. Splitting skills/games into smaller units serves a variety of useful purposes. It avoids the burden of practising elements of the whole, which are

> **KEY QUOTE**
>
> *"It's funny but the more I practice, the luckier I become."*
> **Gary Player**
> (South African golfer)

perhaps too simple, time-wasting or fatiguing (e.g., the run-up in bowling when practice is really focused on ball release). It reduces the information load imposed on the learner and allows for more immediate and precise feedback. And, because part practices are simpler and less dangerous, they serve a useful role in eliminating fear that might otherwise block attempts at the whole skill. They must, of course, not be so simple that the learner becomes bored or frustrated. On the downside, part practices tend to take learners away from what they really want to do which is practice the whole skill, i.e., play the game. Learners must feel challenged and be made aware of the application of individual skills taught out of the game context. Scully (1988) has examined the problems of part practice and suggests that to be effective the cues which are highlighted in a part practice must not be isolated from the whole action. She says:

"... in teaching the jump shot in basketball, the learner's attention may be directed to the arms but only in as much as they relate to what the rest of the body is doing at the same time. Similarly, if cueing the learner to produce more force or speed in a throwing, bowling or kicking action, attention needs to be directed to subtle changes in trunk and other limb motion, in addition to changes in absolute motion components of the limb segments directly involved. All actions are space-time events and to concentrate on one aspect of this relationship to the exclusion of the other would destroy the fundamental unity of action."

The literature is quite clear on this last point. With skills in which performance is concerned not only with the individual components but also their integration and synchrony, then the whole approach is superior. This seems obvious because in such activities as say swimming, success depends on learning the element of co-ordination – when to kick with the legs in relation to the pull of the arms – an element which part practice may not emphasise so well.

In contrast, whole practice methods are supported by Cognitive theories of learning and also recent research on perception-action coupling (Davids, Savelsbergh, Bennett and Van der Kamp, 2002). Perception-action coupling is based on the theory of direct perception promoted by Gibson (1979). Gibson proposed that movements are determined directly from the information contained within the optical array entering the eyes; there is no need for any kind of internal representation of visual input. In this case, actions are coupled directly to perceptions without intermediary processing. This theory supports the whole method of practice because it retains the correct 'sensitive dynamic' and therefore maximises the learner's capacity to use environmental information. In other words, whole methods do not distort or compromise in any way the natural flow of visual information in the way that part methods do. The whole approach gives learners a more immediate picture about what to do and helps them understand more fully the context and relevance of individual skills. But there are potential limitations such as the tendency to overload the learner's attention capacity which, in turn, results in performance errors and possible diminished motivation/self-confidence (William, Davids and Williams, 1999). Further, the whole method would be avoided when the components are too complex or dangerous to allow the beginner to practice the task as a whole. In these cases, the best plan is to program practice so as to develop some proficiency in the separate components choosing components that are as nearly independent of each other as possible and then alternating between part and whole practice. Rink (1999) summarises some of these points:

"... the issue for sport skill instruction becomes an issue of whole part whole learning: should the teacher break down individual skills? Ample evidence exists to support the idea that unless safety is an issue, practice of the whole should precede any attempt to temporarily fragment the skill and practice part of the skill."

Basically, there are no hard and fast rules about choice of method. The following table (*Table 2*) adapted from Scully (1996) lists a number of general guidelines:

	Whole Method	Part Method
Features of the Task	Is simple	Is complex
	Involves little energy expenditure	Is too dangerous or fatiguing
	Has integrated parts	Has highly independent parts
	Is not meaningful in parts	Is made up of individual skills
	Is made up of simultaneously performed parts	If limited practice of parts is essential

	Whole Method	Part Method
Features of the Learner	Is able to remember long sequences of activity	Has limited memory span
	Has a long attention span	Unable to concentrate for long periods
	Is highly skilled	Cannot succeed with the whole method
	Is enthusiastic to do the whole	Is having difficulty with a particular part
	Needs to learn teamwork or group skills	In a group situation, provides more activity for individuals

Table 2: Guidelines for practice methods

IMPLICIT AND EXPLICIT LEARNING

A lot of attention has recently been given to the concept of implicit and explicit learning, especially in regard to the acquisition of language. The concept is equally relevant to skill acquisition. When children acquire language they acquire knowledge about grammatical structure before they can explicitly describe the rules involved. In other words, they can use language before they are actually aware of the fact! This happens quite naturally and shows that learning can sometimes take place without any kind of conscious intervention or knowledge. This is called implicit learning. It has been suggested that knowledge too can exist in either implicit or explicit forms (Hayes and Broadbent, 1984). Magill (1998) defines explicit and implicit knowledge. Explicit knowledge is '... information we can verbally describe, or in some other way give evidence that we are consciously aware of.' Implicit knowledge is '... knowledge that is difficult, if not impossible, to verbalise.' Implicit learning occurs when the accumulation of knowledge about what is being learned is passive and where no conscious analytic strategies are employed. It results in performance gains, but learners are unable to verbalise anything about what or how they have learned – it is automatic and natural. Explicit learning takes place when the learner deliberately uses problem-solving strategies such as generating or testing hypotheses to acquire knowledge – it is consciously controlled and planned. Explicit learning is evident when for example, a skier consciously thinks through their actions and analyses their movements with precision and determination. They might talk to themselves, criticise and analyse why things don't work too well. In contrast, implicit learning is seen in the steady improvement of children playing football during playtime. Their gradual improvement in ball control and tactical awareness takes place quite naturally through playing the game and meeting challenges as they occur. They may not embark on a conscious process of assessing their strengths and weaknesses or analysing how to improve; the learning is implicit to taking part, where, perhaps, enjoyment and motivation are more important.

What is the relevance of this for skill acquisition? Explicit learning is the traditional approach adopted by coaches and teachers. But Magill (1998) and others have questioned whether this is the best approach. A lot of research has demonstrated that people can acquire information critical to skilled performance without being able to verbalise the nature of that information. Some studies have revealed that people are able to perceive important aspects of environmental information critical to skill development without even being conscious of that information. On this basis, it has been suggested that implicit learning should be considered as an alternative to explicit learning. Masters (1992) carried out a study to examine the role of implicit and explicit approaches to learning in the breakdown of complicated skills under pressure. In this study, subjects were required to learn a golf putting skill, either explicitly (with knowledge of how to carry out the task and the rules to consider) or implicitly (without any outside knowledge). They were then required to perform the skill under conditions of stress.

Those who had learned implicitly were less likely to fail under stress than those who learned explicitly. Other researchers have found that when skill acquisition occurs implicitly, learning is more durable and less prone to forgetting. This research suggests that the time-honoured approach to coaching/instruction which consists predominantly of prolonged explicit instruction of how to perform the 'correct' movements, may not be the only or best approach. The distinction has a bearing on the whole/part method issue looked at earlier. It suggests that the part method of learning which relies heavily on explicit practice (focus on rules, principles, movements, feedback) may not be the most effective approach in terms of skill retention or how resistant they are to pressure. The whole method used in the context of implicit learning may be a much more successful approach.

One of the questions raised here is how to teach motor skills implicitly without the learner adopting some form of explicit, analytical problem solving tactic. It is a fact that even when learners are exposed to the whole skill (children playing football in the playground) some will compare their actions with previous attempts and other children to figure out the most effective method – explicit learning. How can this be avoided in order to generate a pure implicit situation? Liao and Masters (2001) have suggested the use of analogies or metaphors. Learners then concentrate on the analogy and in so doing, inadvertently apply the rules of the skill in an implicit manner. There are many situations in skill acquisition where suitable analogies can be devised. For example, in teaching a table tennis backhand drive the learner can be told to "hit the ball as if throwing a Frisbee". In teaching a topspin forehand they can be told to "move the bat along the hypotenuse of a right-angled triangle". In cross-country skiing it is critical to move forward speedily without loosing friction between the skis and the snow; hence it is vital to time precisely downward pressure on the skis. A problem for learners is that in their urge to move forwards, they tend to try to push the skis backwards. This reduces the amount of downward force and consequently increases the chances of the skis slipping. One way around this is to tell learners to "hit their head on the ceiling" every time they weight their skis. In so doing, their concentration is removed from the intricacies of the skill to the analogy.

It should be possible to devise good analogies like this for some situations but it may not always be the most practical approach. It may be very difficult to describe suitable 'analogies' for every whole practice situation. Liao and Masters (2001) make this point when they say:

"Analogy learning is practically feasible on the field and provides an alternative to explicit instructions. Sports coaches may help their pupils develop skills implicitly by using simple analogies that will not interfere with performance. The crucial task for the coach, however, will be to find effective analogies comprehensively integrating the technical structures required to perform the to-be-learned skill."

To conclude this section, it is important to focus on the ideas of Magill (1998). Magill proposes that research on explicit/explicit learning has some particular implications for guidance and practice in skill acquisition. He draws attention to two established findings from the research. Firstly, that the acquisition of knowledge about key environmental variables is critical to the learning process. Secondly, that beginners do not necessarily need to be consciously aware of those variables to the extent that they can verbally describe them. On this basis, he proposes five recommendations for instruction and practice:

• Firstly, he says that if people can learn implicitly then there is no need to ask them questions during their practice about what they see. Thus, it is not important to ask a learner attempting to hit a cricket ball how the ball came out of the bowler's hand. Doing this imposes on the learner an explicit learning strategy that may or may not be effective. Magill suggests the most appropriate question is not what the learner is looking at but where are they looking? This might seem a rather subtle difference, but it has the effect of directing the learner's attention to the 'information rich' area of the display which permits implicit learning (about ball delivery) to take place.

• Secondly, he points to the value of short, concise verbal cues to direct attention to critical information in the display. He suggests there is no need to provide detailed information about what to look for; verbal cues need only specify where to look (e.g., "bowler's hand" or "player's hips"). In this way, the learner implicitly extracts key information and is not told explicitly what to look for.

• Thirdly, Magill suggests that augmented feedback (in addition to specific guidance) should specify where the learner should look rather than exactly what to look at.

• Magill's fourth point relates to practice. Noting that implicit learning only takes place following lengthy periods of practice, Magill highlights the importance of repeated practice in skill learning.

• Magill's final point refers to the nature of practice. He notes that practice should include a variety of performance situations. What this does is enhance the 'distinctiveness' of the key environmental features.

CONTINUITY OF PRACTICE

This section refers to conditions where part practice applies. It has been argued several times in this Chapter that the process of breaking skills into smaller parts must take place within the context of the whole skill. In most sports the elements are dependent upon one another (e.g., in soccer, ball reception might lead to a dribble which in turn leads to passing). In practice therefore, the sequencing of the elements should recognise such patterns. Part practices should form part of a hierarchy in which those taught first 'feed' into more complicated ones which in turn lead the learner to even more detailed ones and finally the whole skill or game. There should be a logical progression from basic, simple skills which are prerequisites for more complicated tasks, through to the final skill or game. This is not to propose a rigid, inflexible approach – deviations, modifications, repetitions, regressions which are needed to solve individual problems will occur – but, the coach or teacher should devise a framework in which effective instruction and progressive learning can take place. The following are examples of this:

Example 1
Introduction of a new footwork movement pattern to a badminton player –

- Use a video of a top player and/or give a shadow demonstration of the new movements
- Allow the players to shadow the movement
- Introduce the shuttle so the player is forced to move across court, play a stroke and recover to base
- Introduce an opponent so the player is put under pressure. etc.

Example 2
Introduction of forward paddling technique to a novice kayaker –

- Beginners stand on shore simulating paddling technique shown by instructor
- Same technique is practiced but with novice in the canoe on dry land
- Beginners practice forward paddling in still water
- Backward paddling technique demonstrated by instructor and novices practice alternate forward and backward paddling, etc.

VARIABILITY OF PRACTICE

Practice variability refers to the practice of a single skill in a variety of situations. Thus, in football, attempts to take a shot at goal from a free kick could be made from a variety of locations close to the goal. Research has shown that in the learning of some skills (e.g., throwing/striking a ball for accuracy as in cricket, basketball and volleyball), variable practice results in greater accuracy and consistency than non-variable practice. This finding is more marked with children than adults. For example, Carson and Wiegand (1979) studied children throwing a beanbag to a target. Children had over 100 trials using either the same beanbag every trial or else using a bag selected on each trial from one of four bags of different weights. After practice it was found that the group which trained with bags of different weights were significantly more accurate using a bag of a novel weight than were the children only exposed to a bag of a single weight. In the learning of a catching task, say slip-fielding in cricket, this would suggest that people should be exposed to deliveries from different angles, at different speeds and varying flight paths and not simply a constant throw to their hands. Why this should be so is explained very well by Schema theory which predicts that when skill learning is concerned with the acquisition of 'rules', the richer and more diverse practice is the more effective it should be. This view fits in well with what we know about open skills, for here the task is always changing and thus the learner needs to be adaptable to new and unexpected things. An interesting thing about Schema theory is that it also predicts variable practice should be better with closed skills. The idea of practice variability does have its critics. Whiting (1982) argues that early learning should be marked by stability so that the learner understands better what is required. He says:

> "... the introduction of variations in environmental conditions should be postponed in the process of learning until an adequate 'image of the act' has been developed under one of the many conditions under which the act has eventually to be executed, i.e., 'the image of the act' has first to be developed as a holistic unit, a gestalt, before it can be manipulated to serve acts under changed conditions."

On the other hand, Rink (1999) argues that:

> "Whilst there may be merit in developing some level of consistency in performance at particular stages of learning, for most situations repetition of the same movement discourages high levels of processing, and in the case of open motor skills reduces the variability of practice essential to prepare the learner to use a skill in a more complex context."

Research by Wulf and her associates (e.g., Lai, Shea, Wulf and Wright, 2000) has shown that practice conditions should change as learning progresses. The suggestion is that practice in early learning should be constant and in later learning varied. Lai et al showed that when introducing variability late in practice, learning was as effective (and in some cases more so) than when practice was varied throughout the learning period. From a practical viewpoint this makes it easier for beginners since it reduces the attentional load that would otherwise be generated through variable conditions.

CONTEXTUAL INTERFERENCE

The suggestions from the last section that variable practice is more effective than constant practice and that the balance should switch from constant to variable practice as the learner becomes more proficient are intuitively appealing. However, they are complicated by other research which has explored the relative benefits of blocked and random practice in terms of skill acquisition (as opposed to practice performance).

Blocked practice involves practicing several different skills, but separately with a given amount of time per skill. Random practice involves practicing a set of skills in a random manner. Take the following example. A mountain rescue team member is required to learn basic life support procedures (A, B, C), how to set up a rope system to lower a casualty down a rock face, and how to lift a badly injured climber onto a stretcher. What is the best way to learn these three new skills? A typical approach would be to dwell on each procedure uninterrupted for a length of time before moving onto the next. In other words, try to consolidate one skill before moving onto the next – blocked practice. Another approach would be to spend time on each procedure within a given training session so that each one is practiced several times – random practice. One might expect blocked practice to be more effective, but research in a number of different areas of skill acquisition shows the random approach is superior (e.g., Wrisberg and Liu, 1991). Specifically, research shows that random practice is less successful than blocked practice when performance is measured during practice, but random practice reveals improved success when performance is measured (remembered) at a later time. The important factor is the moment in time when learning gains are measured. It seems that random practice results in poorer performance than blocked practice at the time of initial practice but it results in superior performance during later practice. Thus, poorer initial performance leads to improved learning! This has been coined the contextual interference effect (Schmidt and Wrisberg, 2000).

> **KEY POINT**
>
> **CONTEXTUAL INTERFERENCE:**
> Random practice results in poorer performance than blocked practice at the time of initial practice but yields superior performance during later practice.

How is this effect explained? Schmidt and Wrisberg (2000) note two explanations. The 'elaboration hypothesis' proposed by Shea and Zimny (1983) argues that random practice allows learners to appreciate more fully the distinctiveness of each learning task/movement which consequently facilitates the transfer to long term memory and hence later recall/practice. The 'spacing hypothesis' proposed by Lee and McGill (1985) proposes that as the learner moves from one task to the next, they forget the one just practiced so that when they return to it, they have to produce a new plan again. Because they are challenged to begin each task anew, their initial performance is poor (compared to blocking), but the benefits of a more rigorous form of practice are realised when they resume practice later.

These findings would appear to challenge the time-honoured practice of repeating a skill (blocking) 'until it becomes natural'. The implications for learning are clear according to Schmidt and Wrisberg (2000). They suggest that in the very early stages of learning (Fitts's cognitive stage) learners should be exposed to a blocked practice regime briefly to assist their initial understanding of the new skill and to permit a basic level of success. Very quickly however, they should move to a random schedule where several different skills are all practiced within the same session. Thus, golfers should practice different shots with different kinds of clubs and aspiring football players should practice different ways of passing and receiving the ball rather than focusing on a single method. One of the downsides of random practice is that it leads to increased errors on the part of the learner with slower initial improvement and potential falls in motivation. These limitations have to be balanced against the long-term gains and, from a practical point of view, learners should be assured of this fact when things do go wrong.

OVERLEARNING

The topic of overlearning deserves mention. It is suggested by many researchers that performers never actually achieve their true physiological and psychological potentials. Their true maximum remains an elusive goal. The only way to approach close to this goal is to train long, hard and in the most appropriate manner. For many people though, the time and effort required is either practically impossible or else limited through boredom, injury or fatigue. The fact is that if people can practice beyond the point when they have apparently reached their maximum level of success – and this could mean working on a skill (e.g., a tennis serve) many thousands of times – then they are rewarded by slight improvements in performance. In addition, overlearning – as it is called – ensures performance becomes more consistent and less resistant to failure under stress. Further, skills which have been consistently practiced to perfection over a very long period (who forgets how to ride a bicycle or swim?) also provide a better platform for skill transfer. It is likely that the technical consistency demonstrated by many world class track and field athletes is partly due to the incredible number of times they have practiced. And it may be that the consistent performance of games players such as Jonny Wilkinson and David Beckham in set situations results from excessive, repetitive practice of the same skills. It goes without saying that only movements which are technically correct should be overlearned – 'Perfect practice makes perfect'!

DISTRIBUTION OF PRACTICE

Overlearning implies practice that in some ways is repetitive or intense. A lot of research has examined the relative merits of practice which is massed (long periods of practice interspersed with short periods of rest) or distributed practice (short periods of practice interspersed with long periods of rest). An example of massed practice would be a learner swimmer practicing the breaststroke for say 45 minutes within a one-hour session. The learner would spend the remaining time on other strokes/rest. An example of distributed practice would be the learner spending 15 minutes on breast stroke followed by three, 15 minute practice periods on different activities. Results from the research have never proved conclusive. One of the problems is that attempts to manipulate time within a practice session is often thwarted by practical considerations such as the fatigue level of learners, the number of people involved, the available facilities and the amount of time available for practice. It seems that the amount of time a learner spends on any single skill or activity and the intensity of that practice is best determined by practical considerations such as those listed below:

• A minimum time is essential for warm up, to establish an appropriate working relationship and level of motivation, and to ensure that some learning has occurred.

• Practice is often limited by finance, time and facilities. A coach for example, may only be free to work with his athletes for a single, two-hour session each week. Or a teacher may be constrained by the school timetable to work with children say only 3 times a week for 45 minutes each session.

• The amount of time spent working with youngsters or beginners should be limited because their attention span is generally limited.

• Some activities are too demanding physically to allow lengthy practice and a minimal recovery period is essential if accidents are not to occur or bad technique grooved.

• There will always be a maximum period dictated by physical and/or psychological fatigue, both of which will depend on the skill in question and the experience of the learner.

Notwithstanding these factors, attention should always be given to the merits of organising random or variable practice (see previous sections). What seems most important is that the coach or teacher gives priority to the 'quality' of practice within the time permitted. This will involve structuring practices correctly (shaping, chaining, variability, etc.) and setting realistic targets – however simple – which can be reached by learners. In addition, learners will naturally pace themselves with regard to fitness and interest and this can serve as a guide for the coach. So long as the learner maintains interest and remembers what they have learned from session to session and is given the encouragement/opportunity to work in between times, then the question of spacing or massing practice probably has little relevance.

OBSERVATIONAL PRACTICE

We have already examined some of the important features about demonstrations in Chapter 3. Watching a demonstration can be defined as observational practice. A question currently being pursued by various researchers is the relative importance of physical and observational practice. It is well known that observation by itself is not as effective as physical practice, and that it is better than no practice at all (e.g., Wright, Li and Coady, 1997). Some findings suggest that a combination of physical and observational

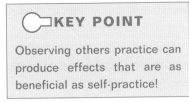

practice is more effective than either physical or observational practice alone (Shea, Wright, Wulf and Whitacre, 2000). Shea et al showed that when a practice regime involving physical practice 100% of the time was replaced with a regime of 50% observational practice and 50% physical practice, there was no deterioration in learning and an enhanced transfer effect. They noted in their studies that as practice progressed, subtle forms of competition, co-operation and goal-setting developed whereby the learners changed how they physically practiced as a result of performing in the presence of and observing other members of the group. From this, they suggested that combined practice has the additional potential to enhance learning through the beneficial medium of social interaction. In related studies, they showed that observational practice alone can be as effective as physical practice if the learning requires some kind of adaptation to new conditions or movement generalisation. Thus, if a teacher is interested in working on principles that apply to a variety of situations (such as the principle of 'moving off the ball', or a 'wall pass'), it may be useful to spend a significant amount of time focusing the learner's attention via demonstrations or video recordings on the principle in question. In this regard, Shea et al (2000) suggest:

"... it is possible that early in physical practice the cognitive sources of the performer are fully occupied in meeting the cognitive and motor demands of the new task. In that situation, observation may give the learner an opportunity either to extract important information concerning appropriate co-ordination patterns and subtle requirements of the task or to evaluate effective or ineffective strategies that would be difficult, if not impossible while he or she concomitantly prepares and executes an impending movement. From that perspective, observational practice offers the learner a chance to conduct processing that could not occur while physically practicing until the skill has become well learned."

They also make the point that if physical practice can be replaced in part by some kind of observational practice, the learner expends less energy which reduces fatigue and the risk of injury.

IMAGERY

One of the curious things about learning is that whilst it is reflected in a change in physical performance, it can apparently take place without recourse to physical practice!

Sometimes, people improve from one practice session to the next even though they have not practised in between times. One reason could be they have 'mentally practised' during the interval – covertly gone through the activity in their mind – and this has supplemented physical practice. Many sports persons testify to the value of mentally going through an action in their 'mind's eye' before an important event or competition. The research literature on imagery (mental practice is a somewhat dated expression) is very extensive and demonstrates quite clearly that under certain conditions it can have a beneficial effect – not so much as actual practice, but certainly more than no practice at all (e.g., Hird, Landers, Thomas and Horan. 1991).

In one particular study three groups of people were required to learn a 'pursuit rotor' task (this requires the person to visually track a target moving in a circular manner with a hand held stylus, and follow the target with the stylus). One group physically practiced over a period of time, one group did not practice at all and the third group were instructed to simply visualise the task in their head. At the end of the training period the visual (mental) practice group had learned to perform almost as successfully as the physical practice group! Why should this be the case? The answer is not entirely clear. It is possible that imagery provides an opportunity for learners to work on cognitive or intellectual parts of a skill (e.g., trying to understand the best way of beating a man-to-man defence system in basketball) – components which might not normally receive the same kind of attention as with physical practice. This view has received some experimental support and is also supported by the finding that imagery sometimes works well with novices when cognitive processing is demanding. Another explanation is that imagery causes a physiological training effect in the sense that it invokes the same physiological processes underlying movement selection, movement execution and feedback. This idea too has received a little scientific support. A more feasible explanation is that imagery has a number of beneficial side effects such as anxiety reduction, goal clarification or psychological preparation. This idea certainly agrees with the views of many athletes, but the exact causes are still unknown.

Imagery is part of a growing subject which centres on psychological training and preparation. It cannot be dealt with seriously in just a couple of paragraphs and will be considered in more depth in Chapter 7. For the present, three issues should be raised:

• The basis of effective imagery is skill transfer (see later). It follows therefore that all the criteria underpinning positive transfer – specificity, reality, etc., – must also be satisfied if imagery is to be of any value.

• Imagery is a complex process. Many expressions are used such as visualisation, imagery, covert rehearsal and they all have different meanings and applications. Different senses can be used for imagery; each for different purposes and in different ways. In addition, one has to learn how to use imagery. It is a skill itself which requires practice and experience. To use it therefore requires a commitment and interest on the part of the coach/teacher as well as the learner.

• Thirdly, the effectiveness of any kind of imagery seems to depend on the sport, situation and the individual. Imagery may work very well for some players before competition whilst others may find it of value only as a training exercise (perhaps during a lay-off through injury). Some people may find that a combination of different forms of imagery is most effective whilst others may struggle to concentrate on any technique. We shall return to this topic in Chapter 7.

EXPERIENTIAL LEARNING

Imagery is a passive form of practice; it does not involve any kind of overt physical activity. Physical practice also has a passive dimension. This happens when learners are told directly what to do and are given little or no opportunity to experiment or assess their own performance. Traditional approaches to teaching and learning are founded almost wholly on (didactic/passive) models like this. Whilst such an approach has a place, especially when risks and the need for safety are high, support for an active or guided

Sometimes it's good to let learners work out things for themselves

approach to learning is very strong. It might be useful for a moment to look at a classic study which examined the perceptual-motor development of young kittens for it highlights the value of 'active' learning. In this study, two kittens were held in a circular carousel arrangement in which one could walk unaided whilst the other was carried around in a basket moved by the first kitten. Because of the mechanical linkage between the two kittens, both received exactly the same kind of visual stimulation during their time in the carousel. Of course the active one also received internal, kinesthetic feedback whereas the passive one did not. At the end of the testing period, the active kittens had developed normal motor co-ordination and could successfully execute simple tasks, whereas the passive ones failed. The point in describing this study – which has also been repeated in modified form with both animals and humans – is to underline the critical importance of allowing the individual to play an active role in their own learning. The broad label given to this is experiential learning (Kraft, 1999).

Dewey (1938) was an early proponent of experiential learning and he outlined the following central principles. He advocated that experiential learning:

• Focuses on the learner and considers their knowledge, skills, interests and needs
• Accepts that learning is a social phenomenon and should involve social interaction
• Involves physical interaction with the environment

- Engages the learner in problem solving tasks
- Engages the learner in a review process
- Predicts that new learning will always be transferred to future situations.

Experiential learning is strongly favoured by outdoor educationalists, but it is also used by many sports coaches and teachers of physical education. The 'Inner Game' approach to coaching which is discussed at length in Chapter 7 adopts some of the key principles listed above. It is an approach to learning which attempts to promote not only skill development but also changes in personal development (such as self-esteem, confidence) and social skills (such as working with others, recognising others' weaknesses).

The principles of experiential learning are supported by a number of theories of learning. Take Association Theory (see Chapter 2). It supports the idea that behaviour changes according to its immediate consequences. The following examples show this. A couple of youngsters presented with the opportunity to paddle an open canoe (without any guidance from a waiting instructor) will quickly determine

KEY QUOTE

"The best way to achieve improved performance is not by the coach dictating to the player, but by co-operation between coach and player."
National Coaching Foundation (1986)

how to propel the craft forwards, turn it around and possibly capsize it! They will adapt and change their actions in direct accordance with the effect those actions have on the canoe. Similarly, a group of primary age children playing touch rugby during their lunch break are very likely to settle into a pattern of play in which rules have been decided, areas have been marked out and teams selected. Their game will have evolved over a period of time during which various permutations of these factors were tried and discarded. These examples serve to illustrate the role of experiential learning within the framework of association learning theory. The same is true of social learning theory. Bandura (1969) suggested that people learn by modelling or imitating the actions and behaviour of other people. Behaviour is directed through the models presented by other people. Information processing theory (see Chapter 2) sees the individual not as a passive receiver of information acting in a stereotyped and predictable manner, but as an active searcher for information anticipating events and actions and making best sense of the data available. Schema theory predicts that learning takes place more effectively against a backdrop of varied practice and experience. Schema are more robust in terms of their generality depending on the richness of the learner's experience. Young children behave in much the same way as they explore the world about them. The child psychologist Piaget (e.g., Piaget and Inhelder, 1967) was of the opinion that a child's intellectual development stems directly from the active contact he has with his immediate environment. He emphasised the importance of active learning and concrete experiences. Finally, it is worth noting Coleman's (1977) distinction between information assimilation and experiential learning. Learning through information assimilation is the traditional teacher directed approach based on the linear transmission of information from teacher to learner; information is presented in various forms in the belief the learner will finally come to understand the principle or concept in question. Coleman suggests that the experiential approach is almost a reverse sequence to information assimilation. The steps in the experiential process involve carrying out an action in a particular instance and noting the effects of that action. Understanding the effects and the consequences of the action, the learner then moves towards an understanding of the general principles involved. Ultimately they are able to apply, through actions, what has been learned in a new setting. From these few examples, the point is hopefully made that experiential learning is a tried and tested approach to learning supported by a wide variety of theoretical approaches. It is therefore a very robust approach to learning and teaching/coaching.

The process of involving learners in their own learning is reflected in a number of strategies, viz., trial and error practice, self analysis, problem solving and peer review. The extent to which learners are permitted to take a full part in their own learning is partly a function of the coach or teacher's learning style. For some coaches (e.g., those who adhere to the 'Inner Game' philosophy) it is important for the learner to take responsibility and play an active part in their own learning. For many coaches however, it may be inappropriate. Thus, for advanced learners working on highly specific movements or in potentially dangerous situations, a direct form of coaching may be more appropriate. We will examine teaching/coaching styles in Chapter 8.

PRACTICE SIMULATION

The individual's involvement in their learning is partly reduced when manual guidance is used to help overcome complex or dangerous movements. Thus, helping a kayaker in a capsize situation by physically manipulating their boat takes some responsibility from the learner. The use of simulators means that almost total responsibility is removed. Simulators attempt to mimic a procedure or movement in an artificial way. Aircraft simulators which mirror the flying conditions experienced in even the largest of jet aircraft are commonly used in pilot training schedules. Devices like this are designed to reduce costs, save time and where appropriate, provide training in safe conditions. Although mainly found in the industrial/commercial fields, they do feature in sport also. Machines have been devised to constrain the club in a golf swing, to project cricket and tennis balls with varying flight characteristics, to teach rowing on dry land and even dummies have been used to provide targets for blocking practice in American football. In addition, windsurfing simulators are very popular,

> **KEY QUOTE**
>
> *"You learn to talk by talking*
> *You learn to walk by walking*
> *You learn golf by golfing*
> *You learn typing by typing*
> *You learn best by doing it."*
> **Nike footwear slogan**

cross-country ski exercisers can be purchased which 'groove' technique and computer games can now be purchased which simulate almost every sport in existence! A commonly used 'ski fit machine' is said to:

"... accurately simulate the motion of downhill skiing, and help to increase aerobic fitness, while improving co-ordination and exercise of the appropriate muscle joints."

(Sports Industry, 1991)

Claims such as these are rarely tested and it would appear there is much scope for research into the actual value of simulators. In terms of skill learning, it is likely that simulators are of value only to the extent that they mirror real conditions and allow transfer to the game or movement proper. Apart from one or two obvious cases (e.g., dry ski matting) the evidence would suggest their value is very limited. And of course there are obvious cost implications with simulators which further reduces their applicability.

Skiing on plastic matting has many similarities to skiing on snow

Playing ice hockey on a road with a ball may not be the best way to simulate practice

TRANSFER OF LEARNING

Practically all learning is based on some form of transfer – the effect of previous experience on present performance/learning. It is thought we rarely learn a totally new skill after the early years of childhood. New skills invariably arise out of previous experiences through the combining of elements learned in the past to form new movement patterns or else the modification of existing patterns. A central assumption in most practice situations is that whatever is learned during practice will have a beneficial effect at a subsequent time. Indeed, it can be argued that the true value of any teaching or coaching programme is the extent to which it serves the learner positively in the future. There are two kinds of transfer – positive and negative.

Positive transfer takes place in many areas of sporting endeavour. For example, physical fitness programmes are designed to make the players fitter for game situations. Feelings and emotions heightened during a pre-match team talk are meant to be carried onto the field of play to motivate players to greater levels of enthusiasm and (hopefully) skill. Techniques practised in isolation are meant to carry over to the whole skill. In contrast, negative transfer is an unwanted agent and refers to the inhibiting

effect that a practice or previous activity has on current learning. An American footballer who takes up rugby may be penalised for 'blocking', which is an integral part of football but is illegal in rugby. Here, a previously learned action intrudes to the detriment of performance in a new sport. A similar type of 'interference' happens in racket sports when players who are proficient in one sport, say tennis, learn another such as say badminton. Initially, they may swing the racket incorrectly and fail to take account of the different flight characteristics of the shuttle. Their performance suffers as a consequence. In situations like this positive transfer often overtakes the initial negative influences.

Several aspects of transfer are little understood and with others there is some confusion (Gass, 1990). Many investigators have attempted to explain why transfer takes place and under what conditions it is maximised. Bruner (1960) proposed two theories to explain how the elements are linked from one learning experience to another. His ideas still have credence today. He referred to specific and non-specific transfer. He said:

"There are two ways in which learning serves the future. One is through its specific applicability to tasks that are highly similar to those we originally learn to perform. Psychologists refer to this specific phenomenon as specific transfer of training; perhaps it should be called the extension of habits or associations. Its utility appears to be limited in the main to what we speak of as skills. A second way in which earlier learning renders later performance more efficient is through what is conveniently called non-specific transfer, or, more accurately, the transfer of principles and attitudes. In essence, it consists of learning, initially, not a skill but a general idea which can then be used as a basis of recognising problems as special cases of the idea originally mastered."

Specific transfer of training proposes that positive carry-over of movements takes place when they are similar or identical from one situation to another. An example would be paddling a canoe on flat water and on moving water. Strokes to propel the canoe forward are identical in both cases albeit slightly different in terms of spatial/force dimensions. With non-specific transfer, carry-over is based on knowledge of principles or ideas that are common to both past and present learning. A good example would be the principle of 'giving' or 'cushioning' the force of a moving ball in order to control its movement. This principle applies in cricket, football, hockey, rugby and many other ball games.

Decisions about how practice is designed must be based in part on the principle of positive transfer. For example, in passing practices the coach expects something to carry over to performance in the game of basketball. In springboard diving, the practice of particular moves on the trampoline is expected to benefit the diver when in the pool situation. It is clear that techniques like this work otherwise they would have been discarded long ago. The interesting question is whether they always work and whether they are the best techniques? It would be useful to know under what conditions transfer is maximised so that best use can be made of practice time. Such knowledge might also minimise the problems of negative transfer where previous learning has a detrimental effect on current learning. Research in the area is considerable and investigators have examined many different kinds of tasks ranging from laboratory-type skills to more realistic sporting skills. The research has yielded different and sometimes contradictory findings, but a number of points do emerge which lean heavily on the two theories mentioned before. Gass (1990) lists the following factors that underline the transfer of learning:

• *Design conditions for transfer* – Here, Gass suggests that learners and teachers/coaches should establish within learners a commitment to look for elements of previous learning which have relevance to current learning. He indicates that for some learners, it may be beneficial to write down how they feel the past may help present learning. The main point is the need for both learner and coach to be actively aware of how the past and present interact and to take advantage of past learning to reduce the effort of new learning that takes place.

• *Create elements in the learning environment similar to those likely to be found in the future* – Here, Bruner's ideas are relevant. The greater the number of common elements the greater the transfer. Elements may refer to physical actions (e.g., arm action in a swimming stroke), stimulus cues in the display (e.g., the manner in which a ball or shuttle travels) or principles of play (e.g., movement off the ball, man to man marking). What seems important is that when the coach analyses a skill for the purpose of breaking it down into part practices, they should assess all possible aspects for relevance and not just the physical movements involved. So, elements such as competition, teamwork or combat which are central to the whole skill should also appear in practice. Skills should be taught so they are transferable from one situation to another. All the variables which appear in the complete skill – movement, speed, form, timing, body control, agility, decision-making, effort, concentration, relaxation, etc. – should be introduced in some form in practice. In addition, it is critical for the coach to underline not only similarities between practice and competition, but also the differences which exist. The learner should be guided into assessing where the similarities begin and end. In this way the learner should become a much more discriminating performer.

• *Provide learners with opportunities to practice close in time to previous experiences* – Transfer is maximised if practice takes place soon after previous relevant learning. There are implications here for how practice is timetabled and scheduled. It is far better to block a number of sessions on one particular skill/activity (within the constraints of boredom and fatigue) than introduce and try to develop a variety of skills in quick succession. Thus, it might be far better to practice for say, six consecutive weeks on a single swimming stroke in order to maximise the transfer effect, than spend the same time on four different strokes. Readers should note previous discussion in regard to blocked versus random practice.

It follows also that transfer is enhanced if previously learned skills are more robust than if they have only been half learned and little practiced. This point is well supported by research evidence.

• *Maximise the naturalness of learning consequences* – Gass suggests that if the outcomes of a learning experience are kept natural and not distorted by, for example, exaggerating the ability of the individual or withholding important feedback, then the potential for that experience to transfer is maximised. He reasons that allowing learners to experience the full consequences of their learning experiences results in stronger formation of skills which, in turn, results in greater transfer to other skills.

• *Provide learners with opportunities to internalise their own learning* – Here, Gass suggests that the process of internalisation (verbalisation, reflection and self awareness) helps the learner form concepts or generalisations which can be later transferred. This is a topic that will be discussed in more detail in Chapter 8.

• *Encourage the learner to take responsibility* – This feature is highlighted throughout this book. Gass draws attention to the benefits gained when learners are actively involved in the learning experience – deciding what to practice, setting goals, self-analysis, peer review, and so on. He suggests that empowering learners like this not only increases their motivation to learn but also their incentive to apply what is learned to future experiences. The well worn adage 'success breeds success' is a good example of this principle at work.

• *Use focused processing techniques* – Key principles involving the use of feedback were discussed in Chapter 4. It is clear that feedback is critical to the learning process, but its influence can be enhanced if particular attention is placed on the reviewing/de-briefing process. Gass suggests a number of useful strategies. He indicates that feedback should be given which his well-intended, specific and directed towards positive change. Feedback should include linking experiences from the past and present learning. He also suggests that when possible, learners should be involved in open reviews on a regular basis during practice; not just at the end of a practice session. All of these strategies assist the positive transfer of learning.

There are three issues that should be reinforced before leaving this section. Firstly, it seems that positive transfer between two skills depends on the degree to which the first skill has been learned. Learners are more able to benefit from relevant past experience if that experience is substantial and if the skills that have been learned are established and well practiced. Thus for example, in order to maximise the trans-

KEY POINT

Positive transfer depends on the:

• Quality of prior learning

• Similarity of prior learning

• Extent to which the learner is involved in their learning.

fer value of any kind of part practice, learners must repeat the part sufficiently to perform the part with confidence and accuracy. Secondly, the degree to which past experience is relevant in terms of movement similarity and commonality of principles, is a major factor determining how quickly a learner progresses with a new skill. Finally, it seems that if the learner can be engaged in the learning process in a positive, analytical manner where they become empowered to 'own' that experience, then the learning that ensues provides a better platform for future learning.

Given these very positive comments, coaches and teachers should always be guarded in expecting transfer to take place automatically. A question mark should always be placed against skill practices that occur out of context or outside the physical environment of the skill or game itself. In addition, if transfer depends on the similarity between present and past learning then the coach or teacher should always seek to determine the learners' past experiences and interests in order to provide a focus for integration. In the practical world where there may be many individuals to coach and where time may be very limited, it may not be practical to delve into the past of every learner; but the principle is still a sound one.

SHAPING SKILLS

Some sports techniques are simple to acquire and can be performed with a degree of success after a relatively few number of attempts (e.g., javelin hand grip, underarm volleyball serve, tying a knot in a climbing rope). It is unlikely these need to be broken down into lesser parts. Others however, cannot be learned easily because they are too complicated or dangerous. Take for example a diving routine, new ball game or new swimming stroke. Invariably, these have to be reduced and simplified in some way.

One way of doing this is to break complex actions into simple steps so the learner can work progressively through each one. Each distinct part of the action is then thought of as a link in a chain. The performer first learns one link, then adds a second link and practices the two together. Then a third link can be added and all three practised in sequence, and so on until the chain is complete. This is the classic notion of progressive-part practice as described previously. Sometimes it is called chaining. In chaining, each part is practised just as it will be performed in the finished technique. This method can only be used effectively with serial-type activities where the degree of integration between parts is minimal. Another method is called shaping and was mentioned in an earlier chapter.

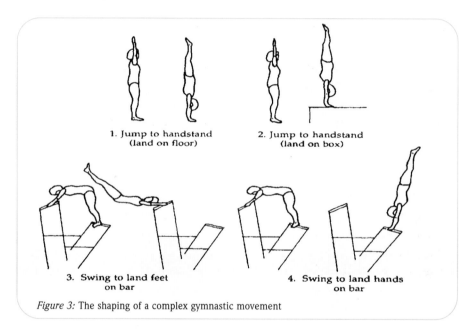

1. Jump to handstand
(land on floor)

2. Jump to handstand
(land on box)

3. Swing to land feet
on bar

4. Swing to land hands
on bar

Figure 3: The shaping of a complex gymnastic movement

Shaping is the method whereby a complex movement is introduced to learners by gradually shaping simpler movements into more complex ones. It is a more continuous process than the step-like approach central to chaining. It is especially appropriate for complicated techniques found in closed sports such as trampolining and gymnastics that are sometimes impossible to break down in a logical manner. Shaping shares some characteristics with trial and error learning; early movements are eliminated and others steadily altered until the desired one is established.

Shaping can be illustrated with a couple of examples. Most skiers aspire to perfect parallel turns but for many, this is too complex to tackle straight away. One way of approaching this is to teach firstly a simple snow plough glide. Once mastered, a turn can be incorporated first in one direction then the other. Following this, the element of 'unweighting' can be introduced which allows the learner to bring the skis together for the turn. With practice the skis can be bought parallel earlier in the turn until both traverse and turn are accomplished with the legs roughly parallel. In this example, the whole skill is gradually formed by successively developing simpler ones.

In women's gymnastics, perfecting new routines on the asymmetric bars presents particular problems of safety, etc. Take for example the 'straddle back to catch' illustrated in the *Figure 3*. In the first stage the gymnast jumps into a handstand to land with hands where the feet were placed, with support from the coach. Secondly, the gymnast attempts the same movement but without support. Next, the gymnast jumps to handstand but moves slightly backward to land higher on a box section. Fourthly, the gymnast tries this without support from the coach. Next, the gymnast transfers to the bars to adopt a position with hands holding the upper bar and feet resting on the lower one. She then swings forward and returns to rest with feet on the lower bar. The next stage is the same swing again but, with the coach standing by, the gymnast releases the high bar to catch the lower one on the return swing. Finally, this is tried without coach support. In this example (see National Coaching Foundation, 1986), the coach has devised a number of simpler actions where each develops naturally from the preceding one thus presenting the learner with small steps in difficulty every time. With careful thought and ingenuity, this method can be applied to most situations and techniques that are too complicated to learn as a whole.

Both of these examples demonstrate how skills can be shaped through the successive development of a simple movement into one that is more complex. For the technique to work, each stage must be attainable and also rewarded. Martens (1997) identifies a number of principles for effective behaviour shaping. He says:

• The steps between stages should be small enough for there to be a good chance of success. It is better to progress successfully in small steps than fail through attempts to progress to quickly.

• Only one aspect of a skill should be practiced/shaped at a time. If for example, a skill requires both speed and accuracy for success, it is better to emphasise one component at a time.

• External feedback from a coach should be scheduled intermittently rather than after every practice attempt. This has the effect of 'driving' performance in the intended direction.

• Technical standards should be relaxed in the knowledge that previous well learned skills may suffer performance decrement when shaped into new ones.

• Methods of shaping behaviour should be sufficiently adaptable to account for individual differences; if one method does not work, it should be exchanged in favour of another.

• If a particular method fails to work, the coach should be prepared to go right back to the start with an entirely new approach.

SPECIFICITY OF SKILL

The importance of transfer has already been highlighted in this chapter. Paradoxically, research and anecdotal evidence shows that motor skills transfer very little between one another, even when they are apparently very similar. In one study for example, people learned how to execute a volleyball pass before they learned a basketball tip for accuracy. They also practised a badminton volley before learning a tennis volley. In both cases, learning the first action had little positive effect in learning the second. The same is also found when actions practised slowly first and then at normal speed show little transfer. The reason for these negative findings centres on the 'specificity of skill' hypothesis. This proposes that skills are defined by a profile of 'abilities' and that a person's ability to learn and perform a skill depends upon whether the person possesses the right mix of abilities appropriate to that skill. Skills which are just slightly different (e.g., crawl leg action in the water and on the pool side) may have little effect on each other because the learner may have the abilities necessary for one but not the other. The same principle applies to the area of fitness. Here, it is known that different sports require different fitness profiles and so whilst a player may be fit for one sport (say football) they may not be fit for another (say hockey) because the required fitness profiles differ.

Within the research literature, specificity has been examined within the context of the 'generality-specificity hypothesis'. Numerous studies have examined whether people transfer specific items from the past to the present or whether they can generalise ideas and principles and apply experience to much wider settings. The 'general' hypothesis predicts for example, that someone who excels in one fast ball (say cricket) game should also achieve in other fast ball games (say lacrosse). The 'specificity' argument disagrees with this and says that skills required across sports are so different as to negate any positive transfer. There is not a clear answer to this question. Evidence supports both views. However, it is widely accepted that as learners become more skilful, techniques and strategies required for success become more distinctive. Consequently, practice should be more specific. At the novice level, it is possible to apply basic skills such as hitting, throwing and passing from one sport to another with a degree of success. Some principles of play common to a number of sports (e.g., wall pass, faking, moving into space) are potentially transferable. Similarly, some attitudes and feelings can be transposed from activity to activity.

The most practical conclusion to be drawn from the literature is that skill is largely specific. Caution should be expressed when extrapolating from practice to game situations. However, teachers and coaches should try to harness the learner's past experience by making realistic links where they exist. The transfer of general actions or principles may be possible in early learning, but as skill develops transfer is overtaken by the acquisition of specific techniques, strategies, etc.

ROLE OF ERRORS IN LEARNING

Few people enjoy failure and most strive to make a success of all they do. The desire in society for efficiency and failure-free operation is reflected in the science of ergonomics which specifically aims to reduce the chances of making errors through good design of equipment and everyday objects. In terms of skill acquisition, the whole point of guidance is to direct learners

to good performance, efficiently and accurately. Learners are not normally forced into error situations intentionally or allowed to repeat mistakes. Indeed, the repetitive practice of mistakes is rarely encouraged because it can lead to the development of habits that are difficult to eradicate. However, an interesting question asks whether teachers and coaches might concentrate on the potential benefits of errors? Can people learn from making errors? What do they learn? Should they be guided into making errors? There are lots of questions surrounding this issue, prompted in part by the fact that guidance is, in a sense, very one-sided. Guidance is primarily concerned with the process of developing correct movements alone and gives learners few direct cues about alternative movements. On this basis, it could be argued that knowledge of correct actions is incomplete if the learner is not given the opportunity to define them against alternatives.

The making of errors has a natural place in trial and error learning; many teachers and coaches argue that people can learn from their errors. This seems especially applicable in outdoor activities such as orienteering, skiing and sailing. For example, in sailing the learner picks up a lot of useful information about a boat's capabilities, wind patterns and emergency drills through capsizing the dinghy – even when unplanned. If they never capsize a boat, then their ability to determine how far they can lean the boat before it capsizes can never be fully achieved. Similarly, orienteering novices learn salient principles of navigation by making fundamental mistakes in say, pace judgement or use of the compass. They associate poor decision making with inappropriate outcomes (e.g., walking into the wrong valley!) and thereby refine their ability on future occasions. To take another example, the confidence of a novice rock climber is increased immeasurably if they relax their hold on the rock and take their weight on the rope above. In this way the climber learns the rope really will hold if they fall! There are similar instances in other sports. For example a beginner to football will probably fail many times to take a successful corner kick; much practice will be required before they understand how to weight the ball for direction, swerve and distance. The important question in these and similar examples is whether teachers and coaches should actively encourage the making of errors? For example, when coaching a volleyball serve, should the learner be made to serve both short into the net and long outside the court, even though the game demands neither of these options? In trampolining would it be a useful lead-up to straight bouncing to give the novice experience of bouncing across the width of the bed rather than just in the centre? It may seem a little strange to answer this question in the affirmative, but schema theory (see Chapter 2) supports the idea of 'error' practice.

Schema theory concentrates on how people change when they learn. The view is that people learn 'rules' which govern the manner in which movements are organised and executed; people do not learn movements per se. Rather, they learn the principles (unconsciously) which define movements. Rules are acquired through active participation, feedback and experience. Furthermore, the more varied the practice, the more strongly the rules are established and the more general they become. In this context, errors are an integral part of the learning process, adding to its variety and so strengthening the basis for skilled movement. This notion is supported by experimental findings as well as anecdotal evidence from coaches. In a much quoted example, an American baseball coach forced his pitchers to aim the ball wide of the plate during practice in the belief that their perception of correct aiming would become more

> ## 🔑 KEY QUOTE
>
> *"Errors can be of two types: learning errors and performance errors. Learning errors are ones that occur because athletes don't know how to perform a skill; that is, they have not yet developed the correct motor program. Performance errors are made not because athletes do not know how to do the skill, but because they made a mistake in executing what they know.*
> *You must be able to distinguish learning errors from performance errors in order to know whether your role is coach-to-learn or coach-to-perform."*
> **Martens (1997)**

acute. Some educational research supports this idea. For example, it is suggested that a good teaching strategy is to present learners not only with the correct way of completing a task, but also with alternative solutions and an opportunity to practice them. This view is based on the premise that knowledge of the correct response is incomplete if there is no opportunity to define it against the alternatives. However, there is an important distinction between errors and alternative movements. It is suggested that guiding learners into alternative ways of solving problems does not imply they have made a mistake, rather, they have just practiced an alternative response pattern. Errors can therefore be viewed as positive learning experiences. Of course, if the position is adopted that errors are good and should be experienced, then the possibility of bad habits being developed through continued error practice should be high in the coach or teacher's mind. This matter is discussed further by Sharp (1988, 2004).

PRACTICAL CONSIDERATIONS

We have examined many principles of practice based on relevant research and informed wisdom. However, in the real world of teaching and coaching skills, there are always practical considerations which, often prevail over theoretical niceties. This section examines some of the key issues.

Safety

If practice is to be effective then it must take place within a well-structured and safe environment. There are a number of considerations that apply to most sports and to all learners. Firstly, practice must be safe. In certain sports – especially outdoor activities – safety is a prime feature and clear guidelines established by the governing body or teaching establishment help the instructor plan practice accordingly (e.g., novice orienteers may work in pairs on their first visit to a forest). In other sports safety factors relating to use of equipment, slipperiness of surfaces, warm up procedures, etc., also play an important part. For example, a number of groups working in the same area should be spread apart so as not to impede each other. Similarly, gymnastic equipment would not be placed close to walls, windows, other items, etc. The current climate in society which tends to focus on litigation, blame and risk assessment, demands that all teachers and coaches dwell seriously on matters of safety.

Planning

Practice must be planned, thought out well in advance and must be given a purpose. Purpose and direction helps to motivate learners and control those who may not be so well motivated. Good planning also ensures that maximum use is made of the time available. Generally, learners should be made aware of why they are practicing certain things (e.g., "This practice will show you why it is vital to take advantage of the space between members of the opposition"). The coach's goals should be in synchrony with the needs and expectations of the learners and practice should be related to the game situation/whole skill. Otherwise, learners may well become very skilled 'jugglers of the ball' but lack the ability to use those skills in the game.

> **KEY QUOTE**
>
> *"Coaching is about improving or sustaining performance towards identified goals, through a structured intervention programme and delivering within constraints of time, place and resource"*
> **Lyle** (2002)

Goal setting

Establishing appropriate goals is based on sound preparation that takes place in advance of actual practice. Knowing what equipment is required, how court areas need to be split, what tasks will be given to learners, how groups should be divided (e.g., groups of three working together initially followed by 3 v 3 practices), etc., are matters which, if dealt with at the right time make for efficiency and go a long way to establishing good learner/coach/teacher relationships. Goals must also be planned ahead. Practice must have clear and simple intentions. Learning is a long-term process: practice sessions that attempt too much will just waste everyone's time.

Flexibility

Having established a set of intentions, the coach or teacher should be prepared to adjust and modify them as appropriate. Through observation, changes may need to be made to say the composition of groups, the layout of equipment or the complexity of the task (e.g., reduce a 3 v 3 practice to a 2 v 2). Good planning should require few major changes, but unexpected things do occur (e.g., a gymnast displays an unusual fault which needs to be avoided) which may require a rethink or change of plan, and the coach must be prepared to modify practice accordingly.

Communication

Once practice is underway, the coach or teacher must consider their ongoing involvement and know how to communicate effectively with individuals or the group. As a guide, continuity of practice should not be broken too frequently. It has already been said that practice is the medium for learning and practice is what learners want to do – they do not wish to have their work interrupted constantly to listen to unnecessary comments. Before practice is stopped, the coach or teacher should know what they are going to say or do next. They should move in advance to a position where all can be seen and heard. The use of clear and obvious commands (e.g., "stop", "begin") directs learners easily, saves time and helps establish a working atmosphere. Simple steps such as kneeling down to ensure the same eye level contact are quite critical. A coach working with few people or perhaps more experienced learners may adopt a 'softer' approach in the way they communicate. However, they must be heard above the normal sounds of practice which are often magnified by poor acoustics in sports halls and swimming pools. If the group has stopped to observe a demonstration then it too must be seen by everyone. And if the angle of observation is critical (e.g., demonstration of height gained in a gymnastic vault from a lateral view) then people must be positioned accordingly. Demonstrations should be preceded by a description and everyone directed to the essential element/s before the demonstration begins.

Ongoing monitoring

Throughout practice, the coach/teacher should be evaluating the work of learners and asking certain questions. Are things safe? Is the equipment appropriate? Are tasks being carried out in accordance with instructions? Do the learners understand what is required? Are they being challenged? Are they working purposefully?, etc. If practice is to be meaningful the coach's role as an observer and analyst is critical. Providing praise, giving feedback, examining the work of individuals, looking for common problems, etc., are part of an ongoing process which helps to make practice effective and interesting.

Attentional matters

Practice serves no useful purpose if learners cannot focus their attention or are confused because of conflicting things to think about or do. If there is one thing that research on human performance is clear on, it is that people are very limited in the amount of information they can process at any one time. People can also be confused by the complexity of the task even when it appears easy to the coach/teacher. The fact is that people, especially beginners, have a limited attention span and memory capacity. This has important implications for the manner in which practice is structured. For example, techniques that are thought by the coach to be too complex or difficult should be broken down into smaller parts or 'shaped' from simpler versions. Given that a technique contains a number of different elements, the coach should identify the sequence in which they should be introduced and then set about presenting them one at a time. For example, a sprint start practice might focus simply on foot placement. The next time it might look at hand positioning. As practice continues and the learner begins to 'handle' a number of items (without prompting from the coach) the learner's attention can be brought back to aspects which may have been forgotten or need refining. An essential skill is the coach's ability to identify, from what may appear to be a multitude of errors, which is the most pertinent and focus the learner's attention on this one alone. The observant coach or teacher who has a sound technical knowledge will be able to isolate errors that may be fundamental to a number of other problems and difficulties. A key skill is to isolate the most important information and present it simply at the right time.

Lastly, thought should be given to whether the learner's attention is being distracted by irrelevant things such as the sun or background noise. The sun may be obscure a demonstration, background noises may mask instructions, equipment may be unsafely positioned, fellow learners may be chatting and so on. The whole practice environment should be geared to ensuring that learners devote complete attention to the task at hand. Practices that are interesting, enjoyable, relevant and safe are fundamental to the skill learning process.

Aids to memory

It seems obvious that the things we commit to storing in memory and our ability to recover vital information from memory has a significant bearing on both learning and performance. Imagine trying to play a game of rugby only to find that you have forgotten the rules or how to pass the ball! Skilled performance is inextricably bound up with memory. The fact that performance improves across time implies that internal representations of those performances have been retained in memory and can be retrieved from memory at the appropriate moment. Learning is obviously bound up with memory. In order to progress from one practice session to the next, it is vital to recall information from previous sessions to use as a platform for skill development. And the transfer of learning also relies on access to previously stored information, principles and movements. If memory is so important, are there methods to help people remember more or recall information better?

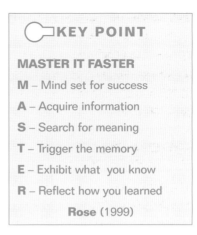

There are a number of established methods for helping people remember things well. It is known that new information can be memorised better if it is associated with things already in memory. Grouping information into logical clusters and the use of mnemonics also helps. Davis, Bull, Roscoe and Roscoe (2000) have identified a variety of principles to aid memory – and consequently the learning process. They suggest:

• It is important for coaches to give meaning to new skills so that learners have a better understanding of skills and why they are important.

• It helps to 'verbalise' movements by associating words with actions (e.g., "reach, pull, twist" describes a canoe 'J' stroke).

• Coaches should take account of the limited capacity of a learner's short-term memory by emphasising only one or two items at a time. Similarly, information feedback should be confined to only one or two salient points.

• Because short-term memory is limited through items 'interfering' with each other, coaches should avoid developing movements or principles that are similar to others. Thus, for example, it would be unwise to introduce a novice rock climber to a variety of different knots each designed to do the same job.

• When it is necessary to present a lot of information, memory retention is assisted if the separate items of information can be linked (or 'chunked') in some way. A useful principle here is the use of mnemonics. An example from climbing serves to illustrate this. To assist learners use a safe system when putting on equipment, they can be told to remember the phrase 'How aBout Climbing Now'. 'H' reminds the climber to fit their Helmet; 'B' to attach their climbing Belt; 'C' to screw up their Carabiner, and 'N' to tie their kNot.

• The use of imagery or visual rehearsal helps organise information in memory which makes it less prone to fading and easier to recall.

• When new skills are linked with previously known skills or knowledge through conscious association, they acquire greater pertinence and meaning. This again facilitates the way in which the information in memory is organised and consequently stored.

• Practice is a vital aid to consolidating information in memory. Practice (physical or imagery) enhances the permanency of the 'memory trace' left by the information.

Most important is the need to question learners about what they have learned. Not only does this confirm whether or not important information has been committed to memory but it also checks on accuracy. Further, the principle of questioning reinforces the importance of learner involvement and empowerment in the learning process; a point which has been emphasised many times throughout this book.

SUMMARY OF THE KEY POINTS

• Breaking skills down into smaller parts has a number of advantages, viz.,

  • information load is reduced
  • attention to vital aspects is enhanced
  • physical fatigue is minimised
  • time is not wasted on the practice of unimportant aspects.

• The successful breakdown of skills depends on the extent to which the parts relate to the whole.

• Research on whole and part learning indicates the following:

  • positive transfer between part and whole skill practice can be expected with skills which are serial in nature.
  • discrete activities should not be broken into smaller parts
  • whole practice is favoured with skills in which the parts are synchronised in time.

• Learners benefit more from practices which resemble the whole game or skill. Improvers and experts are better able to 'bridge the gap' between part and whole practices.

• The design of practices should acknowledge that both learners and coaches have accustomed ways of learning/coaching. Some prefer a part-type of method whilst others the whole approach.

• Methods of guidance, e.g., visual demonstration, direct the learner towards the correct things to do.

• It is argued that learning is incomplete if the learner is only aware of the correct techniques; the learner must have knowledge of alternatives (errors, mistakes) in order to fully define correct technique.

• The schema theory of motor learning focuses on the learning of 'rules' as the basis for skilled performance. The acquisition of sets of rules or schema depends in part upon the variety of experiences gained by the learner. The practice of errors enhances variety and is therefore a positive stage in learning.

• Positive transfer takes place when present learning is enhanced through previous skills. Negative transfer takes place when previous learning has a detrimental effect on current learning.

• Positive transfer is frequently taken for granted. Transfer must be worked for rather than expected. Any expectation of transfer should always recognise the principle of skill specificity; learning of one skill does not necessarily mean that a similar skill will also be learned.

• Research on the transfer of learning reveals that transfer between two skills is often low and positive. The degree of 'similarity' between the two skills is thought to be the most important factor determining the amount of transfer.

• Coaches should be cautious in their expectations of transfer between part practices and whole skills (e.g., breaststroke leg action on land and the complete stroke in water).

• Skill analysis is the process of assessing the important elements that go to make up a skill. The elements may be diffuse in nature and include perceptual, strategic, motor and feedback components.

• Both coaching practice and learning theory support the notion of variability in practice, in contrast to the practice of specific movements in unchanging situations.

• The principle of variability is especially applicable to novices and young children. In addition, it holds true for both open skills in which the display is constantly changing and closed skills where the display is more static.

• Overlearning is the process of repeated practice beyond the stage when the learner has – apparently – reached his/her best performance.

• Overlearning is dictated by practical considerations such as time, expense and motivation, but pays off in terms of increased performance level, consistency of performance and enhanced memory.

• Shaping is a method for developing complex movements from simpler skills in a gradual manner.

• Experiential learning places the learner at the focus of the teaching/learning process. It involves the learner fully in making decisions about what to do and how to do it. Self analysis and self appraisal are key features of the process.

• Passive forms of practice such as imagery and observation have an important part to play in skill acquisition.

• Learning is inextricably bound up with memory. The limitations of memory (especially short term memory) should always be considered when information is expected to be remembered and recalled by learners. There are numerous ways to assist the memory process including the use of metaphors and imagery.

PRACTICAL TASKS

• In many sports there is a need to move quickly and also to move with a high degree of accuracy. Triple jumping is a good example. Both of these variables are often inextricably linked together; if the individual attempts to improve on one, the other falters. Thus, if a triple jumper tries to move much more quickly in the approach run it is likely they will fail to hit the take off board correctly. Problems like this can be overcome with practice, but they take time. This task shows how speed and accuracy work together. Take a sheet of A4 paper and mark on it, two circles 5cm in diameter whose centres are 20cm apart. Now take a pencil and move the point as quickly and accurately as possible from one circle to the next 40 times so that as many dots lie within each circle. You should be able to do this so that very few (if any) dots lie outside either circle. Before you begin this task, get a partner to time your performance to the nearest second. Now take a second piece of paper and describe two circles with centres 20cm apart, but with reduced diameters of only 2cm. Now repeat the task. You will find that your performance in the second task is slower than the first, which demonstrates the fact that increased accuracy results in slowed down performance.

• This task looks at the relative benefits of massed versus distributed practice. Take a lawn tennis ball and stand about 2 metres away from a gymnasium wall. The task is to throw a tennis ball underarm against the wall and catch it in the opposite hand. Then thrown it with this hand and catch it on the rebound with the first hand. Repeat this as accurately as possible. There are two practice conditions. In the first condition (massed practice), ask one person to carry out the task for 2 minutes non-stop. In the second condition (distributed practice) ask a different person to practice for half minute periods with half minute rest intervals to give a total practice time of 2 minutes. It is better if this can be repeated with a small group of people (say 5) taking part in each condition. Once complete, everyone is required to carry out the task for a period of one minute, but this time they are timed for speed. You will find a difference in scores between the two groups showing that one training condition to be better than the other. Discuss the difference in terms of what you have read in this chapter.

• This task compares the relative effectiveness of whole and part learning. The skill is a lay-up shot in basketball. Subjects should have no experience of this skill. Take a group of learners and divide them into two groups. The 'whole' group will practice the whole skill in its entirety whilst the 'part' group will practice first the approach run, then the jump/release and then the whole skill. One person should be involved in teaching both groups. Another person should be tasked to observe the teaching of both groups and to take notes about what they saw. Whilst this is a highly subjective task, it should reveal superiority of the whole method as would be expected from the theory described in the chapter.

• This task looks at the topic of transfer. The skill is to bounce a basketball with the preferred hand as many times as possible in one minute. Identify two recorders who will count the performance of each subject. One can time the minute whilst the other counts the number of bounces. Take 6 people and divide them into three pairs. One pair will practice for five minutes (in their own time and their own pace) using their preferred hand. One pair will do the same but use their non-preferred hand. The final pair will simply watch the others practice but do nothing physical. Once the practice phase is complete, each person is required to perform for one minute with their preferred hand. You should find that the pair which performs best is the one that has practiced with their preferred hand throughout. The 'non-preferred' group will perform next and the 'no practice' pair worst. The fact that the 'non preferred' pair perform better than the 'no practice groups illustrates what is known as bilateral transfer – transfer from one limb to the other.

REVIEW QUESTIONS

In each of the following questions, think of a sport with which you are most familiar, either as a performer or coach/teacher.

• In relation to the whole/part issue:

- Are there accepted methods in your sport where one approach is always adopted?
- Do the textbook methods always work?
- Do you give much thought to the problem of breaking skills down into smaller parts?
- Do you think that some of the accepted procedures used by coaches in your sport are limited, e.g., too much time is devoted to skills practices at the expense of their contribution in the game?
- How difficult is it to introduce beginners to your sport without modifying it considerably?
- Do you ever see people experience difficulties when attempting to put skills which are practiced in isolation, into the game?

• Do you think the normal level of variability which learners experience in your sport (e.g., playing partners, different equipment, varying weather) is sufficient and desirable?.

• Do you think learners would benefit from more effort on the part of coaches or teachers to increase the 'variability' factor?

• Do you think there are any advantages of practicing beyond the point when the athlete has achieved his/your goals?

• What are the disadvantages of too much practice?

• Do you think learners could do a little better given that conditions were slightly different? What conditions would need to change?

• In relation to the matter of errors in learning:

- Are they a natural part of the learning process?
- Are they desirable? Should they be eliminated as much as possible?
- How beneficial is it for learners to examine the reasons for failure?
- Schema theory emphasises the value in coaching 'slightly wrong' movements, e.g., throwing wide of the target. What do you think of this 'active' method of dealing with errors?

• Can you think of an example where a sport learned previously by someone is detrimental to the acquisition of skill in your sport?

• How sure are you that the manner in which you break down skills for practice is the best way of building up skill level?

• In regard to analogy learning can you think of any analogies that are used to describe the movement of body parts or actions involving actions involving other objects – balls, bats, other people?

References

Bandura, A. (1969). *Social learning theory.* London: Prentice Hall.

Bruner, C. (1960). *The process of education.* New York: Vintage Books.

Carson, L.M. and Wiegand, R.L. (1979). Motor schema formation and retention in young children: a test of Schmidt's schema theory. *Journal of Motor Behavior,* 11, 247 - 251.

Coleman, J.A. (1977). *Differences between experiential and classroom learning.* In M.T. Keeton (Ed.), *Experiential learning: rationale characteristics and assessment* (pp. 49 - 61). San Francisco, California: Jossey-Bass Publishers.

Davids, K., Savelsbergh, G., Bennett, S.J. and Van der Kemp, J. (2002). *Interceptive actions in sport: information and movement.* London: Routledge.

Davis, B., Bull, S., Roscoe and Roscoe, D. (2000). *Physical education and the study of sport.* London: Harcourt Publishers Limited.

Dewey, J. (1938). *Experience and education.* London: Collier.

Earle, C. (2003). *How to coach children in sport.* Leeds: Coachwise Solutions.

Gass, M. (1990). *Transfer of learning in adventure education.* In J.C. Miles and S. Priest (Eds.), *Adventure education.* State College, Pennsylvania: Venture Publishing.

Gibson, J.J. (1979). *The ecological approach to visual perception.* Boston: Houghton Mifflin.

Hayes, N.A., and Broadbent, D.E. (1988). *Two modes of learning for interactive tasks.* Cognition, 28, 249 - 276.

Hird, J.S., Landers, D.M., Thomas, J. R., and Horan, J.J. (1991). Physical practice is superior to mental practice in enhancing cognitive and motor task performance. *Journal of Sport and Exercise Psychology.* 8, 281 - 293.

Kraft, R.J. (1990). *Experiential learning.* In J.C. Miles and S. Priest (Eds.), *Adventure education.* State College, Pennsylvania: Venture Publishing.

LeUnes, A. and Nation, J.R. (2002). *Sport psychology: an introduction.* Pacific Grove, California: Wadsworth.

Lai, Q., Shea, C.H., Wulf, G. and Wright, D.L. (2000). Optimizing generalised motor program and parameter learning. *Research Quarterly for Exercise and Sport,* 71, 1, 10 - 24.

Lee, D.N. and Magill, R.A. (1985). *Can forgetting facilitate skill acquisition?* In D. Goodman, R.B. Wilberg and I.M. Franks. (Eds.), *Differing perspectives in motor learning, memory and control.* Amsterdam: North Holland Publishing Company.

Liao, C. and Masters, R.S.W. (2001). Analogy learning: a means to implicit motor learning. *Journal of Sports Sciences,* 19, 307 - 319.

Lyle, J. (2002). *Sports coaching concepts: a framework for coaches' behaviour.* London: Routledge.

Martens, R. (1997). *Successful coaching* (2nd Edition). Champaign, Illinois: Human Kinetics.

Magill, R.A. (1998). Knowledge is more than we can talk about: Implicit learning in motor skill acquisition. *Research Quarterly for Exercise and Sport,* 69, 2, 104 - 110.

Magill, R.A. (2001). *Motor learning: concepts and applications* (6th Edition). London: McGraw Hill.

Masters, R.S.W. (1992). Knowledge, nerves and know-how: the role of explicit versus implicit knowledge in the breakdown of a complex motor skill under pressure. *British Journal of Psychology,* 83, 343 - 358.

Planning and practice (Video, 1986). Leeds: National Coaching Foundation

Pease, D.161 A. (1977). *A teaching model for motor skill acquisition.* Motor skills: Theory into practice, 1, 2, 104 - 112.

Piaget, J. and Inhelder, B. (1967). *The child's conception of space.* New York: W.W. Norton, 1967.

Rink, J. (1999). *Instruction from a learning perspective.* In C. Hardy and M. Mawer. (Eds.). *Learning and teaching in physical education.* London: Falmer Press.

Rose, C. (1999). *Master it faster.* Aylesbury: Accelerated Learning Systems Ltd.

Schmidt, R.A. and Wrisberg, C.A. (2000). *Motor learning and performance.* Champaign, Illinois: Human Kinetics.

Scottish Football Association. (2002). *Early touches.* Glasgow: The Scottish F. A.

Scully, D.M. (1988). Visual perception of human movement: the use of demonstrations in teaching motor skills. *British Journal of Physical Education (Research Supplement),* 19, 6.

Scully, D.M. (1996). Skill acquisition. In P. Beashel and J. Taylor (Eds.), *Advanced studies in physical education and sport.* Walton-on-Thames: Thomas Nelson and Sons Ltd.

Sharp, R.H. (1988). Error is the price of skill. *British Journal of Physical Education,* 3, 19, 127 - 129.

Sharp, R.H. (2004). *Teaching and learning strategies.* In P. Barnes and B. Sharp (Eds.), *The RHP Companion to Outdoor Education.* Lyme Regis: Russell House Publishing.

Shea, C.H., Wright, D.L., Wulf, G., and Whitacre, C. (2000). *Journal of Motor Behaviour,* 32, 1, 27 - 36.

Shea, J.B. and Zimny, S.T. (1983). Contexts effects in memory and learning movement information. In R.A. Magill (Ed.), *Memory and control of action.* Amsterdam: North Holland Publishing Co..

Sports Industry. 88, October, 1991.

Whiting, H.T.A. (1982). *Skill in sport – a descriptive and prescriptive appraisal.* In Salmela, J.H., Partington, J.T., and Orlick, T (Eds.), *New paths of sport learning and excellence.* Ontario: The Coaching Association of Canada.

Williams, A.M., Davids, K. and Williams, J.G. *Visual perception and action in sport.* London: E. and F. N. Spon, 1999.

Wright, L.D., Li, Y. and Coady, W.J. (1997). Cognitive processes related to contextual interference and observational learning: a replication of Blandin, Proteau and Alain (1994). *Research Quarterly for Exercise and Sport,* 68, 106 - 109.

Wrisberg, C.A. and Liu, Z. (1991). The effect of contextual variety on the practice, retention and transfer of an applied motor skill. *Research Quarterly for Exercise and Sport,* 54, 67-74.

"Folk come in all sizes and shapes. They represent different ages, racial groups, genders, and cultural backgrounds. Some individuals have disabilities of a physical or mental nature. People have different temperaments, social influences and types of life experiences. In addition to these kinds of differences, individuals possess capabilities that can influence the quality of their motor performance."

Schmidt and Wrisberg (2000)

INTRODUCTION

This book has covered many principles, but so far, little consideration has been given to how teaching or coaching methods might differ with regard to individual differences. Clearly, we are all different in the way we perform, the things we like to do, our physical make-up and our ultimate potentials. Hence, it seems likely that many of the principles and procedures highlighted in this book may not apply to all learners or with the same degree of emphasis. This chapter looks at different groups and focuses on the approaches considered best suited to each. A discussion like this cannot be exact because of the subjectivity of categorising people. An attempt is made to guide the reader to those approaches which both the literature and anecdotal evidence tend to indicate are favoured for different groups of learners. The same categorisation was adopted as in the first edition of the book.

People come in all shapes and sizes

WORKING WITH CHILDREN

"... children are easily motivated and enjoy a variety of activities and stimulation. These attributes should excite any teacher... It is a matter of capturing this desire to be active and of structuring the learning environment to provide challenging, enjoyable athletic experiences."

O'Neill (1991)

This quotation reflects the importance most adults place on the value of movement, physical activity and sport for young children. Over the years, the subject of children and sport – especially competitive sport – has taken on a particular focus. Several agencies have set up working parties and many publications and conferences have tackled the many and varied concerns regarding sport and

"Start 'em young."

school age children. Issues such as early specialisation, training and overuse injuries, maximising of potential, competition, abuse, giftedness, etc., are just some of the topics investigated. One asks what is the best way to teach youngsters? Are there particular techniques which are appropriate for less experienced learners? Should skills and sports be introduced at specific times? The following sections examine some of these key questions.

Critical periods for learning

A vast literature has examined the physical and performance standards of children of different ages – how fast can they run, how far can they jump, how far can they throw, etc., – (e.g., Brown, 2001; Lee, 1988). Investigators have debated concepts such as 'readiness' and 'critical periods' in learning. Other research has examined the merits of training children much earlier in their lives than would normally be expected, as well as the problems of depriving children of movement experiences.

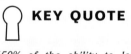 **KEY QUOTE**

"50% of the ability to learn is developed in the first four years of life and another 30% by the age of eight."
Dryden and Vos (2001)

There are many unanswered questions like these as well as many generalisations. One clear message is that children cannot be expected to learn a new activity unless their nervous system has matured sufficiently – they must be 'physiologically' capable. For example, it would be wrong to expect a three year old child who has still to acquire a mature pattern of locomotion, to learn a high hurdle technique. Similarly, a four year old should not be expected to catch a ball successfully. The progressive maturation of a child's physical and nervous make-up lays the foundation for increased learning in sports skills and this process cannot be speeded up. Only when the nervous system is 'ready' can learning occur. This point is echoed in the words of Randy Hill – a member of the US Olympic Committee (quoted in Brown, 2001). He says that:

"Parents and coaches force children to specialize too early. What they should be doing is working on things like agility, co-ordination, balance and speed that will help them develop as athletes. We shouldn't ask them to specialise until after sexual maturity when their bodies normalise."

A frequently asked question is when are children ready to learn specific skills? Research does not help much on this issue (Brown, 2001). One of the difficulties is that whilst children mature in the same progressive manner, they do so at very different rates. In addition, the way in which different sports are introduced varies from one sport to another. MacNab (1986) suggests that with gymnastics four or five might be appropriate; swimming at seven or eight; soccer at nine or ten and athletics at ten to twelve. Brown (2001) has identified a similar programme for a wide variety of sports ranging from tennis to golf and gymnastics to athletics. All of these ideas are based on intuition and informed wisdom; it is impossible to be categorical about when to introduce particular activities to children. Sensitive coaches and teachers should be able to judge fairly carefully when is the correct age and not make the mistake of starting too early. Brown (2001) suggests that both parents and coaches should address a number of practical questions when considering the involvement of their child in sport:

• Are they willing and able to attend regular practice sessions?
• Are they mature enough to understand and play by the rules?
• Are they ready to conform to team goals rather than individual wishes?
• Are they willing to accept coaching and discipline from another person?
• Are they able to keep up with their school work and other non-sport interests?

Not all of these questions will apply to all children/ sports. They do serve to highlight the individual and critical nature of starting in sport and the practical considerations involved.

Whilst it is well recognised that the capacity to learn never stops, it is also accepted that the early years are the most formative. Indeed, it has been suggested that around 50% of a person's ability to learn is developed in the first four years of life and another 30% in the next four years (Dryden and Vos, 2001). These early years lay down the pathways on which all future learning is based. It is also considered that children who, for whatever reason, have a poor start during their first three/four years of life are likely to experience learning problems through childhood and into early adulthood. What seems to be critical from the practitioner's perspective is how activities are

KEY QUOTE

"Coaches should never under-estimate their importance and significance to young athletes in particular. Consequently, they must be well prepared and create a stimulating and challenging practice environment. The quality of the experience and overall impression created will remain with the athlete. Positive experiences stimulate enthusiasm and sustain interest – poor experiences undoubtedly contribute to dropout."
Green (2003)

presented and what form they take. With gymnastics, for example, children as young as four could be introduced to a series of exploratory physical challenges which are stimulating and enjoyable. They may not bear much resemblance to the adult sport. Swimming at seven might be closer to the adult activity and include basic elements of stroke production. Soccer might be a scaled-down version of the full game using grids. Athletics at pre-secondary school age would essentially be experiential rather than technical and only develop into well-defined activities related to the sport proper as the child grows.

KEY QUOTE

"Whatever the sport, participants need to develop as athletes first. Basic motor skills such as running, jumping, throwing and catching, are best learned between the ages of five and twelve. Skills acquired at this stage provide a sound base for continued improvement in sport or other forms of recreation, which in turn provide positive health and social skill benefits."
Earle (2003)

Traditionally, each sport has its own introductory techniques which are well documented in coaching texts or manuals devised by the relevant National Governing Body. The emergence of 'mini' sports where equipment, playing areas and rules are scaled down has given the introduction of sport to children greater character, structure and relevance than was previously the case.

Another way of interpreting the concept of 'readiness' is from a motivational point of view. Does the child want to learn? Is the child interested? Is the individual inspired to take part? What kinds of goals are available for them to strive for? It would seem more important to answer questions like this, because (as was highlighted in Chapter 1) it doesn't matter how mature the learner may be, if they don't possess a desire to learn they will learn very little. The coach should therefore devote their attention to making sure that everything is conducive to establishing the right attitude – safety, enjoyment, length of practice, type of practice, peer approval, rewards, reinforcement, etc.

Many people are of the view that during early childhood (up to five or six years of age) activities should be of a general physical nature and serve as a platform for later experience in specific sports. One school of child psychology underlines the importance of early movement experience as the basis for all development – including social, cognitive and motor dimensions. Paul Fitts (Fitts and Posner, 1967) considered that after the first few years of life, learning an entirely new skill is rare. He suggested that all new skills are built out of already existing skills and that the acquisition of skill is largely the transfer of prior habits to new situations. A widespread philosophy is that specific sports should not be introduced in early childhood but attention should be directed to modified or simplified versions. Thus, gymnastics might revolve around a general 'movement' training whilst many of the traditional team games and sports might lean towards the mini-sport approach. This general strategy was adopted in a longitudinal project carried out in Glasgow in the late 1980's (Pollatschek, 1989). In this study the intention was to examine the merits of daily physical education in the primary school. In the early primary years, pupil practice centred on basic ball handling and manipulative activities. Later, children were introduced to modified activities (e.g., 'king' ball) and then at the age of 10 years they started mini-sports. The project not only produced over-whelming support for daily physical education but

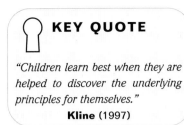

it also supported the general to specific strategy for skill development. The secondary schools receiving the primary pupils involved in the project were forced to rethink the curriculum because the children were 'too skilled' for the existing programme of work!

Such an approach is in tune with the emphasis placed on young children and play. It is well known that early childhood is a period when children like to play, experiment and explore. Psychologists suggest that it is through play that children come to develop many expressive, intellectual, social and emotional abilities. It makes sense to introduce new sporting activities within the context of play by reducing the number of rules, allowing freedom of individual pace and minimising situations which might create anxiety or fear. In addition, children might be allowed some freedom to make up rules and encouraged to understand the objectives of movement/skills rather than acquire mastery of the techniques themselves. The transition from guided play to structured training is a matter for the individual coach or teacher; they should use their experience to decide when the time is right to introduce new skills and when to formalise procedures.

Some researchers have examined the notion of 'critical periods' for learning particular skills. Here, the suggestion is that if a child is not exposed to certain skills before a certain age, they will never be able to achieve full potential. Failure or difficulty to learn a given skill may arise because the child has passed the critical period for learning that skill. Balyi (2002) has suggested that:

"If fundamental motor skill training is not developed between the ages of nine and twelve, skills cannot be recaptured later"

In relation to sports skills, the important experiments to answer this hypothesis have not been undertaken (for ethical reasons). What can be said is that if early childhood is a time for acquiring basic movement skills which form a base for subsequent skill acquisition, then to maximise transfer childhood experiences should be as rich and varied as possible. The last word on this topic is left to Earle (2003). He focuses on a number of age-related principles. He reinforces the finding that very young children learn through play and experimentation; learning should be dictated by fun and enjoyment. Formal teaching should be simple and step-like in nature and praise should be abundant. During the period six to nine years, children begin to distinguish cause and effect in what they do but find it hard to separate effort and success. In this regard, teachers and coaches should be patient, encouraging and praise both effort and achievement. They should also take full advantage of children's enthusiasm to learn new things. From the age 10 to 13 years, children begin to actively judge themselves and are more willing to accept the judgement of others. They may find it difficult to accept their own failures and, as a result, loose interest and motivation to continue. This is a period when teachers, coaches and parents should be supportive, sensitive and help children set realistic goals. Again, it is impossible to be prescriptive in regard to age and the views of Earle should be treated simply as guidelines.

Models for children

A common mistake is to treat children as small adults and impose techniques on them which are really only appropriate for adults. Is would be wrong, for example, to expect a 10 year old to attempt a long jump using the hitch kick. This problem applies to many sports and can be extended to include the misuse of adult size equipment, playing areas and rules. How many readers can remember trying to swing an enormous tennis racquet or kick a soccer ball on a pitch that appeared miles long? Problems like this can be resolved through the use of 'mini-sports'. Mini-sports are scaled down versions of the parent sport where equipment and playing areas are reduced in size and play simplified, to enable children to grasp games more quickly and enjoy greater involvement. Because mini-sports are based upon adult games, they emphasise all the basic skills and methods of play and are a very logical way of preparing young children for senior versions (Sleap, 1981).

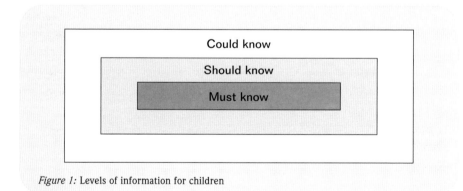

Figure 1: Levels of information for children

Techniques which are right for the expert or adult may be totally inappropriate for the beginner. The sensitive coach should simplify or modify techniques so they 'fit' the age and skill level of the learner. They may even have to do away with 'good' technique altogether. McNab (1986) discusses this matter in relation to the kind and amount of information the child should be given. His ideas are described in *Figure 1*.

In his model, 'Must know' information is absolutely critical. It may include information about safety, rules or key techniques, 'Should know' is of secondary importance and not critical to current learning, but could be imparted given time and learner interest.

Finally, 'Could know' is of minor importance and would only be passed on as a 'bonus'. He gives the example of the long jump and a 15 year old beginner. McNab suggests the youngster must know how to tackle an approach run in the 13-15 strides range, hitting the board accurately and landing with heels in line. He should know the means of holding speed into the take-off board, a vertical trunk and some attempt at lift. And he could know something about flight technique and longer, more structured, approach runs. The problem for the coach/teacher is the task of categorising information like this. In the main, it involves putting most of what they know to one side and extracting just the essence. With youngsters the absolute basics are critical as they are the pillars of future performance.

Learning by imitation

The value of imitation has been underlined several times already. With children especially, imitation is an extremely potent force (Earle, 2003). It really is coaching on the cheap because there is so little for the coach to do except provide a good model. Anyone who watches children at play will note how readily they pick up 'rules' and mimic other people (particularly their sporting heroes) in their movements. An excerpt from Saunders (1986) on teaching children golf is relevant here:

"In a very similar way, the child of eight or nine years can learn to play golf, or ski, or play most other sports, with far less difficulty than an adult pupil. The young child will immediately imitate with reasonable ease the movements he sees his teacher perform. He merely copies what he sees and is quite uninhibited by his initial failure. The child's approach to anything he sets out to learn shows a simplicity and delightful naïveté that is sadly lost in the adult. The child just copies what he sees. He may need gentle words of encouragement occasionally, but as a rule the professional or parents appreciate that all they have to do is to show the child and the child will copy. The young child will watch the professional or parent and develop a kind of picture in his mind of the movements involved, slotting himself into this picture so that in his own mind he becomes the model he is copying."

The coaching and teaching of young children should take full advantage of this medium for learning. This may involve the coach demonstrating or another person – perhaps someone more experienced/older.

The importance of movement

In general, children are restless and enjoy physical activity. Movement is an essential medium for normal, healthy development. Friendships, skills, values and many other qualities are developed as a by-product of movement. Coaching and teaching approaches which keep children stationary soon lead to boredom and unrest on the part of the child. Sessions should be planned which are active and purposeful and which lead to challenge, co-operation with others and success (O'Neill, 1991). Variety is also important. Children tend to have limited spans of attention which makes it difficult to sustain repetitive practice for long periods. Furthermore, it helps if children are not hampered by failure or negative transfer from unwanted skills. It is said that 'nothing succeeds like success', and children especially enjoy satisfaction from praise and reinforcement. The strength behind many proficiency award schemes lies in their capacity to challenge and reward with tangible outcomes.

> **KEY QUOTE**
>
> *"Coaching children well is a most rewarding experience. Children are the sports people of the future and so it is vital that they are coached by those who fully understand their needs. It is important, too, that their experience of sport is enjoyable and rewarding."*
>
> **Pankhurst and Russell** (1991)

It should be remembered, however, that 'success is not the same as winning'. Practices which are geared to winning imply that some children will lose. The child who loses regularly will soon develop a low self-esteem. Lee (1988) discusses in some detail the whole area of competitive sport and young children and says (Lee, 1991):

> *"Perhaps the aim should be to concentrate a little less on competing strongly in childhood and a little more on nurturing the skills, enthusiasm and attributes which develop more effective adult competitors in the future."*

Sensory vocabulary

Youngsters embarking on a new activity soon find out a lot more about their own body. Not only do they realise that muscles can ache, but they also begin to appreciate different ways in which their limbs can move or have to move. Consider for example, the feeling of heaviness experienced by a novice swimmer, the stretching of limbs felt by the gymnast or the imbalance felt by a beginner canoeist. This feel, or sensory awareness is obvious in some activities such as trampolining and diving but less obvious in others such as running or team games – though it may be equally critical. Why are these internal feelings important? For one thing they provide an effective medium for the coach and learner to communicate – a medium which can often compensate for the child's lack of technical knowledge and verbal skill. McNab (1986) expresses this very succinctly:

> *"This 'feel', this sensory awareness, relates not only to body or limb-positioning, but to limb-velocity and the balance of relaxation during movement. Once the athlete starts to 'read' his or her own body, he/she finds the acquisition of skill much less onerous. Equally important, he/she often comes back to the coach with his/her own vocabulary, own expression of movement, which can enrich*

both athlete and coach."

Such a 'movement' vocabulary (words such as strong, hard, effort, fast, etc.) can be very meaningful to the learner and serve to describe how they feel without recourse to technical jargon. The coach can translate expressions like these into their technical equivalents to discover the kinds of problems the learner is experiencing.

Safety and confidence

A strong feature of children's learning is the almost limitless confidence they display. For most children it's as if fear of injury or failure is completely absent. By and large, children have not developed the inhibitions, fears and bad habits that often characterise adult learning. This allows the child of course, to maximise their innate desire to learn and explore the surrounding world in the fullest way possible. Coupled with boundless energy, this makes for very rapid learning. For the coach, however there is a dilemma. On the one hand they have a clear obligation to ensure the safety and well-being of those in their charge, whilst on the other hand the child's confidence provides them with the freedom to challenge the child beyond a point which many parents and onlookers would think safe or desirable. Again, the sensitive coach will decide for themselves, taking into account many other factors such as the goals set for the learner, and pressure from peers and how to balance these two competing tendencies.

Coaching style

Some research has shown that the 'approach' which coaches adopt can significantly determine the satisfaction children gain from sport as well as the likelihood they will drop out. We have looked at various approaches to coaching/teaching in a previous chapter, but let's look once more

KEY QUOTE

"Learning is most effective when it's fun." **Kline** (1997)

at the simple distinction between positive and negative approaches. The positive approach encourages desirable performance by motivating children through positive feedback, praise and reward. A major factor here is development of the learner's self esteem. The negative approach relies on eliminating undesirable behaviours through negative feedback ("Don't do this"), criticism and punishment. The principal factor here is rejection and fear. Research has shown that the most important distinction between coaches who children like most and least is the amount of praise and reward they receive. Children enjoy playing more where coaches are positive. They are more likely to continue in sport if guided by 'positive' coaches. Children respond well to coaches and teachers who are open and friendly and they tend to repeat things which bring approval. It seems the best approach with children is one that is positive and encouraging. Lee (1988) suggests that in order for children to maximise their poten-tial coaches should be guided by three rules:

• They should create a positive setting that encourages confidence and positive self-esteem.

• Children should be made aware that they can all succeed in their own terms – what really matters is the feeling associated with personal attainment rather than particular results.

• Coaches should create an enjoyable inter-personal atmosphere in which children are accepted by the coach and each other.

Earle (2003) provides a highly relevant treatise on working with children. He reinforces these three points but adds a number of others that are worth highlighting. He says there are three stages in skill acquisition – understanding, practicing and performing (this is not very different from the model proposed by Paul Fitts) and suggests a number of key coaching principles at each stage, viz.,:

> ### KEY QUOTE
>
> *"I've tended to coach both children and teenagers and I'll find that I'll adapt my style according to what works best for that age group. The influence, though, is probably the goals of the athletes that I'm coaching. If they are recreational gymnasts they tend to want to enjoy their sport and have fun, and also achieve, but perhaps not to the extent that an elite athlete might do."*
>
> **South** (1999)

• Understanding
  • Assumptions should not be made that children always know what coaches want
  • Demonstrations and explanations should be simple
  • Patience is critical
  • There should be an awareness that children have limited spans of attention.

• Practicing
  • Practice should be fun, appropriate, meaningful and enjoyable
  • Feedback should be given regularly
  • Good performance is based on establishing relevant skills
  • Practice should mirror actual performance, but minus competitive pressure
  • Sports should be adapted (changes to rules, area, equipment) to suit children.

• Performing
  • Plenty of time should be given for children to think about things
  • Develop decision making skills gradually
  • Plan practice sessions that limit choices and focus on skill practice
  • As skill develops increase parameters (speed, space, difficulty)
  • Interest is maintained through involving children in the learning process.

WORKING WITH ADULTS

Learning continues throughout life and doesn't stop when children enter adulthood. It is usual for older people (particularly when they retire) to take on new interests, indulge in different sports and tackle new skills. However, children and adults do learn in different ways. Adults usually learn more slowly than children do. Often they are more fearful and sometimes less overtly enthusiastic. Physically, they may have severe limitations and may be less capable of adapting to change. However, adults have more experience than children and tend to tire or become bored less easily. Their powers of attention are also more capable. What are the implications for coaching and teaching?

Older people are invariably more willing to learn

Previous experience

If new skills are built up from previously learned ones then adults should possess a much richer and wider base on which to build new experiences. It has been suggested that adults are able to learn entirely new skills more easily than children when neither have any background in the specific area. It is believed this is because adults can draw on transferable elements from past experience and apply them to the new situation, whereas youngsters lack this capacity. It's as if adults possess a greater repertoire of individual movement patterns (or schema) which can be adapted for new purposes. Adults are more 'streetwise'. The faster learning by adults assumes of course that all other things, motivation, fitness, etc., are equal, but this is not always the case. The reader will recall that transfer can be negative as well as positive. Sometimes adults display difficulty in picking up new skills because prior habits intrude, as happens, for example, when a different racket sport is learned or when an experienced swimmer tries to correct a faulty stroke pattern. A severe injury or accident can also have long-term negative effects and in such cases a period of uncertainty and interference often precedes solid gains in the new skill.

> ### KEY QUOTE
>
> *"Before you begin to work with any group you must begin to assess why they take part in sport. Not everyone is there for the same reasons. Whatever you are coaching, stand back and consider the needs of the individual or team with whom you are working."*
> **National Coaching Foundation**
> (1986)

With this in mind, the interested coach or teacher should attempt to make some assessment of the adult's background (can they swim? which strokes can they do? how far can they swim? which is their best stroke? what other water sports do they do? etc.) in an attempt to find aspects which may transfer. Adult learners are good at recognising similarities between new skills and previous learning and actively search for experiences on which they 'can hang their coat'. Advantage can be taken of past experience to speed up learning and help solve particular problems. In the case of negative transfer, the coach should highlight differences between previously learned skills and new ones (e.g., how does the flight of a badminton shuttle differ from that of a table tennis ball?) so that new skills can be put into the right perspective.

Confidence

Adults generally display less confidence than children do. Self-esteem can be a stumbling block and, because they are generally less mobile/fit, adults are exposed to a greater risk of injury. The good coach acknowledges these things in a number of ways. They might not be so demanding in their expectations; may work at a slower pace; may give more attention to physical warm up and certainly be more sympathetic to learning difficulties. In addition, they may be more inclined to use manual guidance.

Learning never stops: adults delight in new challenges

Cognitive ability

Research has shown that up to the age of about 25 years, skilled performance (in general terms) increases. There is then a longish period during which there may be a gradual decline or, where experience and accuracy are important to success, progress may continue. However, after the age of about 25 years there is typically a progressive decline in just about every measurable aspect of skilled performance. Movement speed decreases, reaction time increases, anticipation worsens and so on. There are of course exceptions to this, particularly in sports which rely on aerobic endurance such as cycling or walking. Also, with increasing age people generally find it increasingly difficult to comprehend or understand problems, especially when they are new or unfamiliar or when a time stress is imposed. It seems that people become a little slower with age. It is suggested this reflects a slowing in neurological activity and possibly a more 'cautious' approach on the part of older learners. For the coach or teacher the implications are little different to those listed in the last section. They must be more tolerant and prepared to try several ways of approaching a problem, as well as more cautious in their expectations.

Finally, it should be said that many coaches find a number of advantages in working with adults over and above the pleasures of helping children. Coaching can be more sociable. Pressures on goal attainment and winning are lessened and adults are generally more reasonable and appreciative of the coach's efforts. Adults are more analytical and able to draw on their richer experience in order to solve new problems. Whilst this may not compensate for natural declines in fitness, speed, decision making etc. it aids communication with the coach and sometimes provides them with new ideas which can be explored with others. Adults are also more attentive, less distractible and usually prepared to apply themselves for longer periods to repetitive or seemingly trivial tasks.

WORKING WITH BEGINNERS

"Experts do simple things well whilst beginners do difficult things badly"
Forsyth (2003)

As people become more proficient, skilled performance is reflected in a wide variety of changes. For example:

- Errors reduce
- Bad habits are eliminated
- Movement becomes more efficient
- Accuracy, speed, timing, etc., improve
- Performance is more consistent
- Individuals become more adaptable
- Performance is more automatic
- Individual 'style' becomes consolidated
- Self analysis becomes possible
- Attention is more selective
- Irrelevant information becomes redundant
- Anticipatory awareness improves
- Confidence improves
- Technical knowledge becomes greater
- Goal direction becomes clearer and more realistic.

Not all of these apply to every particular sport or activity and some 'kick in' at different stages of the learning process. Some of these are observable and can be seen directly by the onlooker (increased speed, better timing) whilst most are intrinsic to the performer (self-analysis, cue redundancy). If people do change in so many ways on their way to proficiency, then it follows that instructional methods should take account of these changes. What are the key issues when working with beginners?

Reducing the size of the problem

The initial problem with many beginners is simply understanding the task. To help, the coach must simplify matters by trying to extract the most important ingredients of the skill or game in question. It helps to reduce team games to small-side practices where the rules are few and involvement is maximal (e.g., mini-sports). In closed skills such as trampolining, shaping or part techniques can be used to develop complex movements. For example, a somersault might begin with a forward roll on the trampoline bed.

Space: change the	• size of the playing area (length, breadth) • distance that needs to be covered (such as closeness of partners) • height of the working area (such as size of nets) • size of the target area
Task: alter the	• rules to make task easier/harder • methods of scoring • role/position of players • type of challenge (let learner decide activity)
Equipment: consider the	• weight and length of items • colour, size, texture and shape
Position: vary the	• orientation of players • speed of movement of people • space in which players can move
Speed: vary the	• speed with which objects are thrown/propelled • permit slow movements • speed of play (walk rather than run)

Table 1: Some ways in which activities can be adjusted to suit individuals

Skills must be reduced to manageable proportions but still retain their essential ingredients. Beginners, especially youngsters may not possess a complete idea of the sport and know what it is all about. Videos shown briefly of experts in action or a question and answer session on rules, objectives, equipment, etc., can go a long way to helping the novice acquire an initial model. Earle (2003) indicates that sports and practices can be reduced in size in a number of ways – changing the equipment, changing the playing area and modifying the rules. Kerr and Stafford (2003) suggest a very useful model to help adapt or modify activities to make them appropriate to different groups of learners. Their model is based on the acronym STEPS – Space, Task, Equipment, Position, Speed (see *Table 1*).

Information selection

The learner is bombarded with information, most of which is irrelevant and distracting. The coach or teacher must search out the 'key' cues and attempt not to give too much feedback – often a frustrating exercise. The coach's ability to analyse performance and spot underlying causes of problems is critical, although at beginner level this will not present too much of a technical problem for the coach. To take a trampolining example once more, a beginner will display a variety of technical faults only one or two of which need to be identified. The learner might be told to concentrate on where to focus their eyes and this would be reinforced over and over again. Frequently, the teacher or coach will find that directing attention to another fault will cause the learner to 'forget' the first one, which must be returned to fairly soon. Small, but important technical details soon become semi-automatic for the learner, although the coach must be vigilant. Practicing bad habits reinforces them; they must be curtailed early on.

A further way of reducing information load is to ensure that all competing sources of information are excluded. Is the sun shining in the learner's eyes? Can they hear the coach? Are other people distracting the learner? Does the learner feel safe? Do they know exactly what is required? Can they ask questions if unsure? etc. Highlighting cues visually (e.g., drawing hand/foot positions on the gymnastic mat, using brightly coloured balls and other pieces of equipment) helps focus the learner's attention.

The technique of 'hinting' (see Chapter 3) also helps the learner select the correct cues from amongst other distracting features. A few examples illustrate this. With breaststroke leg action a flat foot position can be achieved by asking the learner to 'trap' a ball between their foot and shin. Telling the aspirant soccer player to dribble the ball as if it is attached to their shoelaces encourages better control. Telling the skier to touch their ski tips with their knees helps develop better body posture. And suggesting to the trampolinist that they should bounce as if constrained by a vertical cardboard tube sometimes helps improve technique and overall control.

Another technique used to help learners focus their attention is called 'verbalisation'. Many learners speak to themselves or sometimes aloud when they begin or carry out a movement. This seems to be a natural thing to do and fits in with Paul Fitts's idea that early learning is largely cognitive in nature. The coach can help by providing the learner with a word or series of words to help focus on the important actions in a skill.

For example, a trampolinist attempting a seat drop can say "one, two, three and hips". For a somersault it might be "one, two, three, hips and tuck". In squash, the learner trying to consolidate good backhand positioning when receiving the ball might say to himself "face the side wall". There are numerous situations where a word or two can be linked with a movement to reinforce a specific action.

Presenting the model

For beginners, whether adults or children, imitation is an invaluable aid to learning. The coach often needs to say very little except draw attention to the salient cues (e.g., keep the ball for no longer than five seconds; keep your fingers closed; don't close your eyes). Learners can be directed to the point in question, shown the demonstration and then given the opportunity to practice. The use of one sense at a time (demonstrating and talking simultaneously divides the learner's attention) is critical. The coach or one of the group may demonstrate or a video clip may be shown. In all cases, the model must illustrate the point in question. A world class hurdling action is no good for novices – for imitation to occur, the model must be attainable. In addition, the coach's model of 'correctness' must take account of individual differences in weight, fitness, etc.

Providing feedback

Many learners work better when the amount of praise and feedback is disproportionate in relation to their level of skill. This is because they have a poor basis for knowing whether or not they are correct – especially in activities where the form of the movement as opposed to its outcome is important. The coach may be the only person who can monitor success. This means they must provide guidance and feedback on a regular basis – at least until the learner is sufficiently skilled to take over some of the analysis. Feedback needn't be specific in nature – technical perfection is not the goal in early learning. But, it should be couched in positive terms. Rather than say "no, your legs are in the wrong position", the trampoline coach could say "why don't you bring your legs together when in flight – feel your heels touch?" Fault finding and correction is a large portion of the coach/teacher's work. The key challenge is to make it creative and constructive; it is all too easy to criticise. Time spent deciding what/how to speak to the learner ensures that comments are not only informative but also encouraging. Beginners like to know they are getting better. The adage 'success breeds success' is especially true with beginners.

The point was made in Chapter 3 about the difference between describing errors and explaining their cause. With beginners there is a need to go one step further and inform them how to correct errors. An example from gymnastics shows these steps. A common fault in a backward handspring (back flip) involves the gymnast landing on their feet but then falling forwards. One cause is insufficient backward rotation – the result of bending the arms on contact with the floor. All of this could be summarised by telling the gymnast to "lock your arms throughout the action". This way, the coach doesn't confuse the learner with unnecessary detail; it also translates the problem into a meaningful instruction, which can be acted on by the learner.

Finally, the importance of providing feedback on a regular basis cannot be over-stressed. Beginners are as likely to learn correct actions as they are bad ones. If not halted early on, incorrect actions quickly become bad habits difficult to eradicate. The coach or teacher who is observant picks up faults as they arise and minimises the risks.

Practice considerations

Beginners tire easily because they lack specific fitness requirements and invariably move inefficiently. Experienced coaches recognise that beginners cannot labour as long as those more experienced. They will appreciate that skill breaks down because of for example, limitations in fitness. Poor technique in bowling (cricket) may reflect gross shoulder inflexibility; in skiing, good technique will certainly be compromised through poor anaerobic fitness. Practice should therefore be spaced or reduced accordingly. Practice should also be varied to reduce boredom and fatigue and to maximise the learning of different people.

Learning can be made very meaningful if beginners are given some responsibility for their learning. They might be encouraged to assess why they made mistakes or try out ideas they think will solve particular problems. A problem-solving approach (e.g., in volleyball the coach could say, "Why do you think the ball travels backwards every time you 'dig' it?") involves the learner in a positive way. As an extension of this idea it may be profitable in a group situation to encourage learners to help each other with problems and feedback/peer support. Such a situation has to be treated with tact and sensitivity and will only work with learners who have some experience. Adult learners respond very well to this kind of approach. Finally, practices must be seen by the learner to be relevant to the whole skill or game. What the coach/teacher perceives to be appropriate and what the learner sees as relevant must be in agreement. If practice is isolated and non-game related, learners quickly loose interest.

WORKING WITH EXPERTS

A common misconception is that people who have become proficient (e.g., international athletes) have nothing else to learn. To give an example, most laymen would say that gymnasts competing in the Olympic games couldn't get much better; they had reached a peak of excellence. Paradoxically, those same observers might still criticise the professional footballer and possibly even say they were better themselves. The fact is that even athletes who are talented enough to represent their country may still have the potential to improve. Research has shown that given the right kinds of incentives, people who have practiced a skill many millions (!) of times still have the capacity to improve. It is also a fact that experienced people are sometimes faced with new learning problems. They may become 'rusty' following a long lay-off; a new technique may appear or a new equipment design may demand an adjustment in technique. So what factors are important when working with people who are highly skilled?

It is well known that even expert golfers continue to 'hone' their skills in the expectation of minor improvements

Individual differences

At higher performance levels, no two people perform in exactly the same way. Compared to early learners, the techniques of experts tend to be highly individualistic. Even in those sports where success is dictated by conformity to particular movement patterns (as, for example, in gymnastics and field athletics), people still display personalised forms of movement. Coaches must work within the boundaries imposed by personal style. To try and alter it might cause long-lasting decrements in performance. For example, many years ago an international marathon runner whose running technique was examined by sport scientists was shown to have an asymmetrical arm action which they said was wasting energy. When his coach tried to make changes, the runner began to suffer sore legs and his performance fell away. To change a person's habitual way of performing in order to match a 'textbook' model may take away the single quality that distinguishes the athlete from all the rest! In many other ways too (intellectual, personality, fitness, work ethic, etc.), experts need to be treated as individuals where their particular approach to training and performance has to be respected and considered.

Attentional capacity

Experts perform 'on automatic pilot'. Unlike the novice, they do not have to consciously think through every movement. They use conscious processes for more cognitive activities leaving movements to 'take care of themselves'. This freeing of attention makes it possible for the expert to work on aspects of performance which are irrelevant earlier in learning or else too subtle for the novice to appreciate. In climbing for example, experts are especially interested in practising techniques for protecting themselves as they ascend the rockface. In addition, they come to appreciate how differences in rock texture and type influence the kinds of holds available and hence the hand/foot actions necessary for safe movement. In badminton, the expert will understand that to play successfully at international level, knowledge of different footwork patterns, and how each relates to the kinds of strokes possible, is essential. This means that the coach can help the athlete on fine technical/tactical matters that are inappropriate earlier on. It also means the coach can work with players as they perform without causing a significant loss in performance. Coaching from the sideline – whilst the player is performing – therefore becomes a viable method; one that would be too distracting for a novice.

The coach can help in other ways too. Because skilled performance is largely automatic, it means the performer is often unaware of exactly how they perform particular skills. Experts can become increasingly unaware of their movements and tend to concentrate only on their outcome (did the shuttle land in court, was the somersault spotted correctly, how far was the javelin thrown, etc.). In this way, faulty technique can creep in and lay the foundations for bad habits unless an outsider detects the error. There is a need therefore for vigilance on the part of the coach in detecting small changes in technique that may go unnoticed by the athlete. This is one reason why most top athletes (e.g., in golf and athletics) employ coaches or other professionals. However, this is not a simple task. Forcing an expert to attend to muscular feelings and movements may well inhibit the action of unconscious cues that are necessary for controlled movement ('paralysis from analysis'!). Asking them to step back to an earlier stage in the learning process may well disturb performance dramatically. However, this may be the penalty that has to be paid for improving the athlete's ultimate level of performance. It demonstrates a phenomenon which is known as the 'progression-regression' hypothesis: under unfavourable conditions – such as stress – the performer reverts to an earlier level of control and skill suffers accordingly.

Practice conditions

If the 'whole' method is preferable with novices, then with experts – who are well motivated and understand what they are trying to do – part practices are more meaningful and in fact, highly desirable. As the learner progresses, it follows that techniques become more specialised and practices also become more specialised and suited to the individual. If practice is more specific then the terminology used by coaches will also be more specialised. The skilled performer possesses a much richer vocabulary than the beginner for understanding and communicating with the coach. Instructions such as "shorten/lengthen your backswing", "keep a wide base" are much more meaningful to the expert performer. This makes it possible for the coach and performer to work together on specific game aspects at a level that may be quite inaccessible to the novice.

Skilled athletes tend to possess a number of desirable qualities. They are more capable of listening to detailed instructions, better disposed to sitting down with the coach and analysing problems, and better able to appraise their performance without the immediate help of the coach. Experts can often profit from self analysis (e.g., watching videos of their performance) and experiment with technique without guidance. Their greater experience and sensitivity to what their body is doing permits them to make adjustments without ongoing external feedback.

Imagery

Imagery is mentioned again because it is of particular relevance to experts. More and more elite athletes have adopted imagery as an essential part of their preparation for competition. It is not uncommon to see skiers or long jumpers with their eyes closed making slight movements prior to performance. They are simply playing over in their mind the run or jump they are about to take. It is felt that imagery helps prepare the body and mind for competition, improves confidence and positive thinking and also serves as an important tool in maintaining concentration and attention. Its use is well documented (e.g., Bull et al, 1996) and many outstanding performers from sports as diverse as skiing, golf, lawn tennis and weight lifting testify to its value. As well as an aid to competition, imagery has been shown to act as a learning aid to improve performance, especially with elite or highly skilled individuals. The reasons would seem to be two fold. In the first place, skilled performers possess a model of skill that is conceptually better established than that of learners. As a result imagery has a greater effect with experts because it has a more accurate technical basis. Secondly, experts tend to have clearer goals and search for ways to extract just that little bit more from themselves. As a result, they have an attitude that is more conducive to the use of imagery techniques.

In practice, it is likely that skilled performers – especially those who are highly motivated – spend a substantial amount of time thinking about their sport. A significant proportion of this time will be structured as imagery both on and off the field. Imagery is an acquired activity however and the athlete needs to learn how to do it. One of the problems with imagery techniques is that they take time to learn – time that the athlete may wish to devote to more practical endeavours. In addition, imagery is very susceptible to interference from problems that may occupy the athlete's attention (e.g., personal matters and injury). It therefore requires practice and self-evaluation by the athlete as well as monitoring by the coach to be effective. Its timing must also be appropriate.

Metacognitive ability

The principle of metacognition is pertinent to all learners, but is included in the section because it has special relevance to expert performers. It refers to the knowledge that people have about their cognitive functioning. It also refers to the control they have over cognitive activity during learning. Broadly, it is concerned directly with the degree of awareness people have over the learning process. Some people learn in a very passive manner accepting all they are told and responding without question to the practices set by the teacher or coach. Others adopt a more active stance, questioning what they are told and thinking critically about their own abilities and how they can speed up learning. People who behave like this are said to have greater metacognitive ability. It is reported that people who have efficient metacognitive abilities are able to learn faster, understand better and retain information for longer. Furthermore, the application of metacognitive ability may increase a learner's control and responsibility over their own learning processes.

Metacognitive knowledge (as opposed to ability) includes items such as knowledge of the desired outcomes of a skill, the context in which the skill takes place and the demands of the skill. It also includes knowledge about the learner's own skills, strengths, weaknesses, preferences and goals. An example of this would be the learner who appreciates they can learn better if they watch a demonstration

rather than listen to a lengthy explanation of a technique. It is suggested that this kind of personal awareness is very important since it helps the learner know the kinds of resources or assistance they require to perform efficiently and effectively. Metacognitive knowledge also includes knowledge of other people who may be involved in the learning environment such as the coach or fellow learners. Thus a learner may have a full appreciation of what the coach requires of them, as well as the strengths and limitations of others learners they are working alongside.

Metacognitive ability requires not only the kinds of knowledge just described but also knowledge of cognitive strategies. This is an area in which the expert is more likely to be familiar. Examples of cognitive strategies include the use of analogies (e.g., serving in table tennis is like throwing a frisbee), metaphors (e.g., a basketball free throw can be interpreted as Balance, Elbow up, Extension, Follow through – BEEF), rhythmic counting (e.g., counting strides between hurdles), labelling and rehearsal. Luke and Hardy (1999) suggest that cognitive strategies are any goal-directed cognitive activities, be they obligatory and non-obligatory, conscious or unconscious, efficient or inefficient. Successful performers have a range of such strategies from which they are able to select and adapt flexibly to meet the demands of any given situation. It is suggested that metacognitive ability and the critical thinking it involves:

".... can heighten a learner's awareness of their own thinking and the degree to which their thinking skills can be effective in helping them become more skilful, fit and knowledgeable about physical activity." ~ Schwager and Labate (1993).

An assumption is often made that metacognitive ability takes place without any kind of training or that it is developed as a by product of the skill learning process. Luke and Hardy (1999) make the point that the skill learning process can be significantly enhanced through the use of efficient metacognitive abilities. However, people need to be guided to develop these abilities in the first place. They say:

"... it has been suggested that cognitive strategies may be the key to developing a flexible learner who can adapt to the environment ... it would seem imperative that pupils are encouraged to develop a variety of cognitive strategy types to enhance their potential to learn in a variety of learning situations."

SUMMARY OF THE KEY POINTS

• Many studies have examined the performance standards of children at different ages, but there is little research evidence identifying the most appropriate periods for introducing different sports to children.

• Children must be physiologically mature before they will learn particular skills.

• Childhood is a 'skill hungry' stage; children enjoy activity for its own sake, they are motivated to learn and readily acquire many basic movement patterns. It is suggested that beyond the age of five or six years, children rarely acquire entirely new skills.

• Many sports can be introduced through a form of structured play. Mini-sports are especially useful.

• The research on critical periods in learning and special training has thrown little light on skill development.

• Techniques for children should not be as sophisticated as those for adults, and they should also be adapted to suit the size and shape of the individual.

• Visual guidance should take advantage of imitation and verbal guidance should acknowledge the child's limited technical vocabulary.

• Safety and confidence are critical considerations with youngsters, as is coaching style. Research shows that positive methods are more likely to produce positive results than negative ones.

• Adult learners are able to take advantage of greater experience when learning new sports. The rapid learning which is sometimes found represents the effect of positive transfer.

- Adults may be intrinsically more motivated to learn and are often more analytical in their approach.

- Fear of injury and lack of confidence may impede the learning of adults.

- Teaching beginners has a number of implications for coaching/teaching – skills should be reduced in their information content; relevant cues should be selected; feedback should not be too technical and should be provided regularly; practice should not tire the learner; practice should be varied, interesting and relevant.

- Most experts have the potential to improve and are often faced with new learning problems.

- Experts should be treated as individuals in the way they are coached. Technical proficiency, 'style', fitness requirements, etc., are very personal at high levels of skill.

- Experts are able to respond to highly specific outside advice, often when performing. They are also more able to self-assess their performances.

- Imagery can be a highly useful form of practice for more experienced learners/ performers.

- Metacognition refers to the knowledge and control people have over their cognitive functioning. People who are more aware of their own learning (such as identification of their goals, the requirements of the task, their preferred learning style) are thought to make better learners.

PRACTICAL TASKS

The following tasks are designed to reveal the different ways people perform when confronted with the same task:

- Identify two people who have never tried to juggle with three balls. Provide both people with a simple demonstration (yourself or another person). Then ask both people to 'have a go' whilst you observe their performance. Initially, you may wish to provide them with feedback to keep them motivated and help them improve. But your main task is to observe certain features about the way they perform and learn. Take notes on the following – their relative speed of progress, the kinds of errors they make, their speed of movements, whether they attempt to verbalise their actions, degree of frustration/pleasure. Your task will largely be qualitative in nature (see Chapter 9 for more details on this subject). You may find other criteria useful in describing differences between the two people. Once the two people have practiced for five minutes or so, halt proceedings and examine your notes. It will be very useful to discuss your findings with the two learners. You may wish to question whether your observations were also perceived by the learners. Further, were the two learners conscious of each other whilst they practiced and did they learn from one another?

• The same procedure can be repeated (perhaps with different people) but using different tasks such as throwing or kicking a ball for accuracy. You may wish to examine whether the differences you note in performance between the two people bear any relationship to differences in personality, age, experience, height and so on.

• Watch a video recording of a recent sporting event such as a football match, athletics competition, swimming competition or ski event. Take two competitors and note differences in the way they move. If you watch both people for 10 or more minutes, you will begin to observe significant variations in their actions (speed, fluency, amount, relationships to others). The differences will be more marked in those sports that contain open skills (e.g., football) as opposed to those that contain closed skills (e.g., swimming, skiing).

• Take three people willing to engage in a spell of 'arm wrestling'. Decide on the rules and then set up a mini competition so that everyone competes against everyone else twice (six events). Have a brief discussion at the end and talk about the relative strengths of each other and what marked out the eventual winner. The discussion should reveal that people embark on competition for different reasons and also bring to competition varying qualities such as skill, fitness, motivation and commitment.

REVIEW QUESTIONS

• Take a situation where you introduce a new skill to a youngster, say a forward roll or striking a tennis ball. Suppose the youngster fails to pick up the idea. What are the possible causes of failure? How would you examine the precise problem?

• Youngsters can be very noisy and undisciplined. What steps can be taken to attract their attention to the sport/skills in question?

• Think of an example from your experience, which demonstrates the principle that models for children should be adjusted to accommodate their shape, size, etc.

• Children can imitate both good and bad technique and they may do so with equal success. How would you know whether a child's poor technique was a result of their inability or your own faulty demonstration?

• Children invent games by themselves and in conjunction with others devise rules for playing the game. Examine some of the problems for a teacher/coach in trying to use this natural process as a means of introducing popular sports.

• Children are, by and large, very confident. What do you think to the view that children often put themselves at too great a risk to life and limb?

• Research shows that positive coaching styles are superior in their effect to negative ones. With this in mind, how sensitive/tactful should the coach be when describing errors to children?

• Describe an example from your experience to show that adult learners can be very analytical in their approach to learning.

• To what extent can a coach take advantage of an adult's past experience when introducing a new skill?

• What steps can be taken to overcome the problems of fear and injury when working with adults?

• Take a particular sport and describe the cues, which would be highlighted to a beginner (say, in the first session).

• If expert performers have the potential to improve even further, what steps can be taken to ensure this does happen?

• Comment on the situation where experts are encouraged to practice a technique beyond the point of their physical ability and to a level where skill begins to break down.

• Can you think of examples (viewed on TV or in real life) where top flight performers use techniques of imagery?

• In these examples, what do the performers actually do? And following their performance, do they involve themselves in further imagery?

References

Balyi, I. (2002). *Developing potential.* Quoted in Arena (Newsletter of Sportscotland), 2, p10.

Brown, J. (2001). *Sports talent. How to identify and develop outstanding athletes.* Champaign, Illinois: Human Kinetics.

Bull, S.J., Albinson, J.G. and Shambrook, C.J. (1996). *The mental game plan: getting psyched for sport.* Cheltenham: Sports Dynamics.

Dryden, G. and Vos, J. (2001). *The learning revolution: to change the way the world learns.* Stafford: Network Educational Press Ltd.

Earle, C. (2003). *How to coach children in sport.* Leeds: Coachwise Solutions.

Fitts, P.M. and Posner, M.I. (1967). *Human performance.* Belmont, California: Brooks/Cole.

Forsyth, S. (2003). *Personal communication with SFA Football Coach.* 12th August.

Green, B. (2003). *Personal communication with Scottish Volleyball Association Staff Tutor,* July, 22nd.

Kerr, A. and Stafford, I. (2003). *How to coach disabled people in sport.* Leeds: Coachwise Solutions.

Kline, P. (1997). *The everyday genius.* Arlington, Virginia: Great Ocean Publishers Inc.

Lee, M. (1988). *Coaching Children* (NCF key course resource pack). National Coaching Foundation: Leeds.

Lee, M. (1991). *Coaching children.* Coaching Focus, 16, 3 - 5.

Luke, I., and Hardy, C.A. (1999). *Pupils' metacognition and learning.* In C.A. Hardy and M. Mawer (Eds.). *Learning and teaching in physical education.* London: Falmer Press.

MacNab, T. (1986). *Technique and the young performer.* In Gleeson, G. (Ed.), *The growing child and competitive sport.* Hodder & Stoughton: London.

Planning and practice (Video, 1986). Leeds: National Coaching Foundation.

O'Neill, J. (1991). *Teaching athletics in the primary school.* British Journal of Physical Education, 22, 3, 5 - 6.

Pankhurst, A. and Russell, C. (1991). *Coaching children* (Pre-course workbook). Leeds: The National Coaching Foundation.

Pollatschek, J.L. (1989). *Daily physical education in Scotland.* Unpublished Doctoral Dissertation, University of Strathclyde, Glasgow.

Saunders, L. (1986). Quotation from Sharp, R.H. *Acquiring skill* (Coach Education Modules). Edinburgh: The Scottish Sports Council.

Schmidt, R.A. and Wrisberg, C.A. (2000). *Motor learning and performance.* Champaign, Illinois: Human Kinetics.

Schwager, S. and Labate, C. (1993). Teaching for critical thinking in physical education. *Journal of Health, Physical Education, Recreation and Dance,* 64, 5, 24 - 26.

Sleap, M. (1981). *Mini-sport.* Heinemann Educational Books: London.

"Before a big match I try to visualise myself in different situations in different parts of the field. I will spend a long time practicing kicks from those areas of the field where we plan to attack."

Rob Andrew *(former England International rugby player)*

MIND – BODY DUALISM

The author of this book used to play amateur football. One of his colleagues was an extremely good player whose technical skills marvelled everyone who saw him practice. But when he played in matches, his skill was rarely revealed. Many of us could never understand why his skill in training was not reflected in competition. What was unclear at the time was that he was extremely afraid of injury (high trait anxiety – see later). As a result, he tended to hold himself back in order to avoid any kind of contact with opposition players. His was a classic case of 'mind over matter'. This expression hints at one of the major problems that has dogged sports coaching and teaching for many years, i.e., the unnecessary distinction which is often made between the learner's thoughts, feelings and motivations (the 'mind') and the learner's skills and movements (the 'matter'). The mind-body dualism is well established in western civilisation but many researchers and practitioners have argued strongly for a much more integrated perspective, particularly in regard to an understanding of teaching (e.g., Rintala, 1991).

Historically, teachers and coaches have placed emphasis on the movement dimension of learning – techniques, how they should be broken down, how long they should be practised for and so on. The learner has often been ignored at the expense of over-attention to the psycho-motor dimension of the learning process (see *Figure 1*, Chapter 1). Today, the

> ⌐**KEY POINT**
>
> Feelings, attitudes and motivations not only influence a person's involvement in sport but can also determine their ultimate level of performance.

focus is rapidly changing and the 'psychology' of the individual has assumed a much more important role. Matthews (1991) for example, discusses the important role sports psychologists play in helping athletes overcome problems relating to relaxation, tension, lack of confidence, goal-setting and self-belief. There are increasing references to the psychology of sports performance and the mental side of competition in the popular press (Bull, Albinson and Shambrook, 1996). Hardy (1990) has stressed the importance of psychological parameters as they affect performance. He lists a variety of relevant topics:

"Looking at the preparation of the few world class performers that Britain has produced helps to establish what some of these psychological factors might be. By linking this evidence to the research into the psychological phenomena of peak performance, we can make some educated guesses about what the factors are that we need to bring under control. These include goal-setting, self-confidence, persistence, concentration, relaxation, activation and anxiety."

The Cognitive approach to learning (see Chapter 2) underlines people's perceptions, feelings and goals and the influence of these factors on behaviour. Instances are seen in sport all the time. Take for example, the middle distance runner who fails because he is too anxious, or the tennis player who prepares herself by mentally rehearsing her movements just before she performs. Numerous top performers testify to the value of mental training. Equally, it is

Do you have the right mental attitude to learning?

well established that people fail to meet their potential – especially in competitive situations – through over anxiety, concern about injuries or intimidation from competitors. The fact is that people (competitors and learners alike) do not always behave in a predictable manner. One of the factors is that affective variables such as feelings, motives and attitudes play a significant role in performance. Research and anecdotal evidence has shown that factors like these can have both positive and negative influences. They are relevant to beginners and experts as well as young and older students of learning. The objective in this chapter is to take a look at some of the factors that have particular relevance to learning. We begin with a look at the 'Inner Game' which is an approach to teaching/coaching that was prominent in the mid 1970's. Despite its long history, most of the principles are highly relevant today.

INNER GAME PRINCIPLES

The Inner Game approach to coaching and learning views the learner – their mind, the learning process and their movements – as a whole. It is concerned with the manner in which the coach or teacher approaches skill problems – the 'coaching style' – as well as the way in

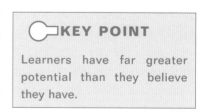
KEY POINT

Learners have far greater potential than they believe they have.

which the learner is involved in the learning process. It addresses both the physical and mental components in sport. A key proponent of the Inner Game, Tim Gallway, noted at the time that his ideas were not novel:

"The Inner Game approach is hardly new. It is similar to the natural way that, as children, we learned to walk, talk or throw a ball. It uses the unconscious, rather than the deliberately self-conscious mind. This process doesn't have to be learned; we already know it. All that is needed is to unlearn the habits and concepts which interfere with our natural learning ability, and to trust the innate intelligence of our bodies."

Gallway and Kriegal (1977)

Gallway drew on several learning theories, but notably the Cognitive and Information Processing models. He argued that traditional coaching and teaching methods have a number of inefficient and negative dimensions. He said that traditional methods are too technically oriented and create barriers between learner and instructor. Crimble (1982) expressed this view in the following quotation:

"Could it be that as teachers and students we are in love with the technicalities and jargon of our sport? If the skill is made to appear too simple it undermines our position of authority and denigrates our efforts to master it. A convenient smokescreen of technicalities reinforces our ego and provides an excuse for our failures."

Gallway suggested that technical orientation focuses the learner's attention on the results of actions rather than the feelings of movements. This presents an obstacle to improvement because the learner is pre-occupied with self analysis and self appraisal and is, therefore, constantly pre-occupied with failure. A knock-on effect is that fear of failure provides a further obstacle to positive achievement. Gallway goes on to suggest that because of an over emphasis on performance-oriented coaching/learning, learners lose interest and cease enjoying sport. Finally, he argued that focusing on performance success and failure encourages aggressive self-instruction and self-criticism. In turn, this leads to anxiety and tension that inhibit the learning process. In addition, the muscular tension created through over-anxiety inhibits technical excellence.

Against this backcloth, Gallway suggested coaches and instructors should adopt a much more positive approach where the learner is not only centrally involved with their own learning, but is also 'de-tuned' to the concepts of success and failure. A major premise is that learners have a potential to succeed and possess inherent talents well beyond their expectations. He based this partly on the finding that sometimes people display 'highs', i.e., occasions when they reveal extreme technical excellence with no lapse in attention and total enjoyment. He gives an example from the world of skiing:

"All of us have had those incredible runs when for some reason everything seems to click and we ski so much better than usual that we surprise ourselves. Turns we've been struggling with are suddenly easy. Frustrations vanish and we

become totally absorbed in the joy of the moment. The usual mental struggle – trying to do everything right, worrying about how we look or about falling and failing – is forgotten. Enjoyment is so intense that we don't even think of making a mistake - and we don't. For a time, self-imposed limitations are forgotten; we are skiing unconsciously."

Gallway suggested that we all possess the ability to perform 'out of our mind', but we don't do it because we build barriers that interfere with the normal mechanisms for success. The release of potential is brought about by an alteration in the state of mind, i.e., when we stop thinking. He said:

"We can only conclude that the reason we don't perform so well is not that we don't have the ability, but that we somehow interfere with it. In the breakthrough run we skied beyond our expectations not because we finally mastered a new technique but because for a few moments our state of mind changed. The mind became quiet, making our movements more natural and co-ordinated. Such occasions indicate that the excellence of our skiing is dependent more on our state of mind than on the self-conscious mastery of memorised techniques."

Self 1 and Self 2

To help clarify these ideas Gallway distinguished between two hypothetical learners – Self 1 and Self 2. Self 1 is the person within the learner who does the talking, judging, worrying and doubting. Self 1 creates self-concepts and fears and is normally in control. Self 2 is the person being instructed who performs the actions. Self 2 has the potential to respond with full capability but is thwarted by the barriers erected by Self 1. Gallway argued that in most cases Self 1 and Self 2 don't get along too well; they 'mistrust' one another and behave as two separate persons. The exception is during childhood when Self 1 has not had time to accumulate distorted and limiting self-concepts. This allows Self 2 the freedom to learn and perform in a natural and confident manner. With adult learners the position is different and conflict exists. The major object is to quieten Self 1 and so free the obstacles which otherwise prevent Self 2's fullest expression and development. How can this be used to help learners achieve their potential and how is it possible to minimise the interference caused by Self 1?

Trust and confidence

Gallway suggests learners can realise their potential and enjoy learning much more by 'taming' Self 1 and 'trusting' Self 2. Recognising the existence of Self 1 and its damaging effects is a start to reducing its effect. Beginning to trust the body and develop confidence is a start to enhancing the efforts of Self 2. What can coaches do to help? Trying to reduce the learner's anxiety helps. By eliminating criticism, listening to learners, respecting their feelings and ideas and generally treating them as partners in a mutual adventure goes a long way to reducing anxiety. Ensuring a safe environment and making instructions relevant and brief obviously gives support. Confidence and self-image can be improved by giving the learner maximum responsibility for their learning. This may require a different style of coaching – one that is more democratic and forgiving – to that which the coach normally adopts. Overall, coaches and teachers should develop the self esteem of learners and minimise the verbal badgering and self-condemnation they often engage in (Matthews, 1991).

Body awareness

To increase learner confidence and belief in potential it is essential to give Self 2 a higher profile. To do this Gallway subscribes to the principles of experiential learning. The nature and merits of experiential learning was described previously. Gallway advocates that 'thinking about doing' is taboo. He says:

> "Self 2 lets experience be the guide. Remaining objective and interested, it grows by absorbing what is happening from moment to moment. In the process of discovery it senses and observes, constantly picking up information and making appropriate adjustments in its actions and direction, thus becoming increasingly able to cope with the situation at hand. The natural learning process is discovery by experience."

Feedback is central to this process. Feedback of all kinds is useful, but feedback from internal sensations is critical. It is through internal feedback that body awareness increases, which in turn brings Self 2 to the fore. Gallway suggests the way to help learners increase body awareness is to make them responsible for their actions and force attention to sensations which might otherwise be ignored. Through being told less what to do and feeling more what is going on in their body, learners become attuned to results and more to the muscular feelings associated with body technique. He gives an example of a coach introducing beginner skiers to the notion of 'edge' control. The coach asks the learners to get used to their skis by shifting their weight from foot to foot, moving them up and down and sideways, etc. He then tells them to follow him up the hill, but he does not mention anything about edge technique. He simply talks to the group, asking them to feel their skis and asking whether they feel flat or inclined. After a short while he asks the group to 'play' with different degrees of edge and see what happens. The learners go through a process of flattening their skis, slipping and correcting. In this way, each learner gains control and increased sensitivity entirely through their own efforts. Gallway argues this goes a long way to helping the learner gain confidence and awareness, which in turn allows the potential of Self 2 to be realised.

In another example, Gallway shows how learners can become sensitised to internal feedback. In this example, a tennis coach tries to correct a bad serving technique in which the learner hits too hard. The coach tells the player to serve the ball as hard as he can, but to ignore where it lands, and to give the effort felt in the arms a score of 10. The player is then asked to serve a soft ball which is given a 1. He is then asked to serve the ball with varying degrees of effort and to give scores from 1 to 10. The net result is that the learner becomes proficient in hitting the ball with less effort, and is able to do so because he is more aware of what his body is telling him. A very useful illustration of this technique is shown in the video published by the National Coaching Foundation (1996).

The Inner Game approach to teaching and learning adds little that is already known about learning but it does underline the critical importance of some principles. These can be listed as:

• Skill potential is often greater than individuals believe
• People learn best when they are directly responsible for what they do
• Focused attention on internal sensations is critical
• Common barriers to skill development (e.g., fear) can be overcome
• Coaching should focus on positive feelings rather than negative outcomes
• The focus is on the learner learning rather than the teacher teaching.

Proponents of the Inner Game attempt to elicit the very best from learners and try to eradicate some of the common hurdles to success such as fear of failure. They switch responsibility for learning from coach to learner and attempt to make learners more aware of what there bodies are doing and telling them.

> "Learning happens best when both instructor and student recognise that experience is the teacher. The role of the instructor is to guide the student into experiences appropriate to his stage of development. At the same time that the student is guided towards attentive appreciation of the sensations of his body, the instructor is learning from him how to best lead him to the next step."
>
> Gallway and Kriegal (1977)

GOAL SETTING

By definition (see Chapter 1) skill is goal oriented; it has purpose and direction. For example, a diver completes a complicated routine aimed at entering the water in a vertical position. Any deviation would be classified as failure; the goal is not achieved. Football players attempt to move the ball past opposing players in order to position it closer to the goal posts. It is usually very clear when you see players in action what are their goals; they are well defined and easily seen by the observer. But goal direction is not just important in skilled performance. For the learner too, targets should be established so that progress can develop logically and successfully. Learners need to have goals to know what to work towards and to realise success.

The need for goals

One of the important determinants of success in sport is self-confidence. Someone who is self-assured and aware of their potential is more likely to succeed than someone who is unsure and lacks confidence. It has been shown that people who believe they have the ability to achieve, actually achieve more and are more persistent in the event of failure than less confident performers. There are a number of factors involved in helping to build confidence, but the most effective way is to ensure that learners succeed in their efforts. The only way this can happen is for learners to strive towards (and realise) achievable goals. The setting of realistic and attainable goals – by the learner and coach/teacher – provides a yardstick against which learners can measure their own performance. And if major goals can be broken into lesser targets, then success occurs throughout learning. The importance of goal setting within the overall teaching/coaching process is highlighted in the model described by Miles (2003) – see *Figure 1*. In this model, goal setting is a key step in the coaching cycle.

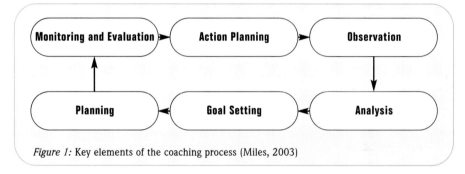

Figure 1: Key elements of the coaching process (Miles, 2003)

There is another reason why goal setting is crucial. Setting goals allows coaches and learners to plan the direction in which they are heading and, as a consequence, the best route taken to get there. A well-thought out plan involving weekly and monthly targets is more likely to result in success than a 'hotchpotch' of ill-conceived ideas lacking overall cohesion. A carefully designed programme of major and secondary goals provides the basis for structured practice – amount, nature, timing, etc. It also makes for efficient use of time and resources. In addition, because goal setting involves establishing specific criteria or targets, it is possible to measure and evaluate the learner's progress in a concrete manner. Evaluation of the learner therefore takes on a much more meaningful dimension and has a sounder basis. Evaluation is discussed more fully in Chapter 9.

Long and short-term goals

If goals are to be effective, they must be specific to the learner and the situation but, they must also lie within the learner's control. For example, it might be inappropriate for a good club table tennis player to set the goal of becoming say National champion. Such a goal would not only be too far away in time (it might be a good long-term goal), but it is also influenced by the skill of other performers. It makes sense to establish goals that can be achieved in the long term, but also to set intermediate goals which are manageable and attainable in the short term. A very detailed example of how long-term intentions can be broken down into smaller goals is seen in the efforts of an international swimmer who wished to win a gold medal at an Olympic games. The swimmer calculated from previous times what performance time might win the gold, and determined that he had to drop four seconds in four years. He then broke the goal down further into one second per year, one tenth of a second per month, one three-hundredth of a second per day, and one twelve hundredth of a second per hour of training! Finally, he made this goal of one twelve-hundredth of a second per hour a little easier to grasp by working out that from the time he began to blink his eyes to the time his eyelids touched was five twelve-hundredths of a second. This was a target he could reach in one hour, and so he set about doing just that. His plan worked and he won the gold medal!

Mutrie (1985) shows how long term or so-called 'dream' goals can be broken down into smaller parts. *Figure 2*, below, shows her approach.

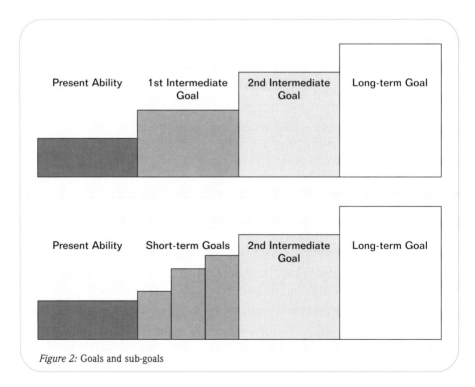

Figure 2: Goals and sub-goals

In the top diagram, the lower step represents the learner's current level of performance and the top step represents the learner's overall goal. The difference has been broken into a number of intermediate goals which help make the long term goal more achievable. The lower diagram shows in turn how the steps between the intermediate goals are further divided by short term goals which are specific and attainable targets. Mutrie makes the point that models like this must be flexible enough to account for unexpected problems (e.g., injuries, eradication of bad habits).

LONG-TERM GOAL	GOALS FOR NEXT MONTH	GOALS AND COURSES OF ACTION FOR THIS WEEK
	1. Learn one new move on each side of horse (Stockli B), parallel bars and high bar	1.1 Learn straddle circle on low bar 1.2 Start work on Stockli B and cast half-turn 1.3 Do not give in if success is not immediate
A. Learn the new World set routines	2. Learn the correct sequencing of all the set routines using mental rehearsal	2.1 Send away for the latest FIG interpretation of the set routines 2.2 Mentally rehearse the four conventional routines at home for 20 minutes each day
	3. Link three moves together from each routine	
B. Score 49.0 on voluntary routines	4. Maintain present perform-ance on all voluntary routines	4.1 Practice full voluntary routines in two halves if necessary on the floor, vault and rings
C. Win a place in the British Men's squad		

Table 1: Breakdown of long and short-term goals – an example

Hardy and Fazey (1986) present a similar, tree-like structure to goal-setting. They suggest coaches and learners should work together to establish a set of say three, long term aims which are realistic and measurable in quantitative terms. Next, they should be ranked in order of importance. For the most important aim, a list of goals which can be attained within a month and which contribute to the achievement of the overall aim should be written down and also ranked. For the second long term aim, one goal should be established which can be attained within a month. Nothing is established for the final long term aim. Now, for the first monthly goal corresponding to the first aim three sub-goals or courses of action should be devised which can be met within a week. For the second monthly goal, two intermediate goals are selected. And so on. *Table 1* shows this scheme applied to a gymnast working towards team selection for a national squad. The same approach is equally applicable to learners just starting off in a new sport. Thus, a youngster wishing to improve their football skills might set the task of learning to trap/receive the ball by breaking it down into various techniques (use of chest, foot, head, etc.), each of which might be practiced on a weekly basis.

The Table shows a hierarchy of aims and goals indicating items of greater or lesser importance. It is important to note that plans within models like this must be seen as dynamic ones which grow and change over time. In the gymnastics example the learner and coach would evaluate success in terms of goal-attainment, re-evaluate monthly goals and set new goals for the following week. So, every week some aims might leave or be adjusted slightly, new ones could appear and others might alter in their importance. It is also important to notice that specific goals need not be skill-oriented. It may be equally valid for the learner to complete a training diary, purchase new equipment or perhaps spectate at a competition. These might be 'easy' goals to attain and help balance more arduous ones. Goal structure is therefore seen as something malleable that develops and changes over time.

Criteria for good goals

Most authorities agree that goal setting should be a joint process between learner and coach/teacher. This is especially true with advanced learners who are more experienced and better able to participate in informed discussion. Goals established in this way are more likely to meet a number of important criteria.

It goes almost without saying that goals must be specific and tailored to suit the individual. Goals that are not specific are likely to cause confusion and lack of direction in the learner's mind. Goals can be derived from the learner's current level of per-formance and might also lean on any special problems they may have. For example, sup-pose a tennis player cannot execute backhand strokes consistently. This could be con-verted into a positive statement such as: "over the next two months, I will improve my backhand by spending half an hour each day on good technique". It is vital the learner expresses negative thoughts and actions as specific, positive goals.

Goals should also be appropriate to each learner. People learn at individual rates and are motivated in different ways. One person may be able to learn a new gymnastic move in a single session whilst another may require several weeks. A good coach/teacher will know exactly how far to push each individual and know what to expect in a given amount of time.

Goals should be challenging and exciting. Targets which are too easy to attain or limited in scope run the risk of de-motivating the learner. People are more likely to persist when faced with a challenge which presents problems but which is not too demanding or impossible. Again, a sensitive coach should know their athletes well enough to determine what is appropriate in any given situation. Goals must also be attainable. Targets which cannot be met in the time allowed or are just impossible to meet will force learners into failure situations and similarly de-motivate. Hardy (1986) suggests that for goals which are under the individual's own control there is an inverse-U relationship between goal difficulty ('attainability') and performance (see *Figure 3*). In this model, as goal difficulty increases so does performance but there a critical point after which performance drops away. The critical point marks the stage at which the individual ceases to accept the goal as attainable. The exact value of the critical point depends on a number of situational influences (e.g., level of competition, type of sport) and subjective factors (e.g., level of anxiety, type of personality), but Hardy indicates that as a rough guideline, goals in practice should be at least 50% achievable.

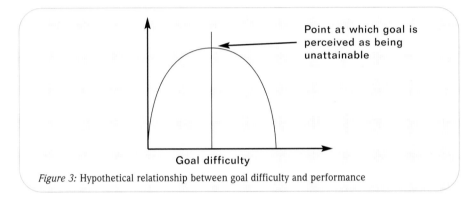

Figure 3: Hypothetical relationship between goal difficulty and performance

Goals must be realistic in the sense that they relate to the overall goals the coach or teacher has in mind. In the swimming example given before, the performer established target times which he considered were attainable. They were also logical steps towards the final time required, i.e., they were realistic. A problem arises when intermediate goals are unattainable or don't fit into the overall pattern of skill development. For example, a gymnastics coach may expect a beginner to learn a movement which is beyond her strength, is too complicated or not seen by the learner to relate to the sequence being learned. This raises the problem that sometimes when goals are not achieved, the coach must determine whether failure is due to the learner or the coach.

Goals must be measurable. The whole process of goal setting breaks down if neither learner nor coach can confirm whether goals have been attained. To help, it makes sense to establish goals that are objective and quantifiable. Measures of time and distance for example, are far better than subjective terms like, 'more', 'enough', 'better', etc. A number of measurement techniques are available and include the use of recognised skill tests (number of free shots out of 20, proficiency award schemes) and notation analysis methods which are particularly appropriate in team sports. One of the difficulties with measurement is that it is easier to concentrate on the 'outcome' of performance than the performance itself (e.g., number of baskets scored as opposed to the quality of the shot). This leads the learner to focus on aspects of performance which are related to the overall goal but not intermediate ones. For example, the beginner swimmer who tries to swim a width of the pool unaided (a very measurable aspect) may display very poor technique and possibly start to develop a bad habit. Somehow, the overall goal to swim unaided has to be broken down into smaller parts which are measurable but which also focus on technique. Use of 'number of strokes' might be a way around this problem.

Mutrie (1985) discusses this problem by suggesting that 'product' goals which relate to the outcome of performance should be used for long-term targets, whilst 'process' goals which refer to the process of improving performance towards the ultimate target, should be set for intermediate or short-term goals. Her reasoning here is that product goals (e.g., to be the national champion), whilst giving direction to a general plan of action, are inappropriate for short-term application because they tend to be influenced by outside factors (e.g., the performance of other people). It is far better in the short-term to set goals which can be controlled by the learner and which refer specifically to the learner's own performance. Finally, it is critical that goals are recorded. The learner may keep a diary and/or the coach might maintain a log of everyone's progress and targets. In this way, it is clear to everyone what is required whilst reviews and evaluation become more objective.

A good way of listing and recalling essential criteria for setting goals is to use one of several mnemonics. Foxon (1999) proposes the word SMARTER:

- Specific
- Measurable
- Agreed/Adjustable
- Realistic
- Time-phased
- Exciting
- Recorded.

McQuade (2003) uses the shorter version 'SMART' and Bull et al (1996) describes further how mnemonics like this can be used to advantage.

IMAGERY

"Find a few minutes and a quiet place to lie down. Imagine the mountains: a specific mountain on a fine, crisp, winter's day. Imagine yourself stepping out of

the cable car, or getting off the chair lift. Visualise yourself putting your skis on, now your sticks, goggles or glasses in place and zip up your collar. Visualise all the little details, and then set off down a well known run."

Sheddon (1982)

Shedden's description of how a skier might mentally rehearse embodies many of the important things known about the subject – the need for quiet, relaxation and the relevance of both the visualisation of performance and imagination of internal feelings and sensations. Imagery (variously called mental practice, symbolic imagination, covert rehearsal, mental rehearsal or visualisation) is not a new subject and is certainly not specific to the sporting world. Salesmen spend time rehearsing encounters with prospective buyers, and military personnel are instructed to spend time visualising potential emergencies so they can react quicker and more safely during actual emergencies. In the world of sport there are many reported cases of top players using imagery to help them prepare for competition. For example, the skier Jean Claude Killy used to 'run every slalom gate in his mind's eye' just before sleeping the night prior to a competition. Rob Andrew (quoted in Bull et al, 1996) indicated that:

"Before a big match I try to visualise myself in different situations in different parts of the field. I will spend a long time practicing kicks from those areas of the field where we plan to attack."

Many competitors in athletics can be seen spending a moment before they participate imagining the action about to take place. A long jumper might rehearsing the approach, take-off and flight technique several times before he actually begins his movement. In fact, performers in many sports – both team and individual sports – spend time thinking about their performance and testify to the value of imagery.

Why does it work?

It is suggested that imagery has a place both as a pre-competition strategy and as an aid to learning. There is common ground in both approaches. Traditionally, imagery has been examined as an adjunct to skill acquisition. Typically, studies have compared the relative benefits of imagery and physical practice. The classic experimental paradigm has used three groups of subjects, one of which learns a new skill with physical practice, one group learns using imagery alone and the third group acts as a control. The typical finding is that the physical practice group performs best overall, followed by the imagery group and then the control group. The bulk of evidence indicates that physical practice is superior to imagery in terms of learning motor skills (e.g., Hird, Landers, Thomas and Horan, 1991).

This is an interesting finding and begs several questions. For example, why is imagery beneficial? How should imagery be carried out? What should be practiced? Are there different kinds of imagery? In relation to the first question, a number of answers have been proffered. It is considered by some investigators that imagery causes the same neural mechanisms to be used as would be employed during physical practice – a neural learning effect. Others propose that imagery is accompanied by minute physical movements that resemble the actions themselves (Bull et al, 1996). In this way physical practice and imagery provide similar kinds of motor output – feedback experiences. And some investigators conclude that imagery primarily serves a perceptual function whereby learners begin to understand more clearly how to avoid distracting stimuli, concentrate their attention or understand how movements are carried out. Ryan (1981) suggests that imagery is an indirect way of mobilising the 'unconscious mind' and thereby provides the learner with a method of solving perceptual problems. He says:

> *"There is the suspicion that the unconscious can attack a problem relentlessly and constantly, even though the approach is not in the traditional manner. After the conscious has been working on a problem (a period of mental practice), it may yield an insight to the unconscious, though we don't know by what process. One of the most famous incidents in which the unconscious produced an insight was that of Archimedes proclaiming 'Eureka' in the bathtub."*

This may apply especially in situations where the learner is having particular perceptual difficulties. For example, the author can remember trying to learn an upstart on the high bar. Despite dozens of attempts and much support from onlookers he could still not manage to raise his body above the bar. Intense imagery did not seem to have an immediate effect. But, following a week's lay off, the first attempt produced success. Somehow, there was a 'Eureka' effect and everything clicked!

Different types of imagery

In its broadest sense imagery constitutes any kind of conscious thinking whether it be of an event, movement, situation or series of actions. It might be a process of re-construction where say a performance which has already been executed is reviewed and 'run again' (either, as it was, or should have been), or it could be a process of construction where a proposed or anticipated performance is 'previewed'. It might be purely visual in nature in which case the learner watches themself or another per-former undertaking an activity (visual imagery) or it might be kinesthetic in which case the learner goes through a technique and tries to imagine muscular and joint sensations, as well as the timing, forces and positions of the various movements. Imagery might also incorporate sensations of hearing, smell and taste. Hale (1998) distinguishes between internal and external imagery. External imagery is where the individual tries to see themselves from an outside perspective (like watching a video performance). With internal imagery, the individual looks are themselves through their own eyes and also feels their own muscular contractions and movement sensations. Hale suggests that external imagery is most appropriate for beginners; internal imagery is best used when skills are well learned.

It is thought that visual imagery is appropriate for less experienced learners because it is much easier to visualise than to recall or construct kinesthetic sensations. The expert is better prepared to use kinesthetic imagery because they possess better defined self-images and are able to recall internal feelings with greater consistency. For the same reason it may be easier for beginners to visualise others performing rather than themselves. Cox (1986) pursues this line by suggesting that it is better for learners to model their imagery on the performance of good technicians, especially those who are personally known to or admired by the learner. The logic here is that mental images formed by observing good performers are likely to be more accurate than those formed from introspection alone.

When is imagery useful?

Competition: Imagery is thought to have a number of desirable benefits. It can be used to help performers psychologically warm-up, especially at times when there is a time lapse between physical warm up and action competition. In this regard imagery helps the performer prepare 'body and mind' for activity and helps control/ focus their attention on the task in hand. Greenbank (1991) suggests mental imagery can be an effective way of reviewing failure and of curing related anxieties – especially in high risk sports. Many authors go as far to suggest that mental rehearsal should be an essential part of the individual's preparation for competition. It may be a particularly valuable aid at times during injury, whilst travelling or at other times when not practicing.

> **KEY QUOTE**
>
> *"Whilst mental practice is not a substitute for physical practice, there is evidence to suggest that it can play a complementary role. It is especially useful for rehearsing more complex movements, for preparing for action, while resting between bouts of physical activity and as an alternative to physical practice when injured."*
> **Archontides et al (1994)**

Learning: Schmidt and Wrisberg (2000) report that imagery is especially effective when the skills being learned contain a large cognitive component involving mental activity centred on strategies, critical cues and complex instructions. Imagery then provides learners with an opportunity to think through the task before they act. It will be recalled that the early stages of learning (see Chapter 2) are heavily influenced by cognitive processes; imagery may therefore be a very natural process for learners. In actual practice, it may be best for learners to visualise just prior to their performance, particularly if the activity is of brief duration as in high jumping or sprint starting. Attention is then focused on crucial elements of a movement and minimises the effects of potentially distracting influences. Thus a child attempting a vault might imagine themselves complete the whole action as well as the three phases – approach, flight on, flight off – in sequence. Following an attempt at the vault, they could imagine once more and compare what was expected with actual performance. The sequence – imagery, practice, imagery – is commonly used by learners and competitors alike and evidence shows that the best strategy for beginners is to alternate imagery with physical practice (Etnier and Landers, 1996).

Imagery is only beneficial if the skill level of the learner is reasonably consistent. This implies the learner must have already undergone an extended period of physical practice. It is therefore of little value for those who have never experienced a skill; learners can only profit from imagery if the input is good! The point here is that models must be technically correct or else the learner rehearses techniques that are wrong with the risk of generating errors in practice. Cox (1986) makes the point that when someone imagines another person performing, the model being rehearsed should be of someone whose performance has been studied many times at close hand. In addition, the model must not be too far removed from the learner's own style and performance level. This would seem to make sense from what was said in Chapter 5 about positive transfer. However, as has been emphasised elsewhere in this book, it is not essential for demonstrations by other learners to be technically perfect; it is sufficient for the essential movement pattern to be conveyed.

> **⊙⊐KEY POINT**
>
> Potential Uses for Imagery:
> • Practice of specific performance skills
> • Improving confidence and positive thinking
> • Tactical rehearsal and problem solving
> • Controlling arousal and anxiety
> • Performance review and analysis
> • Preparation for performance
> • Within pre-performance routines
> • Maintaining mental freshness during injury.
> **Bull et al** (1996)

Imagery is highly dependent on intrinsic motivation. It is extremely difficult to do if the learner doesn't believe in its importance. Highly motivated people automatically think a lot about their sport and are more likely to accept imagery as a viable training aid. For those who are not motivated to improve their skill levels by using imagery techniques, there is little point in trying.

The imagery process

Imagery is a learned skill that takes considerable time and dedication to develop fully.

Some people find it very difficult if not impossible to do. The fact is that one cannot just decide to 'have a go' and expect immediate results. For one thing, imagery demands a relaxed state of mind and this itself demands control and practice (see later). Also, the learner needs to know how to do it. Learning how to rehearse comes about through practice and evaluation. Beginners to imagery can recite to themselves or speak to another person. Another person questions the learner about rehearsal strategies. Bull (1991) argues for individualised mental training programmes. Hale (1998) recommends that imagery can be effective if the 'user' follows a number of criteria. He cites the 4Rs, viz.,:

• *Relaxation.* The individual must be relaxed in mind and body to enable total involvement in imagery exercises.
• *Realism.* Images must be realistic and technically perfect. Practice should be the same as the way the person wants to perform or play. Aspects such as clarity, vividness, control and emotion should all help to make images real.
• *Regularity.* Imagery should be practiced regularly (every day) to have any positive transfer effect.
• *Reinforcement.* The quality and control of imagery is aided using video footage to refine and confirm performance problems.

The problem with any kind of conscious mental activity is that the mind is very limited in the amount of information it can handle at any one time. For example, it is very easy to forget a telephone number before dialling is complete. Imagery therefore, has to be concentrated and focused. This presents problems for activities such as team games which extend over time and generate a considerable amount of changing information. Imagery is still applicable in these circumstances, but the activity must be broken down into smaller segments. Thus a football player might rehearse a series of set plays or attacking tactics (in turn), whilst a swimmer might rehearse each length of a distance swim. Another strategy would be to visualise a lengthy activity in its entirety first (e.g., a long rock climb or a gymnastic tumbling routine) and then start again, but focus only on certain parts. The same problem does not exist for repetitive or short-duration activities such as high jumping, or tennis serving. Here, the learner does not have such an information overload problem and can probably rehearse the action many times before actual practice.

> ### KEY QUOTE
>
> *"... psychological skills are honed and developed in the same way that physical skills are. Exceptionally talented athletes have to practice, work on, and plan how to use their psychological skills just as they do their physical skills."*
> **Brown** (2001)

Most authorities agree that imagery should mirror as closely as possible the exact circumstances which exist in practice, even to using the same equipment, clothing, footwear and working area. In addition, movements should be rehearsed in their entirety (it would be pointless – and perhaps impossible – to stop a somersault in mid-flight or rehearse a high jump approach without the actual jump or follow through) and at the same speed as actual performance. This principle is based on the 'neural model' of imagery mentioned previously which proposes that actual performance and imagery stimulate the same underlying nervous mechanisms. Imagery should also have a successful outcome. The rehearsal of errors is likely to increase the possibility of errors in performance. It is not easy to think always in such a positive manner especially for a learner. Imagery also demands a lot of self-discipline, which again underlines its learned nature.

Imagery is thought to be most effective if it includes sensations of feel as well as the sight. Kinesthetic imagery provides a 'richer' experience than just a visual picture. This technique however, is only useful with advanced learners who are more attuned to the feel of their movements. Finally, it is agreed that imagery must take place when the individual is in a relaxed state of mind. A person who is anxious or thinking about other matters will not be able to focus their attention correctly. Relaxation is an essential foundation upon which the skills required for imagery are built. There are many relaxation techniques each of which is based on focused attention. People can focus on different things such as breathing patterns or alternate contraction and relax-ation of muscles. It is not relevant to discuss these here but it might be useful to quote from Hardy and Fazey (1986) who describe the technique known as Progressive Muscular Relaxation:

"Sit or lie down in your chosen position. Breathe slowly with your lips apart. Concentrate on the slowing of your breathing pattern. I shall begin counting from one to fifteen. As I count, gradually increase the tension in your muscles. One. Two. Three: squeeze your muscles slightly harder, tense as many of the muscles in your body as you can. Four. Five. Six: clench your fists. Seven. Eight. Nine. Ten. Tense your thighs. Eleven. Twelve: squeeze harder. Thirteen: and now really hard. Fourteen: and finally as hard as you can. Fifteen: and relax. Focus on your breathing, and relax for a moment. Feel the relaxation spreading and enjoy the sensation of the easing tension. In a moment or two we shall repeat the exercise. etc."

Methods such as these require both time to learn and time to apply and therefore are not appropriate for beginners. At best, beginners should be encouraged to visualise during practice sessions and especially just before and immediately following activity. As they gain experience they may be introduced to sophisticated methods of relaxation and imagery which can be employed outside the training environment. At advanced skill levels, there is little doubt that athletes benefit from relaxation and imagery techniques, but their complex nature should always be born in mind. Miller (1991) puts forward a good case for an integrated approach to imagery which co-ordinates with the whole competition schedule.

MOTIVATION

"I told this player – 'Listen son, you haven't broken your leg. It's all in the mind'"
Bill Shankly (former Liverpool football team manager)

A simple way to understanding the topic of motivation is to examine the reasons why people take part in sport. Woods (1998) lists five categories:

• To learn and improve motor skills
• For fitness and health benefits
• To make friends or be with like-minded people
• To compete against others and win
• For excitement and challenge.

This list is derived from research evidence as well as reports from teachers, coaches and learners. But it doesn't give a very structured account of motivation.

Motivation is inextricably bound up with attitudes, drives, feelings, expectations, needs and aspirations. Motivation has both long and short-term qualities. It influences a person's decision to take part in sport as well as their will to persevere and practice over many years. In the short term, motivation can be responsible for the intensity or vigour with which a person performs, the momentary quality of their per-

> ## KEY QUOTE
>
> *"Motivation is defined as some inner drive, impulse, intention, etc., that causes a person to do something or act in a certain way."*
> **Matheson And Mace** (2001)

formance, as well as the variability in skill which occurs from one occasion to the next. Many agree that motivation is a major force that attracts people to sport and encourages them to learn and succeed. Highly motivated people tend to devote greater effort to their learning, are more conscientious and prepared to work for longer periods. People who are less motivated or not motivated at all, practice very little and show little interest or enthusiasm to learn. In the long term, motivation is the factor which keeps people involved over many years, often when things are tough or very difficult. So, motivation is something that drives people towards particular goals. It is also useful to think of motivation as something with both intrinsic and extrinsic dimensions. When a person does something for personal satisfaction, feeling of competence or self esteem (e.g., climbing a mountain for the first time) we say they do it for intrinsic reasons. If, on the other hand, a person does something for outside gain (e.g., they climb a mountain to raise funds for a worthy cause) then we say they are motivated for extrinsic reasons. Often, both apply; beginners try hard not only to improve their skills but also to please their peers.

A variety of theories exist which attempt to explain why people behave in the way

that they do. Three are identified by
Matheson and Mace (2001). They refer
to hedonistic, competence and achievement theories. The hedonistic approach
asserts that individuals involve themselves in things because they derive
pleasure and satisfaction. They do not
take part in things that may bring them
discomfort or suffering. Competence
theory argues that people are driven to
acquire sets of skills; they desire to play
the piano or learn how to juggle.
Achievement theory focuses on people's
need to achieve and to be successful in
the presence of others.

Extreme motivation can often overcome
physical (environmental) limitations!

The intention in this section is not to provide a comprehensive analysis of the subject, but
to present some broad ideas that demonstrate the relevance of motivation during learning.

Motivation, arousal and anxiety

Motivation is often linked to the words *arousal* and *anxiety*. Arousal is related to a
state of readiness and anticipation. It involves both physiological activity (e.g., raising
of heart rate and pupil dilation) and cognitive activity (e.g., focusing of attention).
Arousal lies on an intensity continuum from very low (fast asleep) to very high
(responding to a fire alarm). A given degree of arousal is necessary in order to carry
out any task successfully such as kicking a ball, engaging in conversation or coaching
an athlete. It is important to note that arousal is not necessarily positive or negative.
A person can become equally aroused by winning a large sum of money or learning of
the death of a near relative. In contrast, anxiety is a negative emotional state generated by a threatening situation. It is a form of fear or apprehension as experienced
when, for example, a beginner gymnast attempts their first unaided somersault.
Anxiety can be classified in two ways. Trait anxiety is a stable, personality characteristic that reflects an individual's behaviour in many different situations. Thus, someone who becomes anxious easily even when circumstances are non-threatening is considered to have a high trait anxiety. State anxiety is a short-term emotional response
to a particular situation. Someone who feels very apprehensive at the start of a football match experiences high state anxiety. Some one who does not react in the same
manner has low state anxiety. State anxiety has both cognitive and somatic dimensions.
Cognitive anxiety is a feeling of nervousness or apprehension. Somatic anxiety is the
conscious feeling of internal sensations or the heart beating faster.

Arousal, then, is a general (body/mind) response that is neither negative or positive, whereas anxiety is a negative response to potentially threatening situations. There are a number of theories as to how arousal level affects performance. An early theory (Drive Theory) proposed that as someone becomes more aroused, their performance improves. It does so because increased arousal predisposes a person to respond in a particular way. If that

response is a skilful one then the more aroused they are, the more likely they are to respond skilfully. Thus, expert performers are more likely to respond better under pressure because their favoured or dominant response is likely to be a skilful one. On the other hand, beginners are less likely to perform well under pressure since they have fewer (if any) dominant responses. An alternative theory (called the Inverted-U Hypothesis) predicts that performance improves with increasing levels of arousal, but only to a point. If arousal level increases beyond this point then performance begins to deteriorate. This theory is intuitive but is highly simplified (see *Figure 4*).

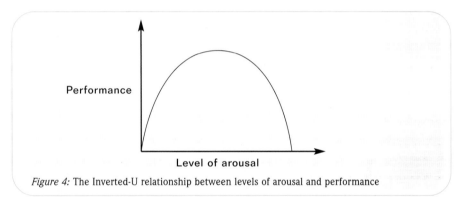

Figure 4: The Inverted-U relationship between levels of arousal and performance

It is argued that the optimal level of arousal depends on many factors such as the individual's personality, stage of learning and type of task. Thus, the optimal level might be much lower if the person is easily stressed or if the task is highly complex. In practice, the relationship between performance and arousal is not always so continuous. Sometimes, performance drops off dramatically with arousal level. Hardy (1990) argues that the relationship is compounded by the level of anxiety experienced by the individual. He suggests that if arousal levels are at their optimum for a given task and if the individual's level of cognitive activity is also high, then any further increase in arousal will result in a large and sudden decrease in performance. Cognitive anxiety or degree of nervousness can have a major impact on a person's performance and that is why it is very important to control such factors when people are performing at crucial events. There are a number of useful texts that give a more detailed treatise on these topics (e.g., Woods, 1998; LeUnes and Nation, 2002).

What are the implications for skill acquisition? There are two key points. If anxiety can have a negative influence on performance then it makes sense to ensure the coaching/

teaching environment does not exaggerate the learner's level of anxiety. This could happen if, for example, a new skill seems unsafe to someone or if the presence of other learners increases their apprehension or worry. The key here lies in the coach's or teacher's power of observation to judge whether the learner appears to be under too much stress. They should be particularly sensitive to individuals whose trait anxiety level is high. Most teachers and coaches usually know their athletes although this shouldn't present too much of a problem. When a problem does surface however, the important

Motivation is often reflected in intense concentration

thing is to do something about it by changing the situation to reduce anxiety levels. The second point bears on the Inverted-U Hypothesis described before. Performance is best when arousal levels are optimal. Arousal level is dictated in part by the interest value of the skill to be practiced. This in turn is a function of factors such as the level of challenge presented by the skill and its relevance to the learner. Thus, if the learner shows little interest because the skill appears unchallenging and irrelevant, then it is likely they will not try very hard to acquire the new skill; practice may be quite meaningless. The important thing is for the teacher or coach to raise arousal levels so they generate maximum effort and performance. How this is done is situation specific, but there are many strategies available:

- Relate new learning to previously learned skills
- Encourage learners to assess their own performance/errors
- Find out from learners what they wish to learn
- Provide positive feedback
- Ensure practice is relevant to the skills being learned
- Maintain constant challenges
- Move on to new skills or different practices before boredom sets in
- Encourage peer learning
- Completely change the activity.

Reinforcement motivation

In Chapter 4 it was noted that feedback plays an informative role as well as a motivational one. Feedback has the power to motivate because it reinforces good performance. There are four types of reinforcers that teachers or coaches can use to assist motivation, viz., social, material, performance and internal reinforcers:

• Social reinforcers encompass the positive benefits that can be gained from the presence or comments of other people. The coach may signal "very well done" or a friend may congratulate the learner on a particularly successful effort. Comments like these or just public displays of performance provide attention and demonstrate approval and recognition by other people. Learners can be drawn to try hard and perform well because they wish to please their coach or teacher, particularly if they have high respect for that person. Social reinforcement is a very powerful motivator.

• Material reinforcers take the form of tangible items such as certificates, badges, etc. Rewards like these, which characterise most proficiency award schemes, are useful because they provide concrete proof of success and recognition of performance. They also help formulate status within peer groups. They are especially valuable when young people embark on a new skill, but their effect diminishes with learning as internal satisfactions take over. They have little value for adult learners.

• Performance reinforcers such as time taken, number of attempts and accuracy achieved, provide learners with specific information about performance and serve to give direction to the learner's efforts. As with material reinforcers they also facilitate social approval. They often have a longer lasting effect than material rewards and are equally powerful with youngsters and adults.

• Internal reinforcers include feelings which learner's experience and the personal goals realised during the learning process. For example, a youngster who learns to swim unaided may feel fitter/healthier or more independent than before. These feelings help the youngster maintain interest in swimming and may generate new goals such as a desire to learn to dive or compete. The sense of satisfaction someone gains from learning a new or challenging skill or finding out they have hidden talents are examples of internal motivators.

These four categories are not mutually exclusive. Any single event may have a number of consequences. For example, swimming the length of a pool for the first time may produce social approval from friends, stimulate internal satisfaction and also provide a yardstick for improvement.

With regard to the impact of reinforcement motivation in learning there are a number of issues. External reinforcement and materialistic rewards such as badges, praise, prestige, etc., (the first three reinforcers as defined above) tend to be less important than internal goals such as self esteem, self expression, personal satisfaction and self fulfilment. It is considered that the development of intrinsic motivation leads to more satisfying and long lasting results. Although internal and external motivators operate together with one sometimes being more dominant, external ones are usually shorter lived in their influence than internal ones. One particular exception is with beginners who are often attracted to sport and stimulated to learn new skills because of tangible external rewards such as certificates and medals. These often bring status, pride and satisfaction to learners. However, in time, external reinforcers are overtaken by internal motivators that keep people engaged and encourage greater persistence and performance. In fact, learning in several ways is reflected in a change from dependence on extrinsic sources of motivation/information to internally generated sources.

There are a number of additional points about reinforcement that should be highlighted at this point. These were first described in Chapter 4. Firstly, it is not essential for reinforcement always to be positive. Reinforcement in the form of praise is beneficial but only to a point. Constant praise soon ceases to have an effect and learners should recognise that from time to time they will be told that things are wrong. How the coach or teacher handles these occasions needs to be treated with care if some learners are not to be discouraged. Secondly, coaches should determine the most effective way of providing reinforcement. A coach may find that personal comments carry more weight than performance scores. Or that the presence of a particular learner within a group spurs on the rest by a disproportionate amount. A sensitive coach should recognise the 'group dynamics' in any situation and maximise those which have the best effect. Thirdly, reinforcement should be individual-based. Comments such as "good work team" or "that's the way to go" are often ineffective, particularly if they are repeated. This applies especially to beginners who are searching for clear, personal signs of success and approval. The coach also needs to be sensitive to how learners react to feedback. Some who do not perform according to expectations will lose self-confidence and motivation. Others who are 'emotionally tougher' will respond to harsh words from the coach. Further, timing is critical. Reinforcement should be supplied immediately success is observed. Every 'teaching moment' should be used to reward learners. Finally, reinforcement should be variable in its type and emphasis. This refers to the richness of the coach's vocabulary, the manner in which his/her voice is used (change in volume, pitch, emphasis) and the extent of non-verbal communication (facial expression, use of gesture, physical contact with the learner).

Achievement motivation

Attempts to encourage motivation should acknowledge individual differences between learners – a sensitivity to differences with regard to personality, reaction to incentives, need to achieve, etc., is critical if the optimal level of arousal (motivation) is to be achieved for each learner.

> **KEY QUOTE**
>
> *"Passion plus vision plus action is the equation for success"*
> **Marilyn King**
> (Olympic pentathlete)

A person's aspiration level – the goals they expect to achieve – often determines the level of performance achieved. In part, aspiration level is dictated by previous successes and failures. It is well known for example, that satisfying experiences lead to continued enthusiasm and success. Coaches and teachers can ensure learners maintain high aspirations by reducing the chances of continual failure. This, in turn, is achieved by making sure learners are confident and aware of their realistic potentials. There are implications here with regard to setting practical and specific goals for learners as well as making true appraisals of their past performance. It is worth mentioning that people sometimes fear success because it brings responsibility and prestige they cannot handle. A shy person who is very skilful may not realise their full potential because they cannot cope with the peer recognition that comes with success. Problems like these will be detected by the perceptive coach and need to be managed in a thoughtful manner. It should also be mentioned that a common reason for failure is low self esteem – those who say they won't do very well, often end up not doing well. Level of aspiration can work both for and against the learner!

Level of aspiration represents an individual's expected or desired performance level. It is linked to the concept of 'need for achievement'. Some investigators have examined the concept of need achievement as a way of measuring differences in motivation between people and also explaining why some people are more highly motivated than others. Need achievement has been defined by LeUnes and Nation (2002) as a person's drive to "… overcome obstacles, to exercise power, to strive to do something difficult as well as quickly as possible." Put simply, a person's need achievement represents their motivation to succeed as well as their desire to avoid failure. It is a combination of both factors. It is considered to be a fairly stable personality trait and is highly specific to both the situation and the individual. People who possess a high need to achieve can be described quite well. They tend to be extremely persistent, work hard and fast, take reasonable risk, enjoy stress, like to take personal responsibility for their actions and need detailed knowledge of the results of their performances. People who possess a strong motive to avoid failure tend to be over-concerned about failure, avoid challenging tasks, perform worse when evaluated by others and often attribute failure to outside situations (e.g., other people, luck). Wood (1998) suggests that everyone possesses each of these motives to a certain degree, but it is the difference between the motive to succeed and the motive to avoid failure that defines the level of a person's achievement motivation.

The concept of need achievement tells something about the manner in which people habitually think about themselves; a person's level of need achievement may indicate how good they perceive themselves to be. It has been argued that the development of need achievement hinges on an interactive process where ideas can be exchanged and understanding improved. Cox (1998) suggests for example, that someone whose fear of failure is high and motive to succeed low can be assisted through some sort of extrinsic motivator. He says that outside rewards can be effectively used to encourage children who are fearful and high in the motive to avoid failure to participate in sport when otherwise they would not. It seems that skill and need achievement can be developed through close learner/coach relationships. The importance of the coach's or teacher's involvement in shaping the motivations of learners and developing a positive attitude to learning can be highly significant.

Teacher/coach expectations

It is well known that factors outside the individual's control can influence their interests in sport and how well they perform. For example, cultural influences create ambitions and encourage interests in particular sports (cricket is popular in Great Britain and India but not N. America). Social expectations created by family, friends and peers can also act as forceful motivators. For example, it has been shown that the presence of other people tends to dampen the performance of lowly skilled individuals and raise the performance of the highly skilled. There are implications here for the way in which groups of beginners are organised; individuals should not see themselves as focal points 'on trial' – especially those with high trait anxiety. The coach has to balance potential difficulties like this with the benefits to be gained by learners working together in a group.

Another potentially important influence on the learner is the nature of the learning context. Research has shown that situations can be contrived in which people think they can do better than expected. As a consequence, they do perform better when in fact there is no scientific basis for them doing so. For instance, in the medical world it has been shown that patients suffering from severe and persistent headaches often improve when they are given medication which they believe to be useful when, in fact, it contains nothing more than an inert substance such as sugar. In education, the same thing happens under the banner of 'teacher expectations'. Here, pupils can often do better than predicted because the teacher 'expects' them to do well. With regard to coaching, there are implications for the attitude adopted by coaches in relation to what they expect of learners. The coach who sets high standards and creates a positive atmosphere that is safe and successful, will 'push' people along to greater effort and skill levels through positive expectation alone. If the coach can encourage learners to believe they have the potential to succeed and surround them with an air of expectancy and success, it is likely the learner will rise to the occasion. This is probably one reason why many successful sports clubs (e.g., Manchester United football club) as well as individuals achieve consistently well over many years – 'success breeds success'!

Attribution theory

Attribution theory is concerned with the reasons people give to explain some aspect of their behaviour (or that of other people). For example, "why did I fail to score from the penalty kick?", "why did he overtake me when he did?" or "why did I beat my opponent today but not the last time we played each other?" The theory attempts to categorise the attributions (reasons) people give for their successes and failures. It is reasoned this can help explain a number of questions – why people persist in their sport, what their expectations are, how satisfied they are and their level of performance. In this sense attribution theory provides some clues about people's motivations. Research has shown that when people are asked to explain why they failed or succeeded, they provide reasons that can be classified as due to ability, effort, task difficulty or simple luck. Further, these attributions can be sub-divided into internal or external and stable or unstable. An internal attribution is one related to the individual, such as "I have poor co-ordination" or "it was a lack of concentration". External attributions relate to the environment, such as "the weather turned sour just at the wrong moment" or "the other player was more skilled". Stable attributions are relatively unchanging, such as "I lack the skill" or "the ground is always in poor condition". Unstable attributions are less stable and may vary greatly, such as "I had a tummy bug" or "it rained in the middle of the race". These four categories are summarised in *Table 2*.

	Internal Attribution	External Attribution
Stable Attribution	Not tall enough	Opposition always fitter
Unstable Attribution	Had a bad cold	Noise from the crowd

Table 2: The four categories of attribution with examples

Interestingly, people do not always offer the correct attributions. There is a tendency for people to attribute success to internal sources and failure to external ones. It is thought that people do this to protect their self esteem. This is a general view that is not true for everyone. For example, high need achievers tend to attribute success to internal sources. They also attribute failure to unstable factors and are more likely to persist after failure in the knowledge that unstable conditions can change. In contrast, low need achievers tend to attribute failure to stable factors and consequently give up in the belief they cannot change anything. Evidence also shows that as athletes mature and become more experienced they tend to internalise their attributions focusing more on their own limitations and strengths and less on outside influences. Interestingly, this also reflects the gradual shift in feedback control as learners become more able to sense and analyse internal sources of feedback with practice (see Chapter 4).

What are the implications of attribution theory for skill acquisition? In general terms it predicts that motivation and high achievement are, in large part, a function of cognitive variables – how people think about situations and understand their strengths and limitations. On this basis, teachers and coaches should facilitate this process by engaging learners in the learning process so they come to understand and accept their potentials and weaknesses. Specifically, attribution theory highlights the value of talking to learners and ascertaining their views about their learning goals, aspirations and difficulties. At higher levels of performance, 'attribution retraining' can be used to help individuals develop attributions that improve performance. This has been shown to be particularly valuable for young and older athletes whose aspirations are lower than their potentials. Further discussion of this topic is outside the scope of this book but is covered in some detail by Woods (1998) and Cox (1998).

SUMMARY OF THE KEY POINTS

• Skilled performance as well as skill learning depends on the refinement of technique and is inextricably linked to 'mental' factors such as imagery, motivation and need achievement.

• The Inner Game approach to learning addresses both the physical and mental components in sport.

• Proponents of the Inner Game advocate that:
  • traditional teaching methods are too technically oriented
  • critical self-analysis by the learner is an obstacle to success
  • learners have a potential to learn which is often never revealed
  • trust and confidence in the learner must be engendered by both the learner and the coach
  • enhancing body awareness is one of the major keys to successful learning.

• Goal setting is an important strategy for learners and coaches.

• Clear goals increase confidence and provide direction for practice.

• Long term goals should be broken down into intermediate and short-term goals.

• Goals should be specific, individually oriented, challenging, attainable, realistic and measurable.

• Product goals are appropriate in the long term whilst process goals are more applicable in the short term.

• Imagery can be a valuable aid to learning. There are a number of theories as to why it works, e.g.,, physiological, perceptual.

• Imagery can be both internal and external in nature and take advantage of all the major senses.

• Imagery is beneficial for learners (especially external imagery) but is especially useful for experts. It is a learned skill in its own right.

• Motivation has both short-term and long-term qualities and is responsible, among other things, for the intensity with which a person performs/learns as well as the extent of their commitment to sport.

• Reinforcement has four dimensions, viz., social, material, performance and internal reinforcement. They are not mutually exclusive.

• Need achievement has been defined as a person's drive to "... overcome obstacles, to exercise power, to strive to do something difficult as well as quickly as possible." Put simply, it represents their motivation to succeed as well as their desire to avoid failure.

• Good teaching/coaching recognises the individual nature of motivation with regard to, e.g., personality, values, achievement need, reaction to incentives, the situation and the task in hand.

• Arousal is neither negative or positive whilst anxiety is a negative agent. The classic relationship between arousal level and performance is inverted-U in nature.

• A person's performance level and 'will to improve' can be influenced greatly by how they are perceived by those around them – coaches, parents, peers. Sometimes people perform as well as they are expected to perform.

• Attribution theory attempts to explain why people succeed/fail in their sport. Typically, when people are asked to explain why they fail or succeed, they provide reasons that can be classified as due to ability, effort, task difficulty or simple luck. Further, these reasons can be sub-divided into internal or external and stable or unstable.

PRACTICAL TASKS

• This task investigates the effect of an audience on performance. Start with a group of four people. One person is a time recorder and the other three are subjects. Each subject – separately – adopts the following position for as long as they can until fatigued (recorder note the time). The position is resting with back to a wall with ankles, knees and hips at 90 degrees and arms hanging to the side. Each person does this separately. The following day, the three subjects do the same, but this time together. A comparison of each subject's time on both days should show improved performance on the second day. This reveals the beneficial influence of an audience which increases arousal and consequently helps to sustain performance.

• This task is designed to illustrate the beneficial effects of imagery. Select three people. Each will learn a simple line drawing task (how to draw a straight line 20 cms in length). Each person is given a sheet of paper on which is drawn a straight line 20 cms long. Their first task is to copy the line by drawing another line the same length under the original one. They repeat this five times. Now, one person continues to do this at their own pace a further 15 times. The second person closes their eyes and imagines doing the task 15 times. The third person does not practice at all but is engaged in distracting conversation by someone else. Following this, each person is required to draw a 20 cm line five times, but with their eyes closed. The average error for each trial is recorded to give an average performance value. According to the theory, the 'physical practice' person should perform best followed by the 'imagery' person followed by the 'no practice' person.

REVIEW QUESTIONS

• Take a sport in which you coach or teach. Would you say you dwell too much on technical matters at the expense of others such as the learner's goals and motivations?

• In your own learning can you remember occasions when you have been too self-critical of your performance? Was this a good or bad thing?

• What are the disadvantages of self criticism? List say, three points.

• Can you think of any evidence to support Gallway's view that the potential of most learners is rarely realised?

• Take a sport familiar to you. What steps would you take to direct the learner's attention to the 'process' of movement instead of the 'product' of movement? In other words, how would you sensitise the learner to internal feedback?

• Is it necessary to talk to learners about the precise goals for every training session?

• How easy is it to establish goals for large groups of learners? Does 'ability grouping' help?

• How would a coach assess whether or not a particular goal was attainable?

• What reasons militate against the use of imagery with beginners?

• When would a player in a team game such as hockey, employ imagery during the game itself?

• Do you think that 'visual' rehearsal is appropriate for open skills such as team games, whereas 'kinesthetic' rehearsal is more appropriate for closed skills such as gymnastics?

• How important is the coach's belief in the learner? Do you think people can be pushed to higher levels if they are made to think they have the potential?

• Think once again of a sport or pursuit you engage in. When your performance is less than expected, how do you explain this? Can you explain it in terms of attribution theory as described in this chapter?

• And with your sport again. What motivates you to take part? Can you explain your involvement in terms of reinforcement motivation. Has this changed over time?

References

Archontides, C., Fazey, J., Smith, N., and Crisfield, P. (1994). *Understanding and improving skill* (Coach resource pack). Leeds: National Coaching Foundation.

Brown, J. (2001). *Sports talent: how to identify and develop outstanding athletes.* Champaign, Illinois: Human Kinetics.

Bull, S.J. (1991). Personal and situational influences on adherence to mental skills training. *Journal of Sport and Exercise Psychology,* 13, 121 - 132.

Bull, S.J., Albinson, J.G. and Shambrook, C.J. (1996). *The mental game plan – getting psyched for sport.* Cheltenham: Sports Dynamics.

Cox, R. (1998). *Sport psychology: Concepts and applications.* London: McGraw Hill.

Cox, R. (1986). *Psychological preparation for competition – mental rehearsal* (Coach Education Module 8). Edinburgh: The Scottish Sports Council.

Cram, S. (2003). *Comment made during World Athletic Championship,* August, 2003.

Crimble, S. (1982). *Inner sport – a look in.* Scottish Journal of Physical Education, 10, 1 - 3.

Foxon, F. (1999). *Improving practices and skill.* Leeds: The National Coaching Foundation.

Gallway, T. and Kriegal, R.(1977) *Inner skiing*. New York: Random House.

Greenbank, A. (1991) *All in the mind*. Climber & Hillwalker, XXX, 12, 40 - 42.

Hale, B. (1998). *Imagery training: a guide for sports coaches and performers*. Leeds: The National Coaching Foundation.

Hardy, L. (1986). *How can we help performers?* Coaching Focus, 4, 2 - 3.

Hardy, L. (1990). *Importance of psychological factors in affect on performance*. Coaching Focus, 15, 4 - 5.

Hardy, L. and Fazey, J. (1986). *Mental preparation for competition* (Key course resource pack). Leeds: National Coaching Foundation.

Hird, J.S., Landers, D.M., Thomas, J.R. and Horan, J.J. (1991). Physical practice is superior to mental practice in enhancing cognitive and motor task performance. *Journal of Sport and Exercise Psychology*, 8, 281 - 293.

LeUnes, A. and Nation, J.R. (2002). *Sport psychology: An introduction*. Pacific Grove, California: Wadsworth.

Matheson, H. and Mace, R. (2001). *Skill in sport*. Droitwich: Sport in Mind.

Matthews, S. (1991). Sports psychology: A consumer perspective. *The Psychologist, 4*, 4, April.

McQuade, S. (2003). *How to coach sports effectively*. Leeds: Coachwise Solutions.

Miller, B. *Mental preparation for competition – a system for success*. (1991). Coaching Focus, 18, 3 - 5.

Miller, B. (1991). *Mental preparation technique for racing and training*. CoDe (Newsletter of the British Canoe Union).

Miles, A. (2003). *What is sports coaching?* Leeds: Coachwise solutions.

Mutrie, N. (1985). *Goal setting*. Coach Education Modules. Edinburgh: The Scottish Sports Council.

National Coaching Foundation. (1986). *Improving Techniques*. Leeds: National

Coaching Foundation.

Rintala, J. (1991). The mind-body revisited. *QUEST,* 43, 260 - 279.

Schmidt, R.A. and Wrisberg, C.A. (2000). *Motor learning and performance* (2nd Edition). Champaign, Illinois: Human Kinetics.

Shedden, J. (1982). *Skilful skiing.* East Ardsley, West Yorks: EP Publishing Ltd.

Woods, B. (1998). *Applying psychology to sport.* London: Hodder and Stoughton Educational.

CHAPTER 8 – TEACHING AND LEARNING STYLES

"As individuals we each have different rules for learning which is driven by our own interpretation of new experiences and knowledge from an early age. How much any individual learns is very much related to whether the educational experience is geared towards their particular style of learning rather than how intelligent they are, or from what social background they may come from. In essence the question to be asked is not 'how bright is the individual' but 'how is the individual bright?'"

Grant (2002)

INTRODUCTION

In the past ten years there has been an increasing interest shown by various organisations (especially Government departments) in teaching 'methods', 'styles' and 'approaches' (Mawer, 1999; Miles, 2003; Williams, 1996). This is especially notable within secondary education and physical education in particular where Mosston (e.g., Mosston and Ashworth, 1986) has taken the lead. Lyle (2002) discusses the importance of this within the context of coaching

> **KEY QUOTE**
>
> *"Whatever it is that dictates our preferred learning style, an understanding of these various styles plays an important role in the instructor's ability to instruct/teach and the learner's ability to learn."*
> **Grant** (2002)

and suggests that coaching style is a fundamental aspect of coaching practice. There are a number of principles common to both teaching and coaching that will be addressed in this chapter.

Why is there an increased focus on teaching styles today? It seems this has arisen for two essential reasons. Firstly, today's society is much more aware of differences between people in terms of their culture, heritage, age, abilities and potentials. As a result, there has arisen a need to adopt strategies to meet these differences. This is part of an increasing concern for the needs of the individual in society, equal opportunities and recognition that individuals and minority groups are as important as larger social groupings. Secondly, education today attaches greater importance to developing skills beyond the retention of subject-based knowledge. Skills involving analysis, critique, judgement and interpretation involve the learner more deeply and can be transferred to situations quite different from the subject being studied. In order to develop and nurture skills like these there has had to be a re-think about the approaches undertaken by teachers and consequently an increased focus on how individuals learn. Consequently, a full discussion of how people acquire skill must also account for the various ways in which people learn and teach. Let's examine learning styles and some current thinking on some of the most commonly used categories.

INDIVIDUAL DIFFERENCES

As a result of heredity, upbringing and environmental demands, different individuals have different talents, interests, life styles and work styles. We all perceive and process information differently and as a result, see the world in different ways. It has even been suggested that we all think differently. To place some order on the subject, Gregorc (1981) has identified four separate groups distinguished in terms of how they think – concrete/abstract and sequential/random. He defines the four categories in the following manner:

• Concrete sequential thinkers process information in an ordered, linear, sequential manner. They focus on details and tend to break problems down into specific steps.

• Concrete random thinkers tend to experiment and adopt a trial and error approach to problem solving. They look at problems from more than one viewpoint and possess a strong desire to find alternatives.

• Abstract random thinkers are strongly guided by feelings and emotions. They operate best in unstructured, people-oriented environments.

• Abstract sequential thinkers are guided by theories and concepts. They think logically with thoroughness and rationality.

It is vital to note that although there are four distinct categories, probably very few people fully meet the descriptions of each one. It is more likely that each of us has a tendency towards one category, with elements of others also present. Some people may not fit a single category very well but reveal elements of all to

 **KEY POINT**

We all seem to adopt characteristic ways of Thinking and Learning that remain relatively stable across time and situations.

varying degrees at different times. Nevertheless, descriptions like these are very useful because they do lead to a better understanding of learners and their behaviour. Readers may care to ponder on this categorisation and judge where they might fit. Hopefully, they will find a 'home' in one of the four categories!

Differences like these go someway to explaining why people learn in different ways at varying rates and to varying levels of skill. We know that some people work best in the morning whilst others are 'night owls'. Some of us are mainly visual learners who like to see pictures and diagrams whilst others prefer to listen to explanations about what to do. Some people are referred to as haptic learners who learn best by using their tactile sense (touch) or through movement (kinesthesis). Others are print-oriented who prefer to learn by reading. It has been suggested that whilst people are able to learn in different ways most have preferences in one direction. Furthermore, it has been suggested that one of the biggest causes of failure by learners is the mismatch between their learning style and the teaching style 'imposed' on them. This is a very important point. It is vital for teachers, coaches and instructors to recognise and value these differences. The modern expression used to describe individual differences is 'differentiation'. Differentiation is a principle well established in both Primary and Secondary Education in the UK. Teachers are required to adopt procedures and practices which recognise differences between pupils and which also try to maximise the individual's potential. Indeed, Rink (1998) emphasises that:

"Instruction, regardless of its roots must meet particular learner needs. The task provided to the learner must be individually appropriate; the learner must have a clear idea of what he or she is expected to do and be motivated to engage at a high level with the task; the learner must have sufficient opportunity to learn the task; and, the learner must receive information on their performance."

In the world of sports coaching it goes without saying that the recognition of differences between people and the desire to improve the skill level of every learner are key aims for all coaches. This is particularly true at the high end of sport where coaches and athletes have very individualistic relationships. How do coaches and teachers differentiate between learners? The first thing for them to do is establish a 'mindset' that individuals are important. In other words, they must adopt a philosophy that individuals are more important than the group. This is a simple principle to understand but much more difficult to put into practice. It is easy teaching a relatively homogeneous group of learners a simple skill such as catching a ball or tying a knot but much more difficult to teach the same skill in a variety of ways suitable to each and every learner. It requires a degree of commitment and effort based on much experience. The second thing is to recognise that whilst everyone learns in different ways, there are certain broad approaches that all people adopt which simplifies the task of differentiation (note the four 'thinking' styles described before). This makes it possible to place individuals into broad categories according to their preferred learning 'style' rather than treat every person as a specific individual. This is not to suggest that members of a group are specifically identified, placed into groups and taught or coached according to their 'style' of learning. This could be divisive and would be highly impractical. Rather, knowing the kinds of ways in which people learn permits the teacher or coach to identify individual learning problems and approach them with strategies appropriate to the individual. It is rather like the teacher possessing a repertoire of approaches and methods, which can be bought in to play as and when required. Most of the time, one approach may be appropriate, but if the situation demands it (say a small group are experiencing a particular difficulty in learning how to execute a gymnastic cartwheel), then the teacher/coach can bring into play a method or tactic tailored to the requirements of that particular group. Let's now examine some of the broad ways in which people learn.

LEARNING STYLES

Honey and Mumford (1992) propose that through experience people display certain behaviour patterns that become habitual. With time, they come to adopt (learn) a particular style of learning that can be classified according to set criteria. It is their view that one of the major barriers to learning is the mismatch between a person's learning style and the teaching style of the coach or teacher. Further, they feel that people can be helped to become more effective learners if they are aware of their learning style preferences. They argue that whilst much research and development has examined teaching methods this has not been balanced by attention to differences in approaches to learning. They describe four learning styles.

Activists

Activists involve themselves fully in new experiences. They are open-minded and enthusiastic about anything new. Their philosophy is 'I'll try anything once'. They tend to act first and consider the consequences afterwards. Their time is filled with activity; as soon as the excitement from one activity has died down they are busy looking for the next. They enjoy high visibility and difficult challenges. In terms of learning, they oppose any kind of passive approach such as lectures or reading. They are not happy to reflect, spend time on preparation or practice the same activity many times.

Reflectors

Reflectors like to ponder experiences and observe problems from many different angles. They are happy to collect data and think about a problem thoroughly before coming to any conclusion. They tend to be cautious and thoughtful and enjoy observing other people in action. They listen to others before making their own points and only act when fully aware of the wide picture. They are unhappy to respond before knowing all there is about a task. They do not like to be rushed or given precise instructions about how to carry out a task.

Theorists

Theorists think problems through in a step by step logical way. They assimilate disparate facts into coherent theories and are keen on principles, theories and models. They tend to be detached and analytical and dislike anything subjective or ambiguous. Their approach to problems is logical and they rigidly reject anything that doesn't fit with it. They feel uncomfortable with subjective judgments and lateral thinking. They are unhappy with open-ended problems and uncertain situations or involvement in any situation that seems to lack depth.

Pragmatists

Pragmatists are keen on trying out ideas and techniques to see if they work in practice. They look for new ideas and are always willing to experiment to see if things work. They like to get on with things and act quickly and confidently on ideas that attract them. They are essentially practical, down to earth people who like making practical decisions and solving problems. They respond to problems and opportunities with energy and enthusiasm. They like to see people demonstrate solutions to problems and receive feedback from credible people and are happy to emulate models of performance. They do not respond well if there is no immediate, practical benefit, reward or clear practical guidelines.

COGNITIVE STYLES

It is well recognised that learners adopt a variety of cognitive strategies when tackling a new skill and that these can have a major influence of the quality of that learning. Cognitive strategies include counting, analogies, rehearsal and labelling. It has been suggested that people tend to adopt a particular 'style' in the way they organise, represent and process information when learning. The manner in which they do this is relatively stable over time. Riding and Cheema (1991) describe two broad dimensions – holistic-analytic and verbaliser-imager dimensions. Both dimensions are independent of one another so that a learner's position along one dimension bears no relation to their position along the other. Holistic learners tend to organise information into wholes whereas analysts prefer to separate information into smaller parts. In contrast, learners towards the verbaliser end of the dimension tend to verbalise when thinking whereas others tend to use visual images.

Most importantly, it has been suggested that a learner's preferred cognitive style influences their learning ability and this is linked to the kinds of cognitive strategies they adopt. Thus, a person's cognitive style predisposes them to adopt a particular kind of strategy. As an example, an individual classified as a holistic learner is more inclined towards holistic strategies when learning a skill. Thus, they would favour a learning environment which focuses on the contextual aspects of that skill – how the skill fits into the game, why it is important, when is it used, and so on. Their opinions and beliefs about the sport might also play a big part in how they approached their learning. Thus, a young boy who was an avid fan of a football club known for their aggressive behaviour, might be inclined to inject the same kind of behaviour into his own learning. In contrast, a learner whose style is analytical would be more inclined to use planning strategies that focus on the parts of a skills and how they link together; they would be less inclined to see the parts as they fit within the game context.

From a practical point of view it seems that learners should be encouraged to determine their own cognitive style and then be guided to developing the cognitive strategies that best suits that style. Luke and Hardy (1999) suggest that for any cognitive strategy to work, learners must fully understand why and how it works. They should also be encouraged to develop a wide repertoire of strategies to maximise success. Finally, they say:

> *"... cognitive strategies may be the key to developing a flexible learner who can adapt to the environment. It would seem imperative that pupils are encouraged to develop a variety of cognitive strategies types to enhance their potential to learn in a variety of learning situations."*

IMPLICATIONS

Readers may wish to examine whether any of these descriptions reflect the way they feel about themselves. No doubt some will identify very clearly with one of the four categories whilst others may see elements of two or more in themselves. How useful is this knowledge? Is it valuable and can the ideas be put into practice? Firstly, any information which helps teachers or coaches understand their learners better must be valuable. The fact that people learn in broadly different ways is a very useful starting point for helping people to learn. It's rather like a cook who is given a recipe to work from. A recipe provides important guidelines about how to proceed. It allows the cook to combine the ingredients in a balanced and structured manner rather than adding them together using guesswork alone. A good analogy can be made with the topic of fitness. We know that physical conditioning involves a number of variables (strength, aerobic capacity, flexibility, etc.) that apply to all athletes regardless of the individual. The task of improving fitness involves addressing each of these variables to a greater or lesser degree depending on the individual's strengths and interests. In the same way, it's extremely valuable for coaches and teachers to know that when confronted with a group of learners, assumptions can be made about the broad requirements of those learners in terms of the way they think, the kinds of information they require and their general attitude to the learning process. Thus, 'activists' like to be involved in a practical manner whereas 'theorists' prefer to absorb lots of factual information before they take part. Coaches can take advantage of this knowledge by adapting their approach to suit.

Another practical use of this knowledge is in helping individuals with particular learning difficulties. The locus of learning problems may not always lie with the learner, but may reflect the approach taken by the teacher or coach. Some people may experience particular difficulties in learning and it may just be that they have not been treated in the most appropriate manner. As Dryden and Voss (1991) mentioned, the problem may lie in a mismatch between learner and coaching styles. And Cross (1999) also suggests that:

> *"Failure to satisfy the needs of athletes can lead them to suffer from lack of confidence, reduced motivation, decreased levels of performance and even to dissatisfaction with their sport."*

Coaches and teachers therefore have an obligation to consider whether the learning needs of all individuals are being met. With particular individuals it might be useful for the coach to determine the learning style of the individual and adapt their methods accordingly. The question this raises is how practical is it to test and monitor the learning styles of every individual? The answer is that it is probably very difficult unless the coach or teacher is working with only a single athlete/learner. Cross (1999) again says that:

> *"Whilst it is inconceivable that a performance coach in any competitive sport would deny the need for individualised training in one way or another, only where the coach/athlete relationship is on a one-to-one basis is it always guaranteed. Thus, the individualization in all team sports is problematical and, even where the sport is an individual one, being responsible for a large number of athletes may make it difficult too."*

The major advantage of knowing something about learning styles is that it helps sensitise teachers and coaches to individual differences and the importance of trying to maximise the potential of all learners. Further it provides an additional source of information to help when learners experience special problems of skill acquisition. Let's now switch from learners to teachers and examine current views about teaching/ coaching styles.

TEACHING/COACHING STYLES

The importance of the individual and the individual's development (technical, physical, attitudinal, etc.) to the coaching/teaching process has been underlined several times. Cross (1999) suggests that 'individualisation' is an essential component of the coaching process. He suggests that:

> *"Athletes may need individualised attention in several different areas. Some athletes will require particular work on technique development, which may involve help from a specialist sports scientist such as a bio-mechanist, etc..."*

Lyle (1996) notes further that:

"Each coaching process is unique for a number of reasons. Athlete aspirations, capabilities and personal circumstances will differ as will the organisational, resource and occupational circumstances within which the coach operates."

Given the importance of the individual within the learning environment and the ensuing need to cater for individual differences, what kinds of teaching approaches can be used to ensure individual needs are met? Indeed, are there differences in method and if so, are some 'better' than others? The educational literature refers to various terms such as 'methods', 'styles', 'strategies' and 'approaches'. Numerous authors have investigated this subject and attempted to clarify the meaning of each of these terms (e.g., Mawer, 1995). It is not the intention to enter this discussion here, but it is worth stating that the focus is always on the nature of the interaction between the learner and the teacher or coach. An essential ingredient of that interaction is the degree of control or involvement the learner has over what is learned, the pace of learning and the nature of relationships with other learners. We will look at this in a moment.

> ## KEY QUOTE
>
> *"It cannot be assumed that, once identified as appropriate, coaching styles can be adopted readily by all coaches. One must assume that a degree of personal preference, idiosyncrasy and the diversity of prior experiences will mean that the coaching practice of all coaches will be recognisably different."*
> **Lyle** (2002)

Firstly, it is important to question whether style is something that is a relatively fixed part of the person rather like their personality, or something that can be adopted to suit the circumstances. In other words, is style something stable that reflects experience, interests, upbringing and personality, or something more transient that can be assumed (selected from a repertoire of styles) as the situation demands? Unfortunately, there isn't a clear answer to this question (Lyle, 2002), but anecdotal evidence suggests that both explanations may be correct. Thus, a teacher may feel most comfortable when adopting a particular approach and this may be the approach they tend to adopt in most situations. On the other hand, it is possible for people to adopt different styles dependent on circumstances. Thus, when working with beginner rock climbers it may be appropriate to adopt a direct, task-oriented approach where the instructor makes all the decisions leaving little room for individual judgement. In contrast, the same person working with an elite performer on fine skill development may adopt a more flexible, supporting approach that pays greater attention to the athlete's feelings and wishes.

What kinds of teaching or coaching styles exist? Many researchers, educationalists and philosophers have tackled this question. Models have been put forward and ideas have changed over the years to explain what approach is 'best'. Interestingly, the past 30 years has seen a general rise in prominence of 'learner-centred' approaches and a move away from traditional approaches that focus more on skills and techniques. An illustration of this change is reflected in the ideas of Bunker and Thorpe (1983) who favoured an 'understanding' approach to teaching games. It was their view that learners should be encouraged to think about the decisions they make when playing games, in addition to how they execute the skills involved. This approach was very different to the more didactic (direct) approach promoted by earlier theorists.

Mawer highlights the relative lack of research evidence in support of any particular approach and this is a point to which we will return. For now, let us examine some of the key thinking in the area. The intention is not to provide an exhaustive picture but to focus on some of the more general ideas. Many authors and practitioners make a simple distinction between two or perhaps three kinds of teaching approach. Let's look at two kinds before moving on to the more differentiated theory of Mosston. Readers should note that whilst the following theories appear to identify only two/three styles, there are, in fact, a wide variety of styles between each end point. It is best to see teaching as a continuum of approaches rather than a small number of well defined approaches.

AUTOCRATIC/DEMOCRATIC

Cooper (1998) refers to two distinct styles of leadership, both of which apply equally to teaching and coaching – 'autocratic' and 'democratic' styles. Autocratic teachers provide information and solutions to challenges; the activity or skill in hand takes priority. Democratic teachers serve as facilitators where the individual is important and the skill is secondary. *Table 1* is adapted from Cooper (1998) and lists the essential characteristics of both approaches. It is important to note again that an individual teacher or coach may habitually adopt one of these styles. Readers may remember from their own experience (school, college or youth group) teachers who were inclined towards one of these two styles. Even though it is possible to adopt different styles, it seems likely that most people possess a habitual or preferred style of

What kind of coach are you?

Autocratic	Democratic
Teacher tells pupils	Teacher shares with learners
Teacher is dominant	Participatory
Teacher passes on skills and knowledge	Encouragement of learners to learn
Learner is passive	Learner is active
Task oriented	People oriented
Competitive environment	Co-operative environment
One approach to teaching	Variety of approaches to learning
Emphasis is on all skills and competencies	Emphasis on experience and reflection
Equipment is an aide to learning	Relationships aid learning

Table 1: Autocratic and democratic styles of teaching/coaching

working with other people. A person's teaching style is the one they feel most comfortable with and which works best for them. It can be argued however, that effective teachers and coaches adopt different styles depending on the situation and the learner/s. Factors influencing the style of teaching include things like degree of risk involved, novelty of the situation, degree of difficulty and the learner's level of expertise and confidence. Cooper gives the following example from a leadership context to illustrate this. He says:

"In reality the experienced outdoor leader will vary the style according to the group, situation and environment. As an example, when taking a group into the mountains for their first overnight camp there will be many occasions where the leader can assign or delegate responsibility. Members of a group may lead sections of the walk, discussing aspects of route finding and deciding stopping places amongst themselves. They might choose their campsite and the particular site for their tent. Later in the afternoon on a high level ridge walk the weather changes, there is heavy rain and poor visibility; the leader's style adapts to the situation. The task of leading the group safely off the ridge and down to camp is paramount and the leader assumes tight control until the group regains safety."

McQuade (2003) and Lyle (2002) draw a distinction between autocratic and democratic approaches to coaching practice, although Lyle urges that such a polarisation is an over-simplification and often, an exaggeration. Lyle describes differences in the two approaches as they relate to five key dimensions of the coaching process (see *Table 2*). Readers will note similarities between the models of Lyle and Cooper.

Autocratic Style	Coaching Facet	Democratic Style
Performance	Feedback	Process
Task Centred	Communication	Person Centred
Coach Led	Decision Making	Performer Led
Directive	Role Orientation	Interactive
Negative	Goal Orientation	Positive

Table 2: Differences between autocratic and democratic coaching practice

Command / co-operative / submissive styles

Martens (1997) suggests that coaching style is all important. It helps determine the kinds of skills and strategies that are taught, how practice is organised and the role learners are given in making decisions. He adds that many coaches tend to adopt one of three styles of coaching. With the command style, the coach makes all the decisions whilst the learner simply responds to all commands. The coach who adopts the submissive style makes few decisions and provides minimal guidance and instruction. Coaches who use a co-operative style share the decision making with their learners; they recognise that an essential part of the learning process is the capacity for learners to make decisions of their own. In evaluating the merits of each style, Martens firstly discounts the submissive style as ineffective and counter-productive. He adds that the command style has historical/traditional significance and may be appropriate for those new to teaching or coaching. The co-operative style he suggests nurtures independence and decision-making ability but permits the coach to give direction and instruction when required. Miles (2003) suggests the style adopted by a coach depends on many factors including the nature of the learner group, the coach or teacher's own personality and teaching philosophy, the activities and the environment. It should be noted that Martens preferences in coaching style accord with many of the principles highlighted in a previous chapter when discussing the merits of experiential learning.

MOSSTON'S TEACHING STYLES

Cooper's classification of teaching styles, whilst logical, is somewhat crude in specifying only two approaches. A different approach is to consider Cooper's two styles as end points of a wide continuum of approaches. The work of Mosston (e.g., Mosston and Ashworth, 1986) has had a significant impact on the approaches adopted by teachers in physical education although is equally applicable to wider situations. Mosston describes a 'spectrum' of approaches, each of which differs in terms of the degree of control the teacher or coach has over the learning environment.

The focus for their ideas centres on key questions such as 'what should teachers teach?' 'What should learners learn?' 'How should ideas and skills be presented?' 'When is the best time to present skills?' The essence of their model is a continuum about who makes the decisions in the teaching/learning situation. At one extreme, the teacher makes all the decisions and at the other end the learner makes all the decisions. In between these two end points there are a range of styles where both teacher and learner are involved in making decisions to a greater or lesser extent *(see Figure 1)*.

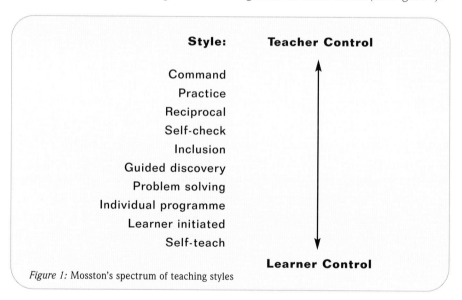

Figure 1: Mosston's spectrum of teaching styles

Mosston identifies ten styles along a continuum. Each one will be described briefly with comment on advantages and limitations.

Command

With the command style the teacher controls every aspect of a session by making relevant decisions in regard to when, where, what and how to practice. Learners are given no freedom of choice but simply respond to commands as given. It is a direct approach that pays no regard to learner's style of learning or individual differences. It has relevance in specific situations, especially where full control is necessitated by

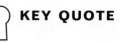

KEY QUOTE

"There is a growing body of evidence to suggest that direct teaching approaches, such as the practical style, may be effective for the learning of motor skills; that peer tutor approaches such as the reciprocal teaching style may positively effect aspects of social development; and that co-operative approaches may facilitate interpersonal and social skill development."
Mawer (1999)

A *teacher directed* approach in action

safety considerations. Thus, an instructor organising an abseiling session for novices would most likely take a commanding role in regard to the actions of everyone concerned. This style may provide a feeling of comfort/ confidence for those who are less able to cope with more relaxed situations and it has the opportunity to maximise activity levels.

Practice

With the practice style learners make some decisions such as where to practice, when to start and how often to practice. The teacher controls the overall period of practice and dictates the task, but has time to provide individual feedback. Using this approach, a coach might describe a particular practice (say a 1 versus 2 passing skill in football) accompanied by a demonstration by two learners. They would then direct the group to practice say 10 times at their own pace in an area chosen by each pair. Research shows this approach is particularly effective when people are developing new skills. It also caters to an extent for differences between individuals. It is a very popular teaching approach.

Reciprocal

With the reciprocal style learners evaluate each other's performance. They usually work in pairs taking turns being the observer; one performs whilst the other observes. The teacher provides simple criteria on one aspect that is to be observed. The teacher chooses the task and may explain and provide a model of performance, but the learners are encouraged to interact with each other and make adjustments to their performance through practice. This approach which is particularly appropriate in display sports, such as gymnastics, where partner work provides frequent rest intervals. It also provides opportunities for learners to support, observe and provide feedback to their partner. It is considered to be particularly effective in assisting personal and social development through learner interaction.

Self-check

This is a development of the reciprocal approach and is appropriate when learners are sufficiently experienced not only to observe and evaluate the performance of others, but also assess and analyse their own efforts. In this situation, it is still important for teachers or coaches to define the task and provide criteria for evaluation. Learners need to be competent enough to assess their own learning against given criteria, so a certain level of technical proficiency is pre-requisite. It is more appropriate to some activities than others. In activities that are fast moving where performance has a qualitative dimension (e.g., tumbling, trampolining) it is difficult for the learner to assess their success or performance. The self check approach is better adopted in sports where performance is more easily quantified such as athletic events and ball games. The use of video is highly relevant with this approach.

Guided discovery or problem solving

These approaches are the exact opposite of the command style and are fully democratic in nature. They place the learner at the centre of the teaching/learning experience. The teacher or coach has a clear idea about what the learner needs to accomplish (e.g., complete a straddle forward roll, pass the ball with perfect accuracy), but leads the learner to it by asking questions,

Youngsters taking an active part in their learning

suggesting strategies and facilitating practice. Answers are not provided but instead, the learner is required to discover and find out for themselves how to progress. It is an approach used in educational dance and gymnastics where precise patterns of movement are less important than the creation of movements that meet underlying principles. It is interesting to speculate whether this approach is useful when the learner is required to acquire a movement which is very precisely defined in terms of its technical requirements, such as a lay-up shot in basketball, a 'j' stroke in canoeing or a forward drive in cricket. These are precisely defined movements and so we might question the value of structuring a situation that permits learners to practice various movements, some of which may be highly inefficient and wasteful of time. The guided discovery approach would not be appropriate where practice and experimentation carry risks.

Individual programme / learner initiated / self teach

With these approaches the teacher decides on the general area of practice and the learner makes decisions about the detail within the general plan. Thus in dance or gymnastics the teacher may set the overall requirements with regard to say tempo and time-scale, but the learner/s is given freedom to create a routine of sequence within these wide constraints. The teacher serves essentially as a facilitator or adviser. All of these approaches have minimal relevance to skill acquisition since, by definition, skill acquisition is goal specific.

DIRECT AND INDIRECT APPROACHES

This is another dichotomous view. Readers will see similarities here with some of Mosston's ideas as well as the approaches described previously by Lyle and Cooper. The direct approach involves the coach or teacher making all or most of the decisions about what is taught (the content), the nature of the practices, how they are progressed and the extent to which the learner is involved in questioning and analysing their performances. There is a clear overlap here between Mosston's command/practice styles and the autocratic approach described before by Cooper. The indirect approach provides a greater opportunity for learners to be involved in the various decisions about the pace of learning, what is practiced and what they feel and think about the learning environment. There is also an overlap here with guided discovery and democratic approaches to teaching/coaching.

IMPLICATIONS

As mentioned before, many investigators have tried to prioritise the effectiveness of different methods, but the research evidence is not always clear on which approach is preferable. This is probably because 'effectiveness' is situation/sport specific. In the context of games playing, Rink (1993) suggests that the best approach to developing essential skills is through the direct approach. An assumption

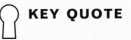

KEY QUOTE

"Good coaches have a range of styles that they have learned over a period of time, usually developed as a result of experience as opposed to anything written in a textbook."
McQuade (2003)

here is that a minimum level of proficiency is necessary before one can 'play the game' and the best way to do this is to introduce skills specifically and directly. In contrast, Bunker and Thorpe (1986) suggest that learners benefit more from being introduced to elements such as tactical awareness and game appreciation, rather than focusing on the skills of the game. They refer to this approach as one of 'teaching games for understanding'. Central to this approach is the use of simplified or modified practices/games that help learners understand the nature of the game; its principles, rules, tactics, and so on. Specific skills are developed later on when learners are ready to use them in context of the game proper. The approach proffered by Bunker and Thorpe plays down giving information to learners about how to execute skills. It relies very much on an indirect teaching approach since it emphasises the importance of learner experience and the discovery of game principles.

Mawer (1999) has analysed the research evidence comparing the tactical/understanding approach with the skill/technical approach to developing games skills. He concurs with the views of Rink, French and Graham (1996) who suggest that it is wrong to determine whether one approach is better than the other. They suggest that direct and indirect approaches are best viewed as end points along a continuum and that teachers should select and apply the method they judge to be most appropriate for the circumstances. This will depend on the individual learner and their stage of development and understanding of the game in question. Indeed, they advocate that a combination of both approaches might sometimes be the most appropriate approach to teaching both skills and tactics. However, they do suggest that in regard to teaching games, an emphasis on initial skill development (before tactical play is introduced) is necessary because it aids the concentration of learners and provides a basis for decision making in the game proper. As skill develops, they advocate skills have to be set within the game context and tactics introduced either directly or indirectly as appropriate. Mawer (1999) highlights that increased attention should be devoted to teaching tactical awareness and for skill development to take place within the game context.

As far as the individual teacher or coach is concerned, it is very wise for them to examine their own practice and identify what style works best for them. As mentioned before, many people seem to adopt a habitual way of working with learners. Knowing what that approach is helps the teacher/coach understand more fully their capabilities. A person who has never given any thought to the way/s they teach is in a poor position to evaluate their own weaknesses (and react accordingly) or identify strengths which can then be developed.

RELATION BETWEEN LEARNING AND TEACHING STYLES

Adopting a particular style will hinge on coach or teacher preferences, but it should also be influenced by the results of careful and professional reflection. A variety of factors should be considered before employing a particular style. Williams (1996) advocates:

> *"... that learning is more effective if the teaching style used is consistent with the preferred learning style of the pupil and that a mismatch will have an adverse effect on learning."*

But there are other, equally relevant factors. Wuest and Lombardo (1994) categorise them as student, teacher, subject and environmental factors. Student characteristics are the most critical variables in the process of style determination and include the skill level, physical maturity, motivational level and learning style. For example, students that are highly motivated and intelligent may benefit better from a style towards the guided-discovery end of the spectrum. A group that is physically immature or that is unable to function well as a small group may benefit more from a direct style.

The need to recognise individual differences and teach/coach accordingly (differentiation or individualisation) has been reinforced in this and other chapters. Does it follow therefore that one kind of teaching approach is more appropriate to a certain way of learning? In other words, are teaching styles and learning styles related? It has been suggested that certain teaching styles may be more appropriate for particular learner characteristics. Mawer (1999) suggests the most critical factor is the way learners interpret the teaching approach being used which, in turn, may depend on the learner's preferred learning style. Thus, an 'activist' may benefit more from a guided discovery or problem solving approach. In contrast, a 'reflector' may find that a direct or reciprocal style is better.

Teacher variables include the ability to manage groups, confidence and personality. Thus, a coach who enjoys and is competent in demonstrating skills may adopt a direct approach. Someone who is highly committed to helping individuals learn and the contribution each makes to their own learning and that of others may adopt a more flexible approach. As mentioned before, it turns out that most people have a preference for one teaching style or similar group of styles rather than another.

Subject variables include the degree of risk involved, complexity of the movements, whether the skills are open or closed, team or individual. Thus, the reciprocal style works well for individual skills whereas skills with a high risk factor are better delivered with a less exploratory style.

The learning context or environment is also important. Relevant factors include the resources available (facilities, equipment, space), time and size of the group. Thus, if space is limited, the practice style might be precluded. If there is an abundance of equipment then a more individualised approach is possible.

The key factor is that coaches and teachers should be fully aware of the various approaches available and be prepared to adapt them as the situation fits. If something doesn't work, they should change approach or adopt a variety of approaches to meet individual requirements. These are skills that take time and experience to develop. Above all, they hinge on an acute sensitivity to the individual learning needs of different people.

SUMMARY OF THE KEY POINTS

• In today's educational climate, great importance is placed on individual differences. Many government policies, teaching resources and learning strategies are geared to supporting the individual in society.

• Individuals can be grouped according to 'how they think'. Concrete sequential thinkers process information in a sequential manner. Concrete random thinkers adopt a trial and error approach. Abstract random thinkers are guided strongly by feelings and emotions. Abstract sequential thinkers are guided by theories and concepts

• One approach to learning styles places people into one of four categories. Activists involve themselves fully in new experiences and are open minded and enthusiastic. Reflectors ponder problems and look at them from various perspectives. Theorists think through problems in a step like manner. Pragmatists try out new ideas and willingly experiment to see if they work in practice.

• Information about the ways people learn and think is useful because it helps teachers and coaches to a fuller understanding of learners in general and also helps deal with particular learning problems.

• A common approach to defining coaching styles is a dichotomous one – autocratic and democratic. An autocratic approach is one that presents the learner with all of the answers to problems; there is no place for individual flare or opinion. In contrast, the democratic approach serves to facilitate learning by creating opportunities for the learner to solve problems.

• The autocratic/democratic dichotomy is best thought of as a continuum of approaches where these are the two ends points.

• Mosston's approach to teaching styles is more sensitive to individual approaches. He describes ten different styles which vary from autocratic (Command style) to democratic (Self teach).

• Whilst a single teaching/coaching style may serve a wide variety of learners, there is a strong view that individual learning is best met when the teaching/coaching style mirrors the learning style. This may be difficult to achieve in practice but more likely when coaching on a one to one basis.

• Teachers and coaches alike should be aware of the various styles (learning and teaching) that exist. Not only does this enrich their ability as practitioners but also provides a practical basis to facilitate the solution of particular learning problems with individuals or small groups of learners.

- The same principle applies to learners. Learners who fully understand their own preferred style of learning/thinking are in a better position to benefit from the teaching/learning environment.

PRACTICAL TASKS

- With reference to Mosston's spectrum of teaching styles, prepare a sheet with the following questions:

  - What style was used?
  - Did the style alter during the session?
  - Comment on why it changed
  - Were you able to associate style with an aspect of improved performance?

Now attend a lecture, class or coaching session with a view to answering the above questions upon completion.

- Attend another lecture or coaching session but this time make sure a different person delivers the lecture/session. Answer the same questions again, and note any differences. Are the differences consistent with your judgements about the relative personalities of the two people (assuming that you know both)?

REVIEW QUESTIONS

- In your capacity as a teacher or coach are you aware of an increasing trend to the recognition of individuals within your subject?

- If so, how has this manifested itself?

- As a learner, can you think of situations or occasions where your particular learning problems were not helped or avoided altogether by the teacher/coach? What were these situations?

- At any point when you have been learning a new skill as part of a group, have you ever experienced problems that others have not?

- How do you account for these differences? Were you less fit? Did you fail to understand, etc?

- In light of information given in this chapter, are you now able to identify with one of the 'thinking' styles described by Gregorc?

- Describe an example to demonstrate why you fit into a particular category.

- In light of information given in this chapter, are you now able to identify with one of the 'learning' styles described by Honey and Mumford?

- Describe an example to demonstrate why you fit into a particular category.

- What kind of teacher/coach are you? Examine this question in relation to the ideas of Cooper, Lyle or Mosston.

- Identify some of the problems in trying to match teaching style with learning style.

References

Archontides, C., Fazey, J., Smith, N. and Crisfield, P. (1994). *Understanding and improving skill* (Coach resource pack). Leeds: National Coaching Foundation.

Bunker, D. and Thorpe, R. (1986). A model for the teaching of games in secondary school. *Bulletin of Physical Education,* 19, 1, 5 - 7.

Cooper, G. (1998). *Outdoors with young people.* Lyme Regis: Russell House Publishing.

Cross, N. (1999). Individualisation of training programmes. In, Cross, N., and Lyle, J. (Eds.), *The coaching process: principles and practice for sport.* London: Butterworth Heinemann.

Gregorc, A. (1982). *An adult's guide to style.* Maynard, Massachusettes.: Gabriel Systems.

Grant, F. (2002). *Learners and learning.* Horizons (Journal of the Institute for Outdoor Learning), 18, 27-29.

Honey, P. and Mumford, A. (1992). *The manual of learning styles.* Maidenhead: Peter Honey.

Luke, I. and Hardy, C.A. (1999). Cognitive strategies. In, C.A. Hardy and M. Mawer (Eds.). *Learning and teaching in physical education.* London: Falmer Press.

Lyle, J. (2002). *Sports coaching concepts: a framework for coaches' behaviour.* London: Routledge.

Martens, R. (1997). Successful coaching. Champaign, Illinois: Human Kinetics.

Mawer, M. (1999). Teaching styles and teaching approaches in physical education: research developments. In, C.A. Hardy and M. Mawer (Eds.). *Learning and teaching in physical education.* London: Falmer Press.

McQuade, S. (2003). *How to coach sports effectively.* Leeds: Coachwise Solutions.

Miles, A. (2003). *What is sports coaching?* Leeds: Coachwise Solutions.

Mosston, M. and Ashworth, S. (1986). *Teaching Physical Education* (3rd Edition). Columbus, Ohio: Merrill.

Riding, R. and Cheema, I. (1991). Cognitive styles. an overview and integration. *Educational psychology,* 11, 3, 4, 193 - 215.

Rink, J. (1993). *Teaching physical education for learning.* St. Louis: Mosby.

Rink, J. (1998). *Teaching physical education for learning* (3rd Edition). Boston: McGraw-Hill.

Rink, J., French. K.E. and Graham, K.C. (1996). Implications for practice and research. *Journal of teaching in physical education,* 15, 490 - 508.

Scottish Consultative Committee on the Curriculum. (1999). *Teaching for effective learning.* Edinburgh: SCCC.

Williams, A. (1996). *Teaching physical education: a guide for mentors and tutors.* London: David Fulton Publishers.

Wuest, D. and Lombardo, B. (1994). *Curriculum and instruction: the Secondary School experience.* London: Mosby.

CHAPTER 9 – EVALUATION OF SKILL

"Often, measurement and evaluation are viewed as a necessary evil, not directly related to the real purpose of the job. However, appropriate measurement and evaluation techniques are essential for all professionals in the exercise and sport science and physical education fields who want to be excellent in the conduct of their job duties."

Baumgartner, Jackson, Mahar and Rowe (2003)

IMPORTANCE OF EVALUATION

Recall the last time you watched a sporting event – football match, swimming competition, tennis match, etc. Do you remember expressing emotion or excitement at what you saw? Were those around you also excited and did they comment on the skill (or lack of skill) of players? We are all very good at passing judgement on the skill levels of others – even though we may never have played the sport ourselves. Spectators often analyse skill and make judgements about what should or should not have taken place. They sometimes try to explain why a player under-performed or why their team failed to win the match. Whenever we watch someone perform we make decisions (often unconsciously) about their ability or skill level. In short, we are all analysts – even though we may not see ourselves as such.

Analysis is central to coaching and teaching. It pervades most things including for example the diagnosis of injuries, the assessment of motivation, appraisal of the 'opposition' and evaluation of performance. Obviously, anyone who is concerned with helping others to improve their skill or knowledge should analyse whether improvement has taken place. However, current literature on skill evaluation is relatively scarce (two exceptions are the excellent texts by Baumgartner, Jackson, Mahar and Rowe, 2003 and Robertson, 1999). One probable explanation is that skill is (apparently) very easy to assess. In many ways this is true. It is simple to note how well a person performs at the start of practice (e.g., an athlete can jump 1.65 ms) and observe their level of attainment sometime later (they can now jump 1.85ms). One just has to look in order to see change! But to adopt this stance is to deny the complexity of human learning and also underplay the value of the

 **KEY QUOTE**

"By analysing and identifying areas for improvement, however big or small, coaches will always be providing performers with knowledge of how they can improve. This can inspire coaches to think about how they themselves can also improve."
Robertson (1999)

numerous methods available for analysis. It is worth highlighting the fact that analysis is relevant to many aspects of sport quite separate from performance – coach/teacher interaction, durability of equipment, footwear and clothing and training methods. These are important although they are not the subject of the present chapter.

The assessment and evaluation of skill is a complex subject and there are a number of important dimensions. Let's examine each in turn.

WHAT ARE THE REASONS FOR EVALUATION?

Why should we evaluate skill in the first place? And what do we do with the outcomes of the evaluation process? A number of reasons have been identified by various authors (e.g., Baumgartner et al, 2003; Strand and Wilson, 1993). Not all of the items listed below are pertinent to all learners at all times and some are more relevant to competition or training situations, but they are listed here for completeness.

• In order to give learners feedback which is accurate and meaningful, the coach/teacher must examine the learner's behaviour and compare performance with either their own model of 'correctness' (some kind of reference of excellence held in memory) or the learner's previous performance. Observation, error diagnosis and rectification are all critical ingredients within this process. And, of course, such information is also an aid to motivation.

• Evaluation helps determine if goals established during a practical session or over a training season have been met. For example, is a new, voluntary trampolining routine ready to be used in competition or has the swimmer who planned to knock one second off their personal best met the mark?

• Evaluation can be used to determine if a particular method of teaching is appropriate (e.g., a procedure for introducing a novel and complicated gymnastic sequence).

• Evaluation can be used to record a learner's progress over a period of time. For example, a coach may examine a high jumper's training diary to assess changes in height jumped over a season.

• Evaluation can be used to provide a record of achievement for the purposes of certification, motivation or selection. For beginners to a new sport, one of the attractions is the attainment of a proficiency award. Awards such as those designed by governing bodies of sport or those designed by the coach or teacher to suit local needs provide tangible recognition of achievement and also help sustain interest and motivation. For experts, a coach may evaluate for the purposes of team selection.

• Evaluation can take the form of assessing excellence in competition (e.g., an ice skating championship, athletics event or swimming gala).

• Evaluation can be used to provide insight into the performance potential of people, as when a talent scout surveys an opponent's players (scouting).

• Another, less obvious reason for evaluation is to provide 'models' of what should be expected in games. For example, in basketball, it is likely that a player or team will not score every attempt at a basket. The coach may wish to determine an acceptable level of performance error in order to provide a basis for evaluating team performance on subsequent occasions. 'Modeling' involves the systematic collection of information over many games. We shall return to this later under the heading of notational analysis.

• Accountability. Accountability is very important in today's society. There is pressure on everyone to quantify systems and expenditure and make the results of analyses public. This is no less true in the world of education and coaching. Parents, teachers, students, officials all require to know 'what is happening'. The evaluation of learning and performance (via practical tests of one kind or another) is simply a reflection of the developing trend in society to make people more accountable.

These are the main reasons why learners and performers are measured. There may be others. Every instance of measurement is unique. The person involved, method chosen and underlying reasons are always specific to the given situation. However, it is possible to categorise the actual things that are measured and the tools available for measurement. Let's look at these two topics.

WHAT CAN BE EVALUATED?

Whatever the purpose behind measurement there is always a critical requirement to monitor the correct things. Decisions have to be made about what element/s of the learner's performance to assess. There are a number of basic skill components which may be relevant such as technique (as exemplified in ski jumping), timing (as in striking a cricket ball), accuracy (as in archery), distance thrown (as in javelin throwing) and frequency (as in soccer – number of goals). In addition, there are tactical and strategic aspects (especially relevant in team games), physical (fitness) and mental (affective) components (motivation, attitude, and values). The emphasis in any given situation will depend on the sport as well as the reason for evaluation and the individual learner. Robertson (1999) provides a useful framework for looking at what to evaluate. He suggests that skilled performance is determined by a wide range of factors that can be grouped into four categories – technical, tactical, behavioural and physical. Each sport or activity places a different emphasis on these components and any kind of comprehensive evaluation should mirror the particular emphasis profile. Let's look briefly at each of these four categories.

Technical

This is the dimension most closely associated with skilled performance. The analysis of technique shows how individual body movements are executed. Good technique is critical in virtually every sport, but in some sports such as diving and gymnastics it is crucial since movements are required to conform to accepted or prescribed movement patterns ('blueprints for action'). Performers attempt to replicate the 'perfect' movement as closely as they can and technique is judged accordingly. In other sports such as dressage, ice dancing and rhythmic gymnastics, good technique is measured according to its aesthetic qualities. Here, facets such as fluency, style and difficulty are monitored. Observation of these kinds of characteristics is often complicated because of the subjective nature about what constitutes excellence.

It is worth adding that in probably every sport, good technique is crucial to success since success depends largely on the efficiency of the movement. It is difficult to think of an example of skilled performance that results from movement inefficiency. Indeed, one of the four features of skilled performance is movement efficiency (see Chapter 1). Thus, good technique and movement efficiency are inextricably linked together. Furthermore, good technique is often 'pleasing' to the eye; this is especially the case when skilled actions are slowed down on video film. Indeed, it can be argued that (mechanical) efficiency, (subjective) style and (movement) technique are each linked together; rarely is performance successful if one area is weak.

Finally, it should be noted that the analysis of technique often hinges on breaking complex movements down into smaller parts. Thus a triple jump could be seen as comprising the run up, take off, flight and landing. Each of these stages could be broken down into even finer steps. Analysis can then focus on each small step one at a time. Analysis is often aided through an understanding of the mechanical principles involved. The kinds of tools used to do this include simple visual observation, bio-mechanics and video technology. We'll look at these topics shortly.

Tactical

Strategies and tactics are important ingredients of many sports, especially team games such as field hockey, basketball and rugby. Strategies are plans designed to achieve an overall goal. They are based on a variety of factors such as particular team strengths, opposition weaknesses, fitness levels and resources such as facilities and equipment. Strategies sometimes change as a game progresses as when a football team decides to adopt a defensive strategy during extra time in order to preserve a potentially winning lead. Strategies are normally designed to take full advantage of a team's special strengths whilst also exploiting the opposition's weak areas. Strategies are placed into effect through the application of 'lower order' tactics. Strategies are defined by the constituent tactics. Thus, a defensive strategy adopted by a football team may be reflected in a revised man-to-man marking system and a decision to play long balls into the opposition's half of the pitch whenever the occasion arises. It might also involve kicking the ball into touch rather than developing attacking play, as well as keeping all players in the team's own half. It is important to note that in sports where strategies and tactics are crucial, technical expertise is sometimes of lesser importance; the outcome of a movement is more important than the way it is executed. The analysis of strategies and tactics can be undertaken at two levels. In a game situation coaches may use personal observation, possibly helped by close colleagues, to judge whether or not a strategy is working. A coach might make changes to team formation or player positions to maintain advantage as the game unfolds based on his/her strategic analysis. Real time analyses like this are very practical but also subjective. As such, they can lend themselves to error. An alternative approach to visual observation is to use some kind of notation system to record the success or otherwise of particular aspects of play. Paper and pencil systems can be used to record the actions of specific players, set moves, movements off the ball, etc., to provide post-match feedback. Or, if the system is simple and quick to use, information can be monitored in real time by a third party and given to the coach to aid his/her judgements. Video and computing technology can also be used to record information (see later). Whatever system or level of technology is used, it is vital for those carrying out the monitoring to specify exactly what game/movement elements require to be monitored.

Behavioural

In Chapter 1, the important point was made that learning has three dimensions – affective, effective and cognitive. The affective or 'mental' dimension frequently plays a key role in sport. People display varying attitudes to training, learning and competition and react differently to the ups and downs of the learning process. Motivation, anxiety and stress all play their part in guiding people to succeed and sustaining interest and enthusiasm. As a result, it is vital for teachers and coaches to understand the impact of these factors on learning and performance and to be aware of the methods available to monitor and measure them. Video can be used to record actions and behaviour and then fed back to show the learner or player aspects which are inhibiting (or enhancing) their performance. For example, a learner repeatedly failing at a new skill may show aggressive tendencies (born out of frustration) that compound their problem. Other methods that can be used include questionnaires to monitor attitudes and anxiety levels, as well as paper and pencil tally sheets to record incidents of particular behaviours. This particular area of evaluation is central to the work of sport psychologists. Bull, Albinson and Shambrook (1996) provide a very practical example. They describe a 'Mental Skills Questionnaire' that is used to measure a variety of dimensions including imagery ability, mental preparation, self-confidence and motivation. The following table *(Table 1)* shows one section from the questionnaire that focuses on relaxation ability. Performers are asked to respond by indicating the extent to which they agree with each statement.

MENTAL SKILLS QUESTIONNAIRE						
	STRONGLY DISAGREE					STRONGLY AGREE
Relaxation Ability						
21. I am able to relax myself before competition	1	2	3	4	5	6
22. I become too tense before competition	6	5	4	3	2	1
23. Being able to calm myself down is one of my strong points	1	2	3	4	5	6
24. I know how to relax in difficult circumstances, etc.	1	2	3	4	5	6

Table 1: Section taken from the Mental Skills Questionnaire

Once every item for each section is completed, a percentage score for each of the seven items is computed. Thus, for example, a person may end up with the kind of profile shown in *Table 2*. This profile is used to show particular strengths and weaknesses, but also as a basis for future comparisons to identify whether improvements (or otherwise) have been made.

MENTAL SKILLS QUESTIONNAIRE RESULTS		
Date: 21st July 2003	SCORE	PERCENTAGE
IMAGERY	15	63
MENTAL PREPARATION	17	70
SELF-CONFIDENCE	17	70
ANXIETY AND WORRY	16	67
CONCENTRATION	9	38
RELAXATION	7	29
MOTIVATION	19	79

MENTAL SKILLS TO FOCUS ON:

1. Need to improve my ability to relax when competing.
2. Need to concentrate more during training.

Table 2: Results sheet from the Mental Skills Questionnaire

Physical

Fitness is crucial in the majority of sports and excellence depends very much on having the right kinds of fitness (e.g., flexibility in gymnastics, strength in sprinting and aerobic capacity in long distance running). In many sports, fitness and technique are inextricably linked together; it is difficult to perform well or sustain good technique if elements of fitness are weak. Indeed, one of the key problems facing many learners is the physical (in)capacity to carry out the desired movements. Often motivation and ability are present, but not the fitness to sustain movement. A good example is seen in trampolining. Many basic moves require sound body tension (especially abdominal strength) but, invariably, many learners are weak in this area. As a result, they struggle to practice for long periods before skill begins to break down through poor fitness. Of course, observant teachers and coaches recognise this and make provision by minimising practice time. All aspects of fitness lend themselves to measurement and in most cases there are many instruments (both field and laboratory based). It is also possible to measure other physical variables such as diet, health and injury. Readers interested in these matters are directed to the excellent text by Baumgartner et al (2003).

METHODS OF EVALUATION

One of the most important topics is how do you measure skill? What methods are available? Are there some that are better than others? Research has shown that both coaches and teachers tend to rely mostly on one technique, i.e., their own personal judgement about a person's skill. There is no doubt that visual observation is practical and appropriate in many circumstances but there are potential problems. The most important is the questionable validity that often accompanies personal observations. When someone makes a judgement about the performance of another person, there can be uncertainty about how accurate or correct is the judgement. Some interesting research many years ago revealed this particular problem. The researchers used a film analysis of the approach run in long jumping and examined aspects of the run as noticed by both the coach and athlete. The film revealed a difference between what the coach noticed and what the athlete actually did. Specifically, the film showed that athletes modify their approach near the take-off board whereas the coach thought that athletes 'programmed' the entire run from the start. How do you ensure against problems like this? One way is through the use of objective techniques (e.g., notation, computer analysis, video, and practical tests). We will investigate some of the more commonly used methods later in this chapter.

THE PROCESS OF EVALUATION

It is important to see evaluation as a structured process. There are many ways this can be

Observation ▶ Analysis ▶ Evaluation

Figure 1: The process of evaluation

evaluation and instruction (see Key Point). For present purposes, a three-stage process is adopted (*see Figure 1*). How does this work? Basically, observation involves monitoring and collecting information, analysis involves summarising and interpreting that information and evaluation is the stage where decisions are made about what to do. Let's take each stage in turn.

Observation

Observation or data gathering must be accurate, relevant and precise. There is no point in spending time and resources gathering information that is not going to be used or which is inappropriate. Methods must be valid, reliable and as objective as possible. Attention must be placed on gathering information that is unbiased and free from prejudice and sentiment. If the teacher or coach relies entirely on visual observation then care must be taken to avoid a number of well known 'human limitations'. Memory limitations make it impossible to accurately recall complicated events, the performance of many people or an activity that takes a long time. Research shows that memory can be very selective; people tend to remember particular aspects such as a very good or poor performance. In situations where the activity takes place in a wide setting (such as on a football pitch) then it is only possible to see action in the central field of vision; peripheral (off the ball activity) events may be missed. Further, it is well known that unless one is highly focused and guided by strict observational criteria, it is very easy to let personal bias and emotion 'add flavour' to what one sees ('you see what you want to see')! All of these factors can threaten the validity and hence usefulness of the observational/ data gathering process. Knowing their existence is one step towards their avoidance. The use of techniques such as video, practical tests and questionnaires may be essential in avoiding some of these problems. Above all, observation must be systematic and focused. And it must be guided by the purpose behind the evaluation process.

> ## ⊂⊐KEY POINT
>
> A qualitative biomechanical analysis to improve technique involves four steps:
>
> 1. Description – Develop a theoretical model of the most effective technique and describe what it would look like.
> 2. Observation – Observe the performance of your student or athlete to determine what their technique actually looks like.
> 3. Evaluation – Compare the ideal technique to the observed performance. Identify and evaluate the errors.
> 4. Instruction – Educate the student or athlete by providing feedback and the instruction necessary to correct those errors.
>
> **McGinnis** (1999)

Analysis

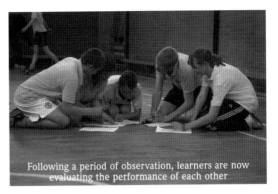

Following a period of observation, learners are now evaluating the performance of each other

Analysis follows data collection and is the process of making sense of the data. It is the process of interpreting the evidence to see what has happened and why it has happened. This stage sometimes has both emotional and informative connotations. Observations may give the coach or teacher pleasure because they see rapid improvement or they may cause them to reflect on a problem whose solution is unclear. They may produce disappointment and suggest something is not right. Analysis usually involves some kind of summary of the data collected. A learner may have been observed attempting a new skill several times. There may be many hours of video footage of the basketball team to analyse or many thousands of figures collected from a notational system. The task of the teacher/coach is to summarise the data and isolate the key problem/s with a view to isolating and informing the learner of the critical factors that will permit progression. Similarly, if the learner has been filmed or written notes have been taken, critical features must be extracted that can be used as a basis for guidance and practice.

Evaluation

Lastly, the coach or teacher must evaluate all the information and, in light of the overall plan (the learner's ability, motivation, goals, etc.), decide how to respond. A conclusion must be drawn about all the data collected. Evaluation usually involves drawing on experience to make changes to the way in which the learner or performer practices. Typically, evaluation results in action of some kind – usually to help move the learner forwards. This results in learners being given information and advice about technical problems and how they can be tackled. Remedial work, further practice or different tasks will be set as a way of rectifying errors, enhancing motivation and solving difficulties. Evaluation is probably the most subjective of the three components as it tends to involve informed judgement. Sometimes, where appropriate, advantage can be taken of the views of other people (other coaches or fellow learners). There may be additional social benefits to be gained from this approach, but it has to be treated with a fine degree of sensitivity (particularly peer assessment) if it is to have a positive effect. A critical part of evaluation is the need for the person carrying out the evaluation to have a model of effective technique so that reliable comparisons can be made between the model and the actual performance.

So far in this chapter, a number of concepts and principles have been mentioned without being fully defined (e.g., validity, objectivity). A key aim is to clarify what these mean; many people use terms such as 'validity' without fully understanding their meaning. The following sections elaborate on the meaning and application of some of the key principles.

CLARIFYING THE TERMINOLOGY

When discussing the assessment of skill, a number of expressions are used, e.g., measurement, evaluation, assessment, analysis. They are often used interchangeably, but do have distinct meanings. A measurement is the actual score or value a person is given to represent their performance (e.g., an athlete runs a mile in 6 mins 30 secs, or a gymnast gains a score of 7 for their high bar performance).

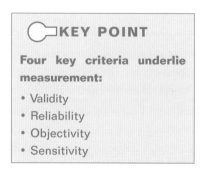

KEY POINT

Four key criteria underlie measurement:

• Validity
• Reliability
• Objectivity
• Sensitivity

Measurements may be quantitative and hence agreed by everyone (15 successful free shots from 20) or qualitative in nature ("She has a very clumsy throwing technique"). Quantitative measurements are typically used to describe the 'outcome' of someone's performance (height jumped, number of goals scored or time taken) and are relatively simple to obtain since they take advantage of commonly available testing instruments (stop watch, measuring tape). In contrast, measurements of movements themselves (e.g., figure skating performance, ski-jumping style) are less easy to obtain as they rely on more sophisticated equipment such as video cameras. Sometimes, measurements do not accurately describe a person's performance. When performance relies on someone's judgement (as in high board diving) people can differ in the score they give the person. Consider for example the varying marks awarded to competitors in Olympic gymnastic or ice skating competitions. This example underlines one of the key problems of evaluation; sometimes the assessment of an individual's skill reflects also the skill of the observer and not just that of the individual!

Another commonly used word is assessment. Assessment refers to the actual process of taking measurements. It is what one does when one takes a measurement. The procedure adopted that makes up the assessment is called a test (e.g., 'Bleep' test, 400 metre run/walk test, Johnson basketball test). A test normally includes a description of the protocol, instructions, equipment required, methods of scoring, etc. The word evaluation is a more encompassing one and includes not only the process of assessment but also that of judgement which involves decision making based on the raw measurements. Coaches and teachers may not always measure learners for the purpose of evaluation, at least not initially. For example, an athlete may keep a training diary recording such things as daily resting pulse, weekly weight, number of hours trained, etc., but the coach may not examine it until some time has passed. At the end of this period, the coach may use the data to identify weaknesses or strengths. Only then is the coach evaluating the athlete.

A distinction is made between formative and summative evaluation. Formative evaluation takes place all the time as the coach monitors players, makes changes, provides feedback and generally deals with moment to moment learning problems as they arise. Formative evaluation is concerned with the provision of information, the diagnosis of errors, and the improvement of skill as well as the improvement of the coach's instructional techniques. In contrast, summative evaluation is concerned with the final or overall evaluation of an individual and is often used for selection or classificatory purposes. The evaluation of a season's conditioning program, the use of a competition to select an Olympic squad or the testing of a new proficiency award scheme following lengthy field monitoring are examples of summative evaluation. Summative evaluation provides a more reliable index of a learner's skill level, but it often lacks detail because it summarises many performances.

Finally, let's look at objectivity and subjectivity. These terms have been mentioned many times already. Broadly, all kinds of evaluations are subjective because they are based on human judgement. They differ, however, in the extent to which the individual's own judgement 'colours' the evaluation. Tests that employ clear methods and efficient measuring instruments are likely to lead to more objective evaluations than those that rely solely on personal impression. The measurement of heart rate provides contrasting examples. For example, heart rate measured using an electronic heart monitor worn on the chest will yield a very accurate measurement. If, however, heart rate is measured by self monitoring the radial pulse, the resulting measurement is likely to be contaminated by the individual's own counting ability. In both cases, the same measurement is taken but one is objective and the other subjective. Generally speaking, all those involved in evaluating the skill of other people, should strive to be as objective as possible.

The next four sections examine four very important measurement criteria. Measurements can easily lose their credibility if certain conditions are not met. Consider for example, the measurement of a person's sprinting ability using a hand-held stopwatch. This technique lends itself to all kinds of errors depending on the skill of the person using the watch, how it is used and the quality of the actual device itself. The usefulness of any data depends on at least four characteristics, viz., validity, reliability, objectivity and sensitivity. The interested reader is directed to Baumgartner et al (2003) for a more in-depth look at these criteria. But here is a summary.

Validity

Validity says something about the relevance of a measurement. It reflects the extent to which a test measures what it sets out to measure. For example, if a coach wishes to examine the sprinting technique of his/her athletes, the method chosen must actually measure the movements involved. If it measures something in addition, e.g., the athlete's motivation or level of fitness then it is not valid.

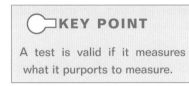

Validity is the most important of all measurement criteria and is often the most difficult one to achieve, especially with regard to skill evaluation which is multi-dimensional. If a coach is measuring say fitness, the problem of validity is easier to resolve because the techniques for measuring fitness are established and better defined.

A test to measure any variable (be it fitness, skill, motivation or something else) will have a validity 'coefficient' associated with it. This will indicate the extent to which the test is valid. The 'strength' of the coefficient (and hence the extent of validity) will depend in part on the sophistication of the methods available to measure the variable in question. In the case of fitness there are numerous methods available to measure the recognised dimensions and several are relatively simple to administer (e.g., local arm endurance – number of pull ups). This is one reason why it is fairly easy to measure the validity of fitness tests. Another reason is that fitness is very well defined and it is simple to isolate the various components. This is not the case with skilled performance. Take the case of assessing skill in volleyball. Volleyball comprises a wide variety of different elements such as service reception or spiking consistency that are simple to isolate. It might be relatively easy to measure these components but doing this does not necessarily provide a valid indicator of volleyball skill. The most important thing about volleyball may be the player's capacity to use the individual components in the game situation. The question is how do you do this? Game related variables such as teamwork, tactical awareness, determination, etc., are much more complicated qualities which do not always lend themselves to objective measurement. These may be as important or more so than skill in the individual components. So a valid test of volleyball may have to include a measure of all of these components with the measurements combined in some way to yield a composite score. This is not a simple matter to resolve.

Basically, when devising a test to measure validity of a particular skill, the technique chosen must be shown to bear a close similarity to some other standard method which already has an established validity (sometimes called a criterion). For example, a coach who selects players for a national badminton squad may decide to use the observations and impressions of other senior coaches. How does the coach know if these measurements are valid? Well, this will only be revealed in retrospect. If it transpires that most of the players chosen succeed at international level, then it can be assumed that the method is valid. Otherwise, the method is not. This technique of assessing players is an example of qualitative measurement. A quantitative method would yield objective data about a person, e.g., number of free shots scored out of 20. Such a test would be a highly valid test of free shooting ability but for reasons mentioned before in regard to the volleyball example; it may not be a valid test of basketball playing ability. In order to assess skill in a game such as basketball it would be necessary to devise a whole battery of tests, each of which measures the essential elements of the game including not only specific techniques but also the many ways in which players work as a team. The battery of tests would then have to be compared against a known test with proven validity to judge if it too was also valid.

A full discussion of validity (of which there are several different kinds) is beyond the scope of this book, but interested readers should examine the texts of Baumgartner et al (2003) or Strand and Wilson (1993) which delve into this subject much more fully. Before leaving this section, it is worth just mentioning two kinds of validity – concurrent and predictive validity. Concurrent validity is the one just mentioned and refers to tests that assess present skill level for the purpose of providing current information (e.g., how good is the backstroke technique of a swimmer). Tests, which have predictive validity, attempt to identify skill level at some future point in time. Scouting is a good example. Tests which attempt to look into the future run obvious risks because many things happen to people in between the time of measurement and the time when they subsequently perform, and these things can influence the manner in which they learn or perform. Predictive validity is consequently very difficult to establish.

Validity is always a matter of degree; tests are neither completely valid nor completely invalid. The assessment of skill is always a function of many factors. The environmental conditions under which the assessment takes place (e.g., the scout watching a potential player in appalling weather conditions) as well as the characteristics of those being assessed (e.g., age, sex, skill level) influence the accuracy and hence validity of assessment.

Reliability

There is often a need to measure skill on two different occasions, e.g., to determine whether and how much learning has taken place. In these cases the method adopted must measure the same thing on different occasions, i.e., it must be reliable or dependable. If a test (which may be simple visual observation) lacks reliability or consistency in what it measures then there is no basis for comparison. To give an example, suppose a coach wished to measure a gymnast's control in performing back flips. The coach might measure the number of sequential back flips that could be completed by laying out a length of gymnastic matting and asking the gymnast to perform as many as possible. This would be a reliable test if the coach ensured that the same conditions prevailed on different occasions (e.g., same time of day, same mat, same gymnasium, same instructions, no injuries etc.) and that the gymnast was allowed a reasonable number attempts on both occasions. Repetition of performance is critical to both validity and reliability. Measurements must yield a 'representative' picture of a person's performance in the same way that opinion polls gather data from many people. In professional football, some teams for example, take potential newcomers to the home ground for a period and watch them train and perform in every possible situation. This is done to maximise the coach's ability to predict correctly good talent. Repeated 'viewing' such

as this is not always possible. At Olympic competitions athletes are typically given one or two attempts to demonstrate their skill. For this reason, it turns out that the 'best' athletes frequently miss out on a medal because their one attempt was not representative of their season's overall performance.

The basis for reliability is the manner in which a test is administered and the procedures adopted to carry out the test. If the test is an objective one (how many baskets scored from 100 free throws) then it is not difficult to ensure that everything (facilities, equipment, layout, instructions, clothing, scoring, etc.) remains constant. With subjective-type assessments such as the scouting example mentioned before, reliability is more difficult to establish because of the varied conditions that often prevail from one occasion to the next. However, reliability can be maximised through the use of a set of guidelines or performance criteria. Judges in gymnastic or trampolining competitions for example work to a preset list of criteria (approach run, technique in flight, control on landing, etc.) so that every athlete is given the same test. Without rigid checklists it is impossible for the judge or coach to be unbiased in their observations. This is also a good principle for learners to adopt when identifying faults in their own performance. If they focus their attention on only a single aspect of their performance as they repeatedly practice, they are more likely to identify errors and correct them accordingly.

It is relatively easy to establish the reliability of a newly devised test providing the methods of measuring skill are not too complex or subjective. Several statistical techniques can be used including test-retest, parallel forms and split-half or odd-even methods (Strand and Wilson, 1993). A test-retest procedure is one where a test is given to a group of people on two separate occasions and the differences noted. If there are no or few differences then the test can be assumed to possess high reliability. Finally, it should be noted that a test may be reliable but not valid. That is, it yields the same measurement every time it is used, but it so happens that the measurement is wrong in the first place (e.g., measuring radial pulse manually may yield the same heart rate on different occasions [high reliability], but it may consistently underestimate true heart rate [low validity]). It should be noted however that a valid test is, by default, also reliable.

Objectivity

Objectivity is a form of reliability in which one possible source of error – that of differences in test administrators – is examined. The best way to explain this term is to give an example. Assume that two different coaches assess a basketball player to decide whether she should be included in the first team. Further, assume that all factors which are

controlled (e.g., the player is watched during the same game for the same length of time and each coach views from the same position). Given this situation, the only reason for differences to exist between the two observations is the fact that two different people are measuring the player.

If there are differences, we say the test lacks objectivity. A test is said to be objective if it yields the same measurements regardless of who carries out the test. Objectivity is important in cases where assessments have to be made by different people. This occurs frequently in skill, especially competitive gymnastics and ice skating. Here, the marks awarded by the various judges often differ (political bias, judging experience?) and the mere fact that they do differ reveals a lack of objectivity. There is a similar problem with National Governing Body proficiency awards. By definition, proficiency schemes are administered by different people and are the responsibility of many coaches. It follows therefore that different standards and criteria may be applied. Thus, depending on the person administering the test, someone may pass the test or even fail it. Hopefully, the tests and procedures for administration are sufficiently robust to minimise this potential problem.

Lack of objectivity may not be a critical problem for beginners to sport where simple badges or certificates are at stake, but higher up the performance ladder where the focus is on prestigious medals or team selection, it is vital that objectivity is as tight as possible. Of course, when the same coach assesses from one occasion to the next, which would be the normal coach/learner relationship, then objectivity is not an issue.

The way you judge a person should not depend on the judge's feelings or beliefs!

Finally, the way to increase objectivity is to ensure that all those people who evaluate players or learners are mindful of the same performance criteria and procedures for carrying out the test. Most proficiency award schemes, for example, provide the user with clear instructions, diagrams and guidelines. However, when evaluation is more subjective it is easier for bias, related for example, to the coach's experience, or nationalism to enter.

Sensitivity/Discrimination

Test sensitivity refers to the extent to which a test distinguishes between two similar performances. For example, a stopwatch that registers only tenths of a second would not be a very sensitive tool for assessing the performance of top level sprinters – they might all achieve

KEY POINT

A test is sensitive if it discriminates between people.

the same score even though positioned quite differently. An electronic system which records to hundredths of a second would be more sensitive (and of course more valid than a handheld stopwatch). A teacher who just remarks "that was good" or "that was poor" is not being very sensitive. Comments like this provide little information on occasions when more detail is required. The issue of sensitivity arises frequently with questionnaires designed to measure opinions. Questions might be phrased to ask a person simply whether they agree or disagree. Or they might be phrased to ask whether the person disagrees/agrees on a much finer scale (see the Mental Skills Questionnaire described earlier). The latter is a more sensitive measurement tool because it provides scope for finer answers. When devising questionnaires, care is required to ensure the right degree of sensitivity is used.

It is easy to devise systems to differentiate performances (the high speed film system used for photo-finishes in athletics is a good example), but for the coach making a visual appraisal it is more difficult. The ability to detect the difference between two athletes (e.g., completing the same diving routine) or two performances from the same person is fraught with problems. The detection of fine differences hinges on a detailed knowledge of technique – what does perfect performance look like, what kinds of errors can occur, how do common faults arise – as well as close attention to specific elements of the technique. The coach cannot simply adopt an overall perspective and hope to isolate particular aspects. Their attention must be selective and consistent. There is also the problem of time lapse between successive performances. A brief interval of time between two successive observations may lead to things being forgotten or distorted in some way. These kinds of problems are helped with the use of video film that provides replay and slow-motion facilities to allow fine discriminations to be made. Video is good because it strengthens all the key measurement criteria – validity, objectivity and reliability. Some sports now employ video replay (cricket, rugby) to assist the referee make valid decisions at times when it is otherwise too difficult to see exactly what has taken place.

In addition to these four key criteria (validity, objectivity, reliability, sensitivity), Strand and Wilson (1993) highlight a number of other criteria that could be used to determine the overall effectiveness of a test. They suggest users might consider the availability of equipment (cost, complexity, availability) and personnel (number, competence), time, safety and space constraints, ease of administration (complexity of instructions and measurement), appropriateness of the tests to the age or gender of those being tested. Users might also consider whether or not the test serves the dual function of both testing and teaching (educational value). Let us now turn our attention to the actual methods used by coaches and teachers to monitor and evaluate skill.

TOOLS FOR MEASURING SKILL

It has already been suggested that skill evaluation is complicated for a number of reasons. Sports differ in many ways; some require teamwork whilst others involve individual performance; skill in some rests on the outcome of performance (time, accuracy, distance) whilst with others performance itself (form, style, agility, co-ordination) is the focal point. In addition, a number of different analytical approaches can be adopted (subjective/objective, quantitative/qualitative, formative/summative).

The method used to measure skills also depends on the aims of making the assessment (e.g., to fault find, to select for a team, to motivate) as well as the resources available. It has been shown that many coaches and teachers favour a single approach to skill measurement (visual observation) for the simple reason they do not have access to or knowledge about more sophisticated methods nor do they have the time to employ them. Hopefully, the following sections will go some way to showing other, practical possibilities.

Movement analysis

Technical analysis is concerned primarily with the mechanical efficiency of movement patterns. This is the domain of the bio-mechanist; it is involved with the study of motion in terms of force, time, energy and distance. How can technique be measured? McGinnis (1999) presents a useful categorisation. He draws attention to two approaches – qualitative and quantitative. Let's take each one in turn.

Qualitative analysis

Qualitative analysis involves breaking down a skill or movement into its basic elements and then subjectively examining those elements. It is based on direct visual observation of the learner or performer and results in a more-or-less subjective evaluation of the movement under consideration. It is typically used (as mentioned before) in teaching and coaching to provide the learner with feedback and also in judging for

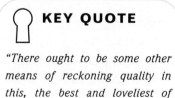

> ## KEY QUOTE
>
> *"There ought to be some other means of reckoning quality in this, the best and loveliest of games; the scoreboard is an ass."*
> **Neville Cardus**
> (Cricket journalist)

the purpose of differentiating between individuals in competition. It is useful to see it as a two-stage process involving the observation and identification of any discrepancies between expected and actual performance and then the diagnosis of the cause of any discrepancies. The ability to observe and know what to look for is critical. If the coach's observations are poor then very general or incorrect instruction will follow. The coach's ability to do this is enhanced if they have personal experience as a performer. Observational ability also hinges on knowledge of what good technique looks like and the mechanical principles that underpin efficient technique. The key to effective observation is the application of mechanical and anatomical knowledge in an organised manner; observation should not be haphazard or ill prepared.

There are many ways in which movement can be observed systematically but in all cases it is essential for the observer to establish clear observational criteria (e.g., noting the distance between the basketball dribbler's body and the ball or the position of the hands in relation to the body in swimming). Radford (1991) argues that the more accurate the teacher's observations the more able they are to provide specific feedback and assessments. A common observational strategy is to formulate a mental checklist of the body configurations at different stages of the movement such as that shown in *Figure 2* (called the 'sequential approach' to analysis).

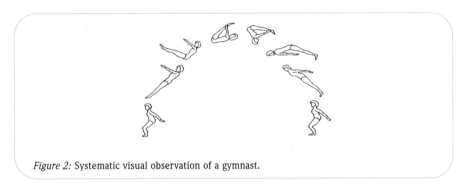

Figure 2: Systematic visual observation of a gymnast.

Once established, this can be compared with the learner's actions. This is a very common method but has certain limitations. Models can be based on elite performers that may not apply to all learners. In addition, whilst this procedure provides a good basis for the identification of errors, it does not provide a systematic basis for diagnosing the cause of movement errors. In a sense, it only provides a description of what went wrong and not an explanation of why it went wrong. This is a critical distinction. For example, it may be clear that a trampolinist's somersault does not result in a successful landing (they keep over-rotating), but the reason for this may not be immediately apparent. There may be a number of underlying causes that generate the same error. In terms of giving learners feedback, the focus should not be on what they did wrong but how they can get it right. Interestingly (and exceptionally useful), learners typically make the same kinds of errors. *Table 3* lists the common errors made by beginners in swimming. This makes the task of technical analysis much easier because it significantly reduces the variety of possible causes of errors. The importance of structure in observation and error analysis is highlighted by the National Coaching Foundation (1987):

"Looking at the world around us is a continuous everyday process and it is all too easy to underrate the importance of a coach developing the skill of systematic observation. To do this you must first of all become familiar with the techniques involved in your sport and the way in which they are applied. Then it is necessary to break down complex movements into simpler elements. You should be aware of how these elements relate to each other – a process of cause and effect. Also, you should know what are the most common faults that beset athletes. As a result of this preparation you will be able to observe an athlete's performance in terms of the relative success at performing each of the elements."

A. Head carried too high or lifted too high to breathe. WHY?
     1. Chest and shoulders too high and facing forward in water
       (Cause – elevation of upper arm and elbow limited during recovery)
     2. Weight of head causes head, shoulders and upper body to sink
       (Cause – hands pushing downwards to support sinking body)
     3. Hips and legs too low in water
       (Cause – straining to keep head out of water)

B. Body fails to pull alternatively to right and left during armstroke. WHY?
     1. Elevation of upper arm and elbow limited during recovery
       (Cause – failure to lift elbow for recovery)
       (Cause – failure to lift elbow above hand)
       (Cause – failure to keep elbow above hand)
       (Cause – holding elbow straight during recovery)

Table 3: Some common errors in the front crawl.

Knowing the mechanical principles involved is of considerable benefit in helping to understand the cause of technical errors. The mechanical approach involves a deeper level of analysis than the sequential approach described previously and involves a thorough knowledge of the principles that govern linear and angular movement. Robertson (1999) highlights a number of relevant principles. He says that:

• Joints must be used in the correct order. Here, if the intention is to produce maximum force (e.g., when a rock climber makes a strenuous move or when a shot putter attempts a personal best) joints should be mobilised in a manner that involves the action of larger muscle groups first, followed by successively smaller ones. Sequencing of action is therefore critical; if one action is out of place then skill breaks down.

• Force must be directed in the same direction as the intended movement. Thus, when a high jumper takes off, they should extend their take-off leg so that force is directed vertically down. Height will be reduced if the angle is any different.

• The speed of rotation depends on the width of the body. If a gymnast wishes to execute a double back somersault, they should adopt a highly tucked position. Similarly, an agile football player will side step an opponent more easily if they keep their arms close to their sides.

• The wider the base of support the greater the balance. In some activities (e.g., judo, fencing, rock climbing) there is a need to maintain balance and stability. Adopting a wide leg stance enhances balance. In other sports there is a need to change position quickly. Thus, in sprint starting or any ball game, rapid changes of direction are helped if the individual moves when their legs are relatively close together.

These are some of the key principles that can be applied to many sporting actions and used to help identify the causes of technical errors or weaknesses. This kind of information provides a very sound basis for evaluating performance and helping learners improve technique. Qualitative approaches to skill evaluation are practical because they demand little use of sophisticated equipment and other resources. The other category of movement analysis – quantitative analysis – is much more objective.

Quantitative analysis

Quantitative analysis is based on the direct (as opposed to indirect) measurement of performance. Teachers and coaches rarely perform sophisticated, quantitative, bio-mechanical analyses. When they are carried out, it is typically with top athletes. There are many ways and approaches to quantitative analysis and the type usually depends on the purpose of the analysis. If it is the end result or outcome of a

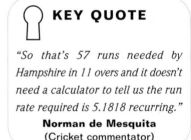

KEY QUOTE

"So that's 57 runs needed by Hampshire in 11 overs and it doesn't need a calculator to tell us the run rate required is 5.1818 recurring."
Norman de Mesquita
(Cricket commentator)

movement or sequence of movements that is required, then direct measures such as time (e.g., as in running or swimming), distance (as in shot putting or long jumping) or number of points scored (e.g., darts, archery) would be recorded. Teachers and coaches are usually involved with this kind of quantitative analysis. If it is the movement pattern itself that is important, then measurements are taken indirectly using cine film, audio recordings or other sophisticated tools such as digital video. Comprehensive quantitative biomechanical analyses require specialised and expensive equipment for recording and measuring the variables of interest. Most rely on some sort of visual recording of movements usually on film or videotape.

Movement sequences are important in many sports (e.g., a routine in gymnastics or the movement of a kayaker uprighting a capsized boat). A quantitative analysis could monitor the nature, duration and/or frequency of discrete movements within a sequence. There are many instances when this is desirable. For example, in football, knowledge of the movements exhibited by players (e.g., jogging, sprinting, and running) and the duration and/or frequency of these movements will help a coach structure specific physical conditioning programmes for different playing positions. Such information would be obtained from film or video recordings of individual players over several games. In the same way, taking a game such as squash, knowledge of the type of strokes and the success rate of the strokes exhibited by an individual player will help the coach plan future technical sessions. These kinds of analyses are referred to as notational analyses and will be discussed in the following section.

Markers attached to an athlete's joints in preparation for film (quantitative) analysis

Returning to movement sequences, it follows that adherence to specific movement patterns tends to be critical in 'closed' skills such as trampolining, diving and gymnastics. Quantitative analysis of movement patterns is more common in these sports. There are two fundamental types of analysis. Kinematic analysis focuses on how the body and/or its segments change their position over time. Variables such as distance moved, speed and acceleration are often measured. To do this requires a permanent recording of the performer, either on regular or digital video or high-speed cine film. This is then replayed frame by frame on a computer monitor and important details such as body positions 'digitised'. Some examples might help to illustrate the value of this approach. In one study the speed/ time curve of a novice sprinter, when compared with that of an international athlete, showed that whilst the novice's start was good, he was weak on maximum speed and the ability to maintain speed (see *Figure 3*). This information helped the coach plan a suitable conditioning work to strengthen the weak areas.

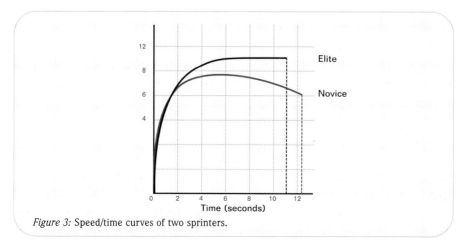

Figure 3: Speed/time curves of two sprinters.

In another study, three-dimensional video technology was used to monitor the joint positions of archers before the arrow was released. The study revealed variations in technique that could not be perceived by the coach's eye or detected by a standard video camera. The data was used to good effect to reduce the archers' errors and improve performance consistency. In studies of swimming technique, it has been shown from film analysis that swimmers tire during a race almost wholly because of reduced stroke length. A longitudinal study found that regardless of swimming stroke and race distance, improvement in swimming speeds is due mainly to increases in stroke length. This information has obvious implications for physical conditioning but also for the manner in which coaches work on technique production under stress.

The other type of movement pattern analysis is kinetic analysis. Kinetic analysis is concerned with the measurement of forces acting on the body or between body parts and how forces affect movement over time. Film and other techniques are employed to estimate values for force and energy. In one study, the forces exerted by a novice sprinter against the starting blocks were monitored and described. A graph depicting the amount of force over time

There are many methods available for quantifying skilled performance

showed that whilst one leg exerted the expected amount of force, the other was very weak and lacked power. This difference was not evident from a visual observation of the athlete. These findings allowed the coach to rectify a problem in technique that may have gone undetected. Another study revealed an important difference in the stroke technique adopted by top swimmers and the technique coaches believed were used by the swimmers. Researchers filmed world class swimmers underwater and examined the patterns of movement as well as the lift and drag forces exerted by the hand throughout the stroke cycle. Analysis revealed that the critical factor propelling the body forward was not the action of pulling the hand backward but rather a sculling motion of the hand! In addition, it showed that skilled swimmers display very different movement patterns – the only similarity being the sculling action. This research suggested that high level skill in swimming is not so much the ability to learn a strict set of movement patterns, but rather the requirement to develop a stroke pattern which maximises the swimmer's morphology (size, shape, proportions, etc.).

In recent years there have been significant developments in the use of computer technology integrated with digital video to assist with quantitative analysis of technique. A number of companies have devised video analysis software that permits the capture of digital video images on computer screen. Portable hardware systems make it possible to carry out highly accurate analyses of high-speed actions and also overlay multiple images to highlight differences in technique. Images can be 'trimmed' to remove unwanted footage and compressed to speed up Internet transmission. Movie files can be generated that contain video footage, measurements, graphics and audio comments. These can be used not only to assist performance analysis but also to help with teaching and coaching.

Measurement techniques such as these are increasingly impacting on coaching with the availability of suitable/portable equipment and the increasing recognition (through funding and support agencies) of the value of sport science in coaching. Several other sophisticated techniques exist for examining the fine detail of a person's performance. Electromiography is a technique for recording the changes in electrical activity of muscles when they contract and is used to establish the exact role that muscles fulfil when generating specific movements. Electrogoniometry is used to record the action of particular joints and can be adapted for both laboratory or field situations. There are several other methods including single-plate photography, accelerometry and pressure measurement, but a discussion of these is beyond the scope of this book. The interested reader is directed to Bartlett (1997) for further information.

Notational analysis

Hughes and Franks (1997) report on the findings of several studies which reveal the often unreliable nature of observations made by coaches – sometimes highly experienced coaches. One study revealed that international level football coaches were only able to report on less than 50% of the key factors that determined successful performance in a football match; they had forgotten more than half of what they saw! The view of Hughes and Franks is that people can be very limited when making judgements based on visual observation. They suggest the way to obtain objective, unbiased accounts of sporting events is to devise ways to collect relevant details of performance during a live event and then recall the details upon termination of the event.

In recent years, a growing interest and body of literature has focused on the subject of notational analysis. The media especially have taken advantage of computerised technology to present viewers with match facts and statistics on screen whilst the action of a player or team is in progress. This is found in sports such as volleyball, basketball, cricket and so on. Match facts may be relatively comprehensive, as in volleyball where the viewer is given information on serving, control of service, blocking, and smash/dump success rates, etc., or quite simple, as in downhill skiing where the computer provides split and final times plus an update of race position. The gathering and accumulation of such information, whether it relates to an individual player or

KEY QUOTE

"Traditionally, coaching intervention has been based upon subjective observations of athletes. However, several recent studies have shown that such observations are not only unreliable but also inaccurate."
Hughes and Franks (1997)

a whole team is known as notational analysis. For the coach, notational analyses invariably use simple techniques and low technology (often just paper and pencil), together with some kind of notational system for observing action in a structured way. Hughes and Franks (1997) describe how systems are devised – both hand notation and more sophisticated ones using computers. They suggest there are four basic purposes of notation, viz., analysis of movement, tactical evaluation, technical evaluation and statistical compilation. A similar way of summarising the purposes of notation has been provided by Brackenridge and Alderson (1985):

• *Modeling.* Modeling is the drawing-up of a 'picture of expectation' of a particular sport. Models are used to aid to understanding about what is acceptable and expected under certain circumstances. For example what level of error is acceptable in, say, penalty kicking in football or slip-field catching in cricket? Or how often should a striker be on target when he shoots at goal? If there is evidence to show how well a team plays (the model) then that evidence can be used as a basis for making comparisons. Notation can be used to compile data (statistical compilation to use the phraseology of Hughes and Franks) over a number of games to provide an objective model of 'correctness'. This idea can be applied to the way teams perform (e.g., number of fouls committed at away games) or the performance of individual players (e.g., how many free shots taken by David Beckham should result in a goal).

• *Post mortems.* Typically, notation is used to provide feedback for players or a team, either as a stimulus to alter strategy or as feedback to improve techniques and tactics. As a tool to aid tactical awareness, notational analysis is especially useful because it provides a means of objectively recording sequences of actions over a number of games. Computer technology can be especially valuable here (see later).

• *Selection.* Player selection is frequently a controversial matter, especially in team sports that involve high levels of judgement and decision making. Notational analysis helps supplement the coach's intuition by providing an objective framework for deciding who plays and who does not. An example is seen in athletics where performance is easily and objectively assessed, which provides selectors with clear data for team or international selection. In a team game, the coach may monitor elements such as number of ball possessions, successful passes, goals scored, etc.

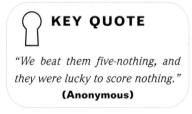

KEY QUOTE

"We beat them five-nothing, and they were lucky to score nothing."
(Anonymous)

• *Scouting.* Notational analysis is an excellent back-up tool for supplementing subjective opinion about prospective new players. It provides information that can be used to predict the future performance of individual players.

The essence of notational analysis is quantification. Visual observation is used as a basis for data collection, but in contrast to qualitative analysis (see before); a permanent record is kept of specific movements or movement outcomes. Typically, a record is kept of the frequency of certain events (e.g., number of winning strokes played from the back court) which is held in some permanent form (e.g., handwritten recording, computer memory). In addition, the analyst is guided in their observations by a list of specific game elements (e.g., forehand or backhand strokes; strokes only in the front court). The need to permanently store data is crucial and reflects, quite simply, the individual's inability to observe, store and recall vast amounts of information without losing it or biasing it in any way. When stored in electronic form it is also possible to quickly analyse information in ways not possible by hand or in the head.

Methods of notational analysis

The essence of any notational method lies in knowing what questions to ask and therefore what data to collect. Only then can a system be selected or devised to collect the data. For example, suppose a badminton coach wished to know something about the relative success of the various ways a player moved on court (with a view to introducing different types of movement patterns or changing the emphasis on existing ones). A number of questions would be asked, such as:

- How many movements are possible?
- What are the possible movements?
- Where abouts on court do they occur?
- How successful is each movement pattern? etc.

Listing questions like this clarifies the various categories of information to be taken from the game. Hughes and Franks (1997) suggest that most forms of notation tend to record data about – a player's position, the player's identity, their movement or action together with the subsequent outcome, and the time of the movement/action. Usually, only two or three of these variables are necessary. Once the aims have been established, a system can be devised to monitor the relevant variables. The most common technique is to use a hand notation

> ### KEY QUOTE
>
> *"You must first decide what you want from your system before you design the system ... Unless you have a crystal clear idea about what data you wish to collect, then you will find that your system will be collecting confusing, and sometimes irrelevant, information."*
> **Hughes and Franks** (1997)

system. It is worth looking at a system described by Hughes and Franks used to examine the shooting patterns of players in field hockey. This example shows the various stages involved in devising and using a system of notation.

Hand notation systems

A coach was concerned about the build-up leading up to shooting in field hockey and wished to know something about the shooting patterns (or lack of them) of her team.

To examine this problem required information from the game about:

1. Position of the pass preceding the shot (the assist)
2. The player's identity who made the pass
3. The type of pass
4. The position from where the shot was taken
5. The player's identity who made the shot
6. The outcome of the shot (goal, save, block, miss, corner, etc.)

The next stage involved the coach devising a notation system to record each of these variables. Variables 1 and 4 were dealt with by splitting the pitch into segments as shown in *Figure 4*.

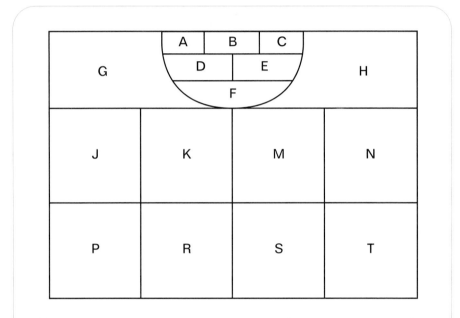

Figure 4: Schematic representation of the playing area divided for notation.

The pitch could have been divided into 18 equal areas (or even more to provide more precise information about position, but the coach decided that unequal divisions would make definition finer in the areas of most interest. Note that each area is given a unique letter of the alphabet. Variables 2 and 5 were dealt with by simply recording the player's shirt number. Variable 3 was dealt with by noting the four possible types of pass and defining them as Flick (F), Push (P), Arial (A) and Hit (H). Finally, the outcome of a shot was recorded as Goal (G), Saved (S), Wide (W), High (H), Blocked (B) and Rebound (R).

This system of notation accounts for all the variables and permits the game to be notated by the coach or operator to record the position from which the shot is made, who made it and the outcome. A sample of the collected data is given in *Table 4*.

Position	Player	Pass (Assist)	Position	Player	Outcome
H	7	P	D	9	S
M	6	F	F	9	B
K	11	P	E	7	W
G	10	P	A	8	G
H	7	P	D	9	B
etc.	*etc.*	*etc.*	*etc.*	*etc.*	*etc.*

Table 4: Sample data from assist/shot analysis in field hockey

It shows for example that the first shot was assisted by player number 7 who pushed the ball from position H. It was received by player number 9 whose shot at goal from position D was saved by the goalkeeper. Each row in the table represents a similar sequence of events. In order for data like this to make any sense, enough has to be collected to be significant. The coach would probably notate several games where the team played against different levels of opposition. The distribution of shots and their assist could then be explored in detail. Data analysis is not a simple process and can be very time consuming. Data expressed in the form shown in the table could be examined relatively easily if it was inputted into some kind of electronic spreadsheet such as 'Excel'. Simple 'macros' could then be designed to reveal frequency distributions (who makes most assists, where do most shots come from, etc.) as well as sequences of actions (what area of the field do most successful shots begin from).

Hand notation systems like this can be devised for any game or activity. Hughes and Franks (1997) describe systems for cricket, tennis, boxing, squash, basketball, volleyball, football, netball and rugby union. It is vital to stress that systems are only worthwhile if they are kept simple, are easy to operate, require minimal learning and answer the right questions. Depending on complexity, systems can be used in real time. But if a lot of information is required in a short period of time a video recording will have to be taken of the action and then played back slowly.

Computerised notation systems

The use of computers to assist notation has a history extending back almost 20 years. There are situations when it is desirable to use computers to obtain and process information. Computers enable large sets of data to be processed very quickly and also permit more searching questions to be asked of the data. Certain kinds of hardware (e.g., specially designed keyboards, touch sensitive screens) can be used to enable data coding and input to take place very easily. Data can be inputted directly to the computer and sophisticated analyses presented in real time. Further, computers can be interfaced with video in order to show sequences of footage that relate to particular kinds of analyses. For example, one system designed to reveal the weaknesses of a basketball team showed they had a tendency to loose the ball whenever their attack began in the right hand side of the court. By using the computer/video link to search for examples, the coach was able to examine instances and identify the locus of the problem. It should be recognised that computers do have some disadvantages. There are added cost factors (hardware plus software) compared to hand notation methods and many lap top machines are not as portable as required (batteries drain very quickly). The process of data entry lends itself to error and can sometimes take a long time to learn. There are also sensitive issues in regard to data protection; any data stored in electronic form about an individual has to comply with data protection legislation. Software can also be very time consuming and costly to develop, especially if it is bespoke in nature.

All notational analysis methods are quantitative in nature and focus basically on either the outcome of a movement (was the attack successful?) or else the frequency with which it occurred (how many times did the player play an unsuccessful backhand volley?). Their application depends on the coach or user clarifying the purpose for which they are used and also the efficiency or 'user-friendliness' of the actual system for gathering information. It is vital that hard data gained in this manner be tempered by the coach's own judgement. This point is well made by Brackenridge and Alderson (1985) who say:

> "The best of all possible worlds, of course, is to combine the knowledge, experience and intuitive judgement of the coach with the accuracy, objectivity and rigour of a good match-analysis system."

Video and skill evaluation

Video is a very accessible and practical medium and is ideal for filming sporting action. In recent years video cameras have reduced in price significantly. VHS (standard and digital) systems can be purchased by the home user and coach/club alike for a relatively small financial outlay. There have been enormous technological developments in recent years. Modern video cameras employ electronic shutters that reduce the smearing or blurring of images that occur when recording moving objects. High quality slow motion or freeze frame devices allow two fields that make up an interlaced video frame to be displayed sequentially. Resolution has also increased which enables video clips to be captured and stored in a computer for subsequent, detailed processing. Most cameras can be held in the hand and footage can be viewed via an integral monitor. For these reasons video has become

KEY QUOTE

"Video is an important tool for analysis. High quality video equipment and video images are making fine grain analysis increasingly possible. Video gives us a chance to record, observe, reflect and check performance accurately."
Hughes and Franks (1997)

widely adopted by coaches, teachers and instructors for analysis and performance feedback in a variety of sports. For example, many ski instructors use video cameras on the ski slope to record the actions of beginner and expert skiers. The integral monitor allows the performer to view themselves and obtain information almost immediately. In canoeing, one system is available which employs two cameras together with a large monitor and is directed to helping national-level slalomists choose the correct path between gates. The canoeist is filmed as they paddle down an artificial course. They then make their way back, but en route draws into the side to observe their actions on a time-delayed monitor. In this way the canoeist can paddle continuously (until fatigued!), attempt gates, receive immediate feedback and try different lines/techniques to improve performance. In other sports it may not be possible to provide immediate feedback (e.g., during a game of football or volleyball) in which case viewing must wait until the game or competition is over.

Video has many potential benefits. It is highly objective and therefore more acceptable to those who might otherwise doubt what they are told. It offers a permanent record and allows learners to observe their performance repeatedly. It allows game details to be recorded which might otherwise go unnoticed such as action off the ball. It allows movements to be slowed down, reviewed or frozen for detailed analysis. Actions can be filmed from different angles and particular aspects can be identified for particular examination. It provides an additional source of information to support the teacher's or coaches observations. It is also a natural and dynamic means of communication that provides individualised feedback.

> ### KEY QUOTE
>
> *"Computer video has many benefits. Coaches can access simple technical images … The images will help them detect exactly where a technique may be inefficient and show the ideal action for comparison."*
> **Robertson** (1999)

Most important, video can be used to assist with technical, tactical, behavioural and (to a lesser extent) fitness aspects of performance. Through recording and reviewing the movement of performers, it is possible to observe and identify improvements and errors in technical performance. Freeze frame and slow motion replay are particularly useful as is the use of computer video in which digital video images can be processed. Computer control over video images provides refined control over slow motion/reviewing as well as multi-screen playback where several images can be viewed in parallel. Computer video also permits images to be quantified in terms of biomechanical features to reveal errors or inefficiencies in movement. Through recording full game situations, coaches and players can take account of strategic and tactical aspects of play. This can take place at team and individual player levels. Video can also be used to provide data for post match/performance notational analysis as well as behavioural (body language, facial expression, verbal comments) and physical analyses. In regard to the latter, some work has been carried out notating the movements of games players to reveal the fitness requirements of various playing positions. This has led to a much greater understanding about how players in offensive/defensive positions (and even playing officials) should train.

Balanced against all this however, are some disadvantages. There are practical problems associated with choosing the right kind of model, technical awareness and actual use (where to shoot from, when to zoom, etc.). The fact that technology changes on a regular basis together with the plethora of makes/models on the market at any one time can make purchasing the correct model problematic. Robertson (1999) suggests many people fail to capitalise on the potential of video for these kinds of reasons. There are also concerns about the conditions under which video really works. This matter was addressed in Chapter 3; readers may recall that video only 'works' if certain criteria are met. For example, learners in the early stages of acquiring a new skill may not benefit as much as those who are more experienced. Video must be accompanied by feedback that draws the learner's attention to important cues for it to have full effect. Also, there is the ever present danger that video will provide too much information, much of which is irrelevant. Video often encourages a very analytical approach that tends to highlight errors at the expense of success. And it has been suggested that video – particularly when used in slow motion mode – may not be very helpful as a demonstration medium. Slow motion film may help learners understand the 'relative' motion of body parts (e.g., how the arms move in relation to the trunk), but it may not help the learner perceive absolute information concerned with speed and forces. This point is highlighted in the comments of Smith (1991) who says:

> *"Although video taped examples of dance performance are on the increase, they are poor alternatives to live demonstration. Qualitative details of time, energy and space seem to dissipate or become lost in the flat two-dimensional projected sketch of the original. Moreover, there are many problems in 'taking movement off' a video performance which has to be stopped, started, slowed and rewound manually and is often shown as a front view performance only."*

Coaches and teachers must balance for themselves the pros and cons of video technology. It may be that video is best used with particular sports and higher level of skill. What does seem clear is that as a tool for skill evaluation, the video camera is, potentially, a significant aid in helping the coach make accurate and informative decisions about how people perform and learn. Highly useful summaries of video use are given by Treadwell and Lyons (1997) and Robertson (1999).

Sports skill tests

Historically, the emphasis on skill evaluation has been placed on the assessment of ability in particular sports through the use of purpose-designed skill tests or batteries of tests (e.g., Strand and Wilson, 1993). A number of tests have been used to measure the notion of 'motor ability' – supposedly a quality which predisposes those who possess it to success in many sports. Such a notion has fallen into disrepute since the acceptance that skill is, by-and-large, specific. Tests have also been devised to predict skill in military, industrial and sporting contexts. These too have proved to have limited success – with, perhaps, the exception of tests employed by the military to assess flying personnel – probably because the criteria or abilities required for prediction are not fully understood. Burton and Miller (1998) explore the concept of motor ability/s and its assessment further.

Sports skills tests are rather dated in concept today although their use in North America is fairly widespread (see Hastad and Lacy, 1998 or Baumgartner et al, 2003 for a more detailed examination). In the UK, they serve the British coach or teacher primarily as a basis for the design of proficiency award schemes and for evaluating performance in specific skill situations. In a school setting they have limited application as a means of evaluating the progress of physical education pupils and providing targets to achieve. A brief discussion will illustrate these points.

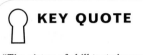 **KEY QUOTE**

"The virtue of skill tests is a subject of ongoing debate. Many skill tests offer a method for evaluating motor skill objectives, that lead to valid interpretations of ability, while others do not. Do not use a skill test that fails your evaluation needs or the important criteria of reliability, validity and feasibility for mass testing."
Baumgartner et al (2003)

A typical sports skill battery includes a series of tests each designed to measure performance in a particular component of the game. For example, one particular basketball test includes items such as a front shot, side shot, foul shot, speed pass, jump and reach test, over arm pass for accuracy and dribble test. A skill battery for football includes tests to measure dribbling, heading and volleying. Some test batteries also include items that would more correctly be labelled as fitness tests. Hastad and Lacy (1998) and Baumgartner et al (2003) describe many other tests designed to measure skill in particular sports. How are such tests designed? The items that make up a test are selected on the basis of complicated statistical procedures and designed to reflect the game in the most accurate way possible. Most test batteries are published with clear instructions and equipment requirements. Some provide the user with normative data (usually American in origin) for comparing the scores of individuals. Many tests have questionable validity, i.e., they fail to measure what they purport to measure. They may be reliable, but many do not accurately reflect the game in its fullest sense. This is because they only include technical components that are simple to define (e.g., penalty corner hit, wall pass) and which are relatively easy and objective to assess. They tend to exclude critical elements such as tactical play, decision-making ability, anticipation and game awareness, which are often the essence of the game.

The value of such tests is limited to instances where the user wishes an approximate measure of sporting skill. They certainly provide motivation and success through the attainment of clear and well-defined goals and in this sense they may serve to encourage beginners in a new sport because they do provide tangible aims and realistic goals to achieve. Any user however, must bear in mind whether the test is a valid indicator of overall skill level and also consider whether the time spent testing would be better devoted to purposeful practice. One positive way in which sports skill tests have been applied is in the area of proficiency award schemes.

Proficiency award schemes

Proficiency schemes have a long history and are well established in most sports (e.g., British Gymnastics Awards in gymnastics and the Kayak Star tests in canoeing). Just as sports skill tests are based on performance of selected components, proficiency tests examine technical competence in a range of areas. For example, the Britoil scheme assesses competence in basic rolling and balancing activities. The Scottish Basketball scheme examines skill in a number of activities such as free shooting, passing and dribbling. Most schemes are tiered to suit different age groups and/or sexes and graded to allow progression from easy to more challenging tasks. Assessment may be a combination of visual observation (qualitative assessment) and objective scoring (e.g., time to complete a shuttle run) and is carried out usually by a teacher or youth leader at the lower levels and a more experienced coach at higher levels. By and large, proficiency schemes have evolved through the desire of governing bodies to encourage participation and the belief that a 'wider base' may produce increased excellence at the top end of the sport. Through the selling of badges, medals, certificates and the like there is also a financial return for governing bodies. As far as the learner is concerned, proficiency awards serve a number of purposes. They provide tangible recognition of achievement and a common yardstick for comparing individuals as well as providing realistic goals for beginners. They also provide the coach with targets and materials to aid their own planning. In addition, because award schemes are progressive in their challenge, they are intrinsically motivating and encourage beginners to develop their interests to higher levels. The expectation is that by the time an individual completes the scheme, they have a strong enough intrinsic desire to improve and continue without further outside reward. These are very laudable intentions but the extent to which they are achieved hinges on a number of factors. They should cater for divergent groups – different sexes, ages, and possibly people with disabilities; they should provide challenge and interest and therefore be sport-related; they should be simple, reliable and quick to administer; and the rewards should encourage learners to work through the scheme.

COMPARATIVE MEASUREMENTS

For a measurement to have any meaning it must be compared with something else. For example, if a sprinter runs 100m in 10.00 seconds, what does that say about the sprinter? Are they very fast or relatively slow? Well, most of us know that 10 seconds is a very fast time. But we only know this because we have knowledge about how other people perform through watching athletics events and keeping a note of World/International records. In recognising that 10 seconds is very fast, we have actually made a comparison with the performances of other people. Take another example. Suppose

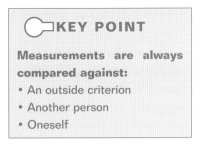

a novice swimmer manages to swim a width of the pool for the first time. How good is this? It depends on the context. Compared to a world record feat, it is meaningless. But compared to the novice's previous (failed) attempt it is an exceptional performance. It follows that measurements of skill only have full meaning when set in context. To have any meaning measurements have to be referenced against something else. There are three ways this can take place.

Norm referencing

Norm referencing takes place when comparisons are made with other people. This approach is typical of competitive situations where one person's skill or the performance of a team is matched against another. Any ranking or league system employs norm referencing. A squash ladder is a good example. Any one player's performance is indicated and judged by their position on the ladder. It doesn't say exactly how good a player is but merely indicates their performance in relation to others in the table. The Olympic games provides another example. An athlete who wins a gold medal is not necessarily the best performer; they are simply the best performer on the day relative to those who took part in the competition.

Norm referencing can achieve two purposes: selection and motivation. Selection plays a part in both amateur and professional sport. Members of International teams are often selected on a 'first past the line' principle. Professional soccer teams are promoted or demoted depending on whether they end up in the top or bottom positions of the division. In these and similar situations, selection is a very powerful force. Vast amounts of money, status and career prospects hinge on such decisions. Norm referenced evaluation provides a strong sense of motivation and competition. It follows that when people are compared and evaluated with respect to others they will often compete vigorously to do better.

Norm referencing clearly has a key role to play in many situations but it does have limitations. Norm referencing always results in people being ranked with regard to their achievements or performance. This means that some people will always fail; for some people to succeed implies that others must fall by the wayside! This is particularly unfair if those who do fail are still good performers as measured in other ways (e.g., the athlete who misses Olympic selection because they are injured on selection day, but otherwise hold the best performance that year). In a school context, norm referencing means that half of all children will always perform less well than the average, despite the strengths and qualities of those in the lower half. And it says nothing about their strengths or weaknesses. Norm referencing provides no information which a teacher or coach can use in deciding how to take remedial action to improve performance or the effectiveness of teaching/coaching. It only provides relative information. It is natural, of course, for people – especially sports people – to compare themselves with others. In terms of skill learning however, apart from providing additional motivation there is little value in norm referencing. It is the learner who is important and how they measure up against themselves which should be the focus of attention.

Self referencing

Self referencing takes place when the learner's performance is compared against a previous performance. Clearly, this is the normal course of events when a coach or teacher works with an athlete on matters such as technique or fitness. An athlete who monitors their weekly resting pulse or keeps a record of their personal best performance over each season is adopting a self-referencing model. Self referencing is especially meaningful with specific groups of learners. For example, teachers, physiotherapists and coaches who work with disabled people are only concerned with the individual's rate of progress. Because of the special nature of some injuries and disabilities, it is meaningless to make comparisons with others, even those similarly handicapped. For similar reasons, the assessment of young and old learners as well as beginners should focus on the individual and not others. So, in regard to skill acquisition, self referencing is the most important way to judge performance and improvement.

Criterion referencing

In contrast to norm referencing, criterion referencing describes exactly what a learner has achieved. Comparisons with one's own performance with another's is irrelevant. Criterion referencing measures an individual's performance against previously determined targets or external standards. In competitive sport there are a number of examples. An athlete's performance may be compared with an Olympic qualifying standard or a world record. In these situations, it does not matter how the person fares with regard to others (many others may meet the qualifying standard, or they may not); it is the relation of the althlete's performance to the standard which counts. Tests, which contain a safety element often, use criterion referencing. One example is a motor car driving test where the examiner is concerned that the candidate reaches a minimum level of mastery to ensure road safety. Examiners work to agreed check lists of skills the driver has to meet. If they fail any one then they automatically fail the overall test. Another is the life-saving award where assessment has to ensure the individual has the minimum knowledge and skill to save life. In the same way, to gain the coaching awards of many governing bodies, the candidate has to meet criteria relating to knowledge and understanding as well as technical execution.

Criterion referencing applies to skill acquisition. It follows that in order to provide learners with informative and relevant feedback, the coach or teacher must focus on specific criteria. Criteria must relate to the technique in question (e.g., how should the feet be positioned, where should the ball be struck, how should the ball be trapped). They may also be established externally. For example, a long jump coach might set a distance of 6.50ms as the goal to be reached before the end of the season. The attainment of such a goal will be the result of meeting many other interim targets or criteria throughout the training season.

Criterion and self referencing should be the models adopted by teachers and coaches. They provide the learner with clear targets to strive for, provide encouragement through the achievement of tangible goals and make for clear communication between coach and learner. In both cases, however, criteria have to be established. Furthermore, criteria have to pitched at the appropriate level (e.g., the criteria for a successful handstand at club level will differ from those at national level). Criterion referencing implies an ongoing, formative kind of evaluation as each target is worked towards and achieved.

Finally, it is worth mentioning that the selection of criteria by a coach/teacher should take account of the fact that when people learn, not only do technical changes take place, but also intellectual, physical and attitudinal changes (see Chapter 1). In other words, the technical model and its requirements will alter as the learner becomes more skilled but so too will the coach's expectations of the learner's acquisition of related knowledge (rules, history of the sport, league organisation, etc.) as well as changes in attitude (punctuality, sportsmanship, helping others, etc.). Evaluation of the learner's improvements should account for achievements along all three dimensions (psychomotor, cognitive and attitudinal).

EVALUATION IN PRACTICE

The role of coaches and teachers is a demanding and responsible one. It is questionable whether many have the time or access to modern technology that enables them to evaluate learners in the most effective (valid) manner. Many may have immediate access to video cameras but fewer will have the scientific back up provided by a national coaching centre or university sports science laboratory. And it may well be that most people do not have the time to learn how to use high-tech methods or indeed the time available during a coaching session to introduce complex and highly individualised approaches. However, there are many approaches to evaluation including those shown in *Table 5* (Sharp, 1988).

Method of evaluation	Percentage of coaches	
	Technique	Tactics
Visual observation	73	68
Views of other people	54	51
Written recordings	52	41
Competition results	51	54
Video recordings	42	33
Self designed tests	39	16
Notational analysis	34	45
Training diaries	20	16
Sports tests	19	8
Audio recordings	10	7

Table 5: Methods used to monitor tactical/technical aspects of performance

The table shows the relative popularity of different methods. Clearly, it would seem that in practice coaches tend to adopt a qualitative approach to skill evaluation relying on their own experience, judgement and intuition. For example, some 73% use visual observation to assess technical skills. They do use other methods as seen in the table but by and large, the subjective approach – which is very cost effective in terms of time and resources – is the mainstay of their work. This is not surprising since it involves little or no equipment and is a very practical approach. A more recent study shows an increasing trend for athletes to monitor and record their own performance and sporting development through diaries or personal logbooks. This idea is entirely in alignment with the message that has been conveyed throughout this book to involve learners fully in their own learning. Personal diaries can include many different kinds of information. The list below identifies some items of a general nature that would apply to most sports/activities:

• Attendance at training sessions, including reasons for lateness/absence
• Aims of preparation; reasons for selection; goals set
• Competitions entered plus entry qualifications
• Amount of physical training, viz., days, sessions, rest periods, totals proposed for the year
• Details of technical preparation, tactical preparation, mental preparation, theoretical concepts acquired
• Comments on progressions and weaknesses.

Permanent records containing information like this help identify the progress made by learners. They also help to give direction to future work.

One of the most important things coaches and teachers can do to ensure their evaluations are practical and effective is to give structure to what they do. It is worth repeating that one way to do this is to adopt the three - part process of observation, analysis and evaluation. Recall that observation is the process of taking in information about the learner's performance. For observation to be effective it should be reliable (repeated viewing; views from various angles; time to absorb the information; etc.), focused (select particular parts of the performance; pre-setting through prior knowledge; etc.) and accurate (aid memory by taking written notes or using a video camera). Analysis is the process of assessing why errors have arisen. The importance of working with people of varying abilities, which helps the coach or teacher develop a repertoire of potential solutions, should be noted here. Analysis is further aided through video and should focus on identification of root problems and not merely the effects of underlying problems. Evaluation is the end stage and is concerned with decision making and action. Action can include additional practice, attempts at a new skill, rest or change of activity. The outcome must be positive, informative and motivating. These three stages – observation, analysis, and evaluation – normally work together, but it is good practice to reflect on the accuracy of these stages from time to time, if only to confirm good practice.

Finally, it is vital for teachers and coaches to monitor their own performance and evaluate whether or not they are achieving their aims and objectives. Bunyan (1991) makes this point when he says:

"To effectively evaluate their teaching performance instructors must sys-tematically appraise what they have done in a variety of ways. They must learn to be self critical, analysing their personal attributes such as voice and non-verbal communication, the appropriateness of the material they have presented, the methods employed to deliver it. Without evaluation a deeper understanding of the teaching situation is unlikely and as a result success and enjoyment will not be optimised."

A further discussion of this particular topic is beyond the scope of this book (see Cross, 1999 and McQuade, 2003 for further details), but it is worth concluding by listing some of the characteristics, which identify effective coaches. The following list is taken from Douge and Hastie (1993). It is notable that many of these relate directly to the process of skill acquisition. They say that effective coaches:

• Provide feedback on a frequent basis
• Provide high quality information to assist correction and further practice
• Adopt high levels of questioning techniques

• Engage primarily in the process of instruction.

SUMMARY OF THE KEY POINTS

• There are a number of reasons for evaluation – to provide learners with feedback, to establish if the coach's goals have been attained, to determine the success of teaching methods, to examine the long term progress of learners, to provide records of achievement, to assess competitive performance, to determine potential, to establish 'models' of sport.

• A number of elements can be measured such as technique, timing, accuracy, amount and frequency.

• Measurements are the actual values indicating skill level. Tests are the procedures used to obtain scores. Evaluation is the judgement the coach/teacher places on measurements.

• Formative evaluation is ongoing and designed to provide feedback. Summative evaluation summarises many performances over a period of time.

• Validity refers to whether a test measures what it purports to measure. Reliability refers to the consistency of a measurement. Objectivity refers to whether a test yields the same measurements with different testers. A test is sensitive if it discriminates between people.

• Qualitative measurements refer to the direct visual observation of movement and tend to be subjective in nature. Quantitative measurements involve the precise monitoring of specific aspects of a movement, normally using some kind of technical recording device.

• Notational analysis is the process of recording particular aspects of a game or player – usually in a team game situation. It has a number of values. To provide the coach with comprehensive 'models' of the game. To provide feedback. To scout and to select team members.

• Methods of notational analysis range from paper and pencil notation to computerised techniques.

• Sports skill tests attempt to measure playing ability in sports through testing the individual on a number of specific skills. They tend to lack validity.

• Proficiency award schemes are popular with learners and serve a number of purposes. For the learner they help motivate, maintain enthusiasm and also provide tangible evidence of achievement.

• Video technology is used increasingly to monitor the skill of learners. It has a number of merits including objectivity, permanent recording, slow down/freeze facilities, etc. Amongst the disadvantages are cost, accessibility, technical operation and poor resolution.

• Learners can be evaluated with reference to themselves (self referencing), other people (norm referencing) or external criteria (criterion referencing).

• Effective evaluation is often compromised through lack of time, inadequate resources and poor knowledge.

• Coaches and teachers should recognise that the evaluation process includes not only the learner but also themselves.

PRACTICAL TASKS

• Take two or three friends to a football match. Each needs to have a stopwatch and pen/pad. Decide at the beginning of the match which player you are each going to monitor. Make sure you monitor at least one forward player and one defender. The task for each person is to monitor the general movements of 'their' player for a period of 30 minutes. Using your stopwatch, keep a record of the number of seconds your player carries out the following general categories of movement:

- Standing still
- Running at less than full speed
- Running at full speed
- Walking/jogging

It is best to start/stop the watch at the beginning/end of each burst of activity. Some practice will be required to do this properly. It may help if four people each record one of the four categories of movement for a single player, by way of practice. Once the data is collected, work out the proportions of time for each category of movement. This should tell you something about the kinds of fitness required of the player. If you have time, carry out the same task for a player in different positions and compare the relative scores for each category.

Finally, comment on some of the problems involved in this kind of analysis and how improvements could be made.

• Select a specific sport and go to the web site for the National Governing Body (NGB) that represents that sport. Examine the awards scheme designed for newcomers to the sport. Many NGBs run short courses or schemes that lead to various kinds of certification. Note the kinds of assessment involved in the scheme. Comment on whether they are quantitative/qualitative or subjective/objective. Comment also on the nature of those components/skills measured. To what extent do they relate fully to the sport?

• Suppose you are required to devise a test to measure the skill of football players at shooting for goal. Consider all the factors needed to devise a test which is valid and reliable. This will involve making decisions about the nature of the task (or tasks), the scoring system, equipment and space requirements, instructions and so on. Carry out a simple validity test by testing two players who are known to differ in their football ability (e.g., one may be a novice and the other may play for a team). The results of your test should reveal the experienced player to perform better than the novice.

• Select a video that shows performers taking part in a 'display' sport such as trampolining or gymnastics. Ask a friend to 'rate' one of the performers with a score out of 10 (10 is high, 1 is low). You do the same. After the performance, compare notes to see whether the two scores agree. The main point of this exercise is to highlight some of the key issues raised by the process of observation. You should discuss topics such as the criteria used to make observations, how often you made observations and the basis for awarding a given score. You should also find a need to discuss both validity and reliability.

REVIEW QUESTIONS

• In your sport, what is the major technique used for evaluation by coaches?

• Are your methods the same as other coaches?

• Is evaluation in your sport given a high enough profile? If not, what do you think are the problems?

• What is the difference between a qualitative and a quantitative analysis?

• Do you think that high technology (computers, videos, etc.) has a part to play in the evaluation of learners in your sport?

• Do you ever examine whether your analysis of learners is correct? For example, is your ability to spot faults as good as it could be?

• Do you encourage learners to examine their own performances? If so, how do you go about it?

• Are you ever conscious of telling learners what they are doing wrong instead of telling them how to improve?

• When you make a comment such as "good" or "well done", are you aware of the point of reference (e.g.,, the learner's previous performance, someone else's performance, your own model)?

• If you were to give feedback to a long jumper about their take off position, where would you position yourself?

References

Bartlett, R. (1997). *Introduction to sports biomechanics.* London: E & F Spon.

Baumgartner, T., Jackson, A.S., Mahar. M.T. and Rowe, D.A. (2003). *Measurement for evaluation in physical education and exercise science* (7th Edition). London: McGraw-Hill.

Brackenridge, C.H. and Alderson, G.J.K. (1985). *Match analysis.* Occasional Paper, Leeds: National Coaching Foundation: Leeds.

Bull, S.J., Albinson, J.G. and Shambrook, C.J. (1996). *The mental game plan: getting psyched for sport.* Cheltenham: Sports Dynamics.

Bunyan, P. (1991). Making the most of our teaching. *Adventure Education,* 8, 1, 5 - 6.

Burton, A.W. and Miller, D.E. (1998). *Movement skill assessment.* Champaign, Illinois: Human Kinetics.

Cross, N. (1999). Coaching effectiveness. In, N. Cross and J. Lyle (Eds.), *The coaching process: principles and practice of sport.* London: Butterworth Heinemann.

Douge, B., and Hastie, P. (1993). Coaching effectiveness. *Sport Science Review,* 2, 2, 14 - 29.

Hastad, D.N. and Lacy, A.C. (1998). *Measurement and evaluation in physical education and exercise science.* Needham Heights, Massachusettes: Allyn and Bacon.

Hughes, M. and Franks, I. (1997). *Notational analysis of sport.* London: E & F Spon.

McQuade, A. (2003). *How to coach sports effectively.* Leeds: Coachwise Solutions.

McGinnis, P.M. (1999). *Biomechanics of sport and exercise.* Champaign, Illinois: Human Kinetics.

Improving techniques – Level 1 (Video, 1987). The National Coaching Foundation: Leeds.

Robertson, K. (1999). *Observation, analysis and video.* Leeds: The National Coaching Foundation.

Sharp, R.H. (1988). *How do coaches monitor their player?* Scottish Sports Coach, January.

Smith, J. (1991). Teaching dance performance in secondary education. *British Journal of Physical Education,* 22, 4, 14 - 17.

Strand, B.N., and Wilson, R. (1993). *Assessing sport skills.* Campaign, Illinois: Human Kinetics.

Treadwell, P. and Lyons, K. (1997). The use of video in notational analysis. In, M. Hughes and Franks, I. (Eds.), *Notational analysis of sport.* London: E & F Spon.

KEY INFORMATION SOURCES

Over the years I have come across many 100's of references relevant to skill acquisition. Many of these are now dated and out of print. Others have been superseded by more recent sources. The list below describes some of the most valuable and practical sources that are still in print and relevant to final year school pupils and first year undergraduates.

Texts:

Baumgartner, T., Jackson, A. S., Mahar. M. T. and Rowe, D. A. (2003). *Measurement for evaluation in physical education and exercise science* (7th Ed.). London: McGraw-Hill.

Black, P., Cruikshank, W. and Ledingham, D. (1995). *Physical education: standard grade course notes.* St. Andrews: Leckie & Leckie.

Bull, S. J., Albinson, J. G., and Shambrook, C. J. (1996). *The mental game plan: getting psyched for sport.* Cheltenham: Sports Dynamics.

Davis, D., Kimmet. and Auty, M. (1995). *Physical education: theory and practice.* South Melbourne, Australia: Macmillan Education.

Davis, B., Bull, S., Roscoe, J and Roscoe, D. (2000). *Physical education and the study of sport.* London: Harcourt Publishers Limited.

Earle, C. (2003). *How to coach children in sport.* Leeds: Coachwise Solutions.

Foxon, F. (1999). *Improving practices and skill.* Leeds: The National Coaching Foundation.

Hale, B. (1998). *Imagery training: a guide for sportspeople.* Leeds: Coachwise Solutions.

Honeybourne. J., Hill, M. and Moors, H. (2000). *Advanced physical education and sport for A-level* (2nd ed.). Cheltenham: Stanley Thornes.

Honeybourne. J., Hill, M. and Moors, H. (2000). *Advanced physical education and sport for SA-level* (2nd ed.). Cheltenham: Stanley Thornes.

Hughes, M. & Franks, I. (1997). *Notational analysis of sport.* London: E & F Spon.

Martens, R. (1997). *Successful coaching* (2nd ed.). Champaign, Illinois: Human Kinetics.

McQuade, S. (2003). *How to coach sports effectively.* Leeds: Coachwise Solutions.

Robertson, K. (1999). *Observation, analysis and video.* Leeds: The National Coaching Foundation.

Schmidt, D. and Wrisberg, C. (1999). *Motor learning and performance* (2nd ed.). Champaign, Illinois: Human Kinetics.

Scully, D. (1996). Skill acquisition. In P. Beashel & J. Taylor (Eds.), *Advanced studies in physical education and sport.* Walton-on-Thames: Thomas Nelson and Sons Ltd.

Sports Coach UK. (1996). *Coaching sessions.* Leeds: The National Coaching Foundation.

Thorburn, M. (2000). *Physical education: Intermediate 1 course notes.* St. Andrews: Leckie & Leckie.

Thorburn, M. (1999). *Physical education: Intermediate 2 and Higher Level course notes.* St. Andrews: Leckie & Leckie.

Thorburn, M. (1997). *Physical education: Higher Grade course notes.* St. Andrews: Leckie & Leckie.

Wesson, K., Wiggins, N., Thompson, G. and Hartigan, S. (2000). *Sport and PE: A complete guide to advanced level study.* London: Hodder and Stoughton Educational.

Websites

Standard Grade Physical Education: Skills & Techniques –
www.bbc.co.uk/scotland/education/bitesize/pe

GCSE Physical Education: Training & Performance –
www.bbc.co.uk/schools/gcsebitesize/pe/training

Also –
www.bbc.co.uk/scotland/revision

Videos

Video Education. (1996). *Analysing physical activity – the learning of skills* (The fitness series). Video Education: Australia.

National Coaching Foundation. (1986). *Improving techniques.* Leeds: National Coaching Foundation. (Currently available from Sports Coach UK)

CD ROMs

Adolos. (2001). *Physical education* (Student) CD-Rom. Edinburgh: Higher Still Development Unit.

Adolos. (2001). *Physical education* (Teacher) CD-Rom. Edinburgh: Higher Still Development Unit.

Mace, R. (2002). *With sport in mind: An introduction to mental skills training for coaches.* Droitwich: Sport in Mind.

Matheson, H. & Mace, R. (2001). *Skill in sport.* Droitwich: Sport in Mind.

AUTHOR INDEX

SUBJECT INDEX

The Mental Game Plan: Getting Psyched for Sport
Bull, Albinson and Shambrook   ISBN 0951954236

This book is ideal for helping students to see how sport psychology theory gets turned into practice. The Mental Game Plan has been used worldwide by coaches, performers and sport psychologists alike, to help with the mental preparation of emerging youngsters to Olympic Gold Medallists. With chapters on anxiety, concentration, imagery, goal setting, team cohesion, injury recovery, confidence and adherence to mental skills training, this book provides simple to follow, easy to implement interventions that are designed to help performers take control of their thinking and produce consistent approaches to developing a winning mentality.

Play Better Cricket
Bull, Fleming and Doust   ISBN 095195430X

A down to earth and common sense approach to mental and physical preparation for cricket. Essential reading for every seriously committed cricket coach or player. An ideal text for helping students who are planning on going into teaching sport.

Coaching Top Club Cricket: Pathways to Success
John Moore   ISBN 0951954334

A simply presented and easy to follow book that offers coaches and players advice on how to develop the physical, technical, tactical and psychological elements of cricket. The book uses real life experiences to provide simple systems for developing excellent coaching.

Sports Dynamics
8 Skillicorne Mews, Queens Road,
Cheltenham, Gloucestershire,
GL50 2NJ

tel/fax: 01242 522638

www.sportsdynamics.co.uk
orders@sportsdynamics.co.uk